Educating the Masses

EDUCATING THE MASSES

The Unfolding History of Black
School Administrators in Arkansas,
1900–2000

Editor: C. Calvin Smith

Contributing Editor: Linda Walls Joshua

Researched and prepared by the Research Committee of the
Retired Educators of Little Rock and Other Public Schools

The University of Arkansas Press
Fayetteville
2003

07 06 05 04 03   5 4 3 2 1

Designer: John Coghlan

⊗ The paper used in this publication meets the minimum requirements of the American National Standard for Permanence of Paper for Printed Library Materials Z39.48-1984.

Library of Congress Cataloging-in-Publication Data

Educating the masses : the unfolding history of Black school administrators in Arkansas, 1900–2000 / editor, C. Calvin Smith ; contributing editor, Linda Walls Joshua ; researched and prepared by the Research Committee of the Retired Educators of Little Rock and Other Public Schools.
    p. cm.
Includes bibliographical references and index.
   ISBN 1-55728-744-9 (cloth : alk. paper)
   1. African Americans—Education—Arkansas—History. 2. African American school administrators—Arkansas—History. 3. School management and organization—Arkansas—History. I. Smith, C. Calvin, 1943– II. Joshua, Linda Walls. III. Retired Educators of Little Rock and Other Public Schools. Research Committee.
   LC2802.A8E39 2003
   371.2'011'08996—dc21

                                                2003007847

to all the black administrators, supervisors, and others who dedicated and continue to dedicate their professional lives to the education of Arkansans

Contents

Preface

It was once said that "definitions belong to definers." Those who define people tremendously influence the culture, history, goals, and aspirations of the defined. This small volume is dedicated to the men and women, primarily black public school principals, who helped generations of black public school students define themselves and discover who they were before the desegregation of the public schools in Arkansas in the 1960s and 1970s, and to those who continue the process in the current desegregated public school environment. Much of the history of these educational pioneers has been lost, but the concerns of Mrs. Frances Johnson and other members of the Retired Educators of Little Rock and Other Public Schools that the remaining history of these people not be lost provided the motivation for this book. They felt that the story of the challenges, struggles, and accomplishments of these people who labored, often under the most adverse circumstances, to educate black youth and direct them toward a brighter future should be recorded, so that future generations would not be uninformed or misinformed about their achievements. Many of the people chronicled in this volume will be readily recognized by some readers, others will not because they labored in relative obscurity. All of them, however, made valuable contributions to the education and life-long successes of thousands of black Arkansans. They constructed the foundations and their story is an integral part of the history of Arkansas, and knowledge of one's history not only connects one with the past but also serves as a guide to the future.

This is not an all-inclusive work because the records of many of those who helped to mold and shape the future of black Arkansans have not been preserved for historical prosperity and are forever lost.

This volume, however, is an attempt at preservation of what remains. Much of the information recorded here has been taken from questionnaires sent to former and active public school principals, to their coworkers and families, and to those in the communities in which they served. Sadly, many of the questionnaires were not returned, thus creating a vacuum in the historical record of black public school administrators prior to the 1960s. Therefore, if readers discover missing noteworthy personalities, it is because the question-naires were not returned or because they cannot be found in the few surviving documents chronicling the history of black public school education in Arkansas.

To acknowledge those blacks who were not public school admin-istrators, but who made significant contributions to the education of Arkansas's black youths prior to desegregation, a chapter is devoted to their labors. Others will be listed in the appendix because there was not enough information available to adequately tell their stories. Responsibility for the accuracy of the information presented here lies with those who completed and returned the questionnaires, but the researchers/preliminary writers and editors of this volume made every effort to verify the authenticity of the information and to fill in gaps through their own research efforts.

CHAPTER 1

The Unfolding History of Black Educational Administrators in Arkansas

Reconstruction to Progressivism, 1865–1895

Education for the masses of black Arkansans had its origin during the Civil War when Union troops captured Little Rock, Fort Smith, and Helena in 1863. As the Union armies moved through Arkansas, thousands of illiterate ex-slaves flocked into Union lines. The Union armies were ill-equipped to handle the volume of refugees and called upon abolitionist organizations and missionary organizations for help in meeting their educational and physical needs. Responding to the call were the American Missionary Association, the Society of Friends, and the Western Freedmen's Aid Commission which sent picture books, freedmen's newspapers, and abolitionist literature to teach spelling, word recognition, and reading. The Northwestern Freedmen's Aid Commission sent teachers and additional educational materials, and the Northern Presbyterian Church and the Western Sanitary Commission also answered the call.[1]

The northern missionary societies that were most active in Arkansas in providing education for the freedmen were the American Missionary Association (AMA) and the Indiana-based Society of Friends (Quakers). In 1863 the AMA established a new district that included all of Arkansas and the Mississippi islands below Helena, and early in 1864 the association opened schools for freedmen in Little Rock, Pine Bluff, Helena, and several other Arkansas cities.[2]

During the same year, the Friends, at their yearly meeting, established a special freedmen's committee to address "the relief of the physical necessities of freedmen and their advancement in knowledge and religion."[3] Before the friends arrived in Arkansas to begin work, blacks in Little Rock, who recognized the value of education, had already begun the process of trying to educate their people. Wallace Andrews, a black minister in the city, had opened a school in his church in 1863. When the Friends arrived, Andrews turned his school over to the organization,[4] which operated the institution until they founded their own school, the Union School, at Sixth and State Street in 1867. When Arkansas established its own public school system in 1868, Andrews's daughter, Charlotte Andrews Stephens, became the first black teacher hired by the state.[5] Although the Friends operated the Union School in Little Rock, they focused most of their efforts in Arkansas on Phillips County, which had a significant black population.

In 1864 one of the Friends working in Helena, the largest city in Phillips County and its county seat, was ordered by the commander of Union troops in the area to provide asylum for the abandoned children of freedmen in the area. As ordered, and willingly, the Friends, under the leadership of Alida Clark, established an asylum and orphanage school in the county in April of 1864. This facility, located nine miles northwest of Helena, grew into what became known as Southland College.[6] The early efforts of the AMA and the Friends to provide education for the freedmen was often supported by black Union troops who guarded the schools from hostile whites, donated part of their meager pay to help support the schools and, during their "free time," attended classes taught by the missionaries. The soldiers were often seen studying their lessons while on duty. After observing the soldiers desire to learn, one newspaper reporter commented: "Notwithstanding the heavy guard and fatigue duties they have to perform, they are making rapid strides toward the attainment of knowledge, and knowledge is power."[7] The local black population in those areas where freedmen's schools were located also thirsted for "knowledge" and enthusiastically attended the schools. Students of all ages, including grandparents, attended the classes.[8] Local whites also realized that education was power and did little to support the freedmen's schools. Daniel T. Allen, an AMA missionary, said that local whites were "bitterly opposed to the [black education] movement, so much so that we are advised by friends to not be out evenings."[9] Another AMA teacher in Lewisburg, Arkansas, was warned by the local chapter of the Ku Klux Klan to quit teaching "niggers" and leave or be killed.[10] And Alida Clark, the leading Friends missionary in Helena, said that in over twenty years of service in the area "only three white women of this Southern land have ever given me a friendly shake of a hand, or an invitation to their homes or noticed me."[11] White teachers in the Arkansas Ozark mountains,

where there were few blacks when compared to the swamps and cotton fields of Helena and Phillips County in the Arkansas delta, were
also ostracized when they attempted to educate the freedmen. In 1866
the Quakers opened schools for blacks in the city of Fayetteville
(county seat for Washington County) and surrounding areas. The vast
majority of teachers in these schools were northern white women who
the locals referred to as "Yankee School marms" and were "ignored
by the local community."[12]

The hostile reception they encountered due to their efforts to
educate blacks did not deter the missionaries from their mission.
However, they were distracted by the sectarian rivalries and preju-
dices that often led them to clash with one another. This friction
among the missionaries led to the takeover of their educational efforts
by the government-operated Freedmen's Bureau. The bureau had
been created by Congress in March of 1865 to help thousands of
people, former slaves and poor white unionists, find transportation,
home, jobs, and food. To pay the cost of operating the schools, the
bureau assessed black families $1.25 per month in order to supple-
ment the fifteen-dollar monthly salary paid to teachers. Although the
Freedmen's Bureau took the responsibility for educating freedmen,
the missionaries continued to raise funds and provide teachers for the
schools. Freedmen also raised funds to help pay for their education
because they believed that education held the keys to their future.
This willingness of blacks to help shoulder the educational financial
burden was clearly revealed in 1867 when the Arkansas reconstruction legislature authorized white-only public schools. Blacks in Little
Rock, who were perhaps the most affluent in the state, responded by
establishing the Colored Education Association, which raised funds
to pay teachers and to operate its own free schools for blacks.[13]

In 1868 the Arkansas legislature under the leadership of "Radical
Republicans" adopted a new state constitution that authorized separate, but free, public education for black and white citizens. The
schools were funded by a levy of one dollar per annum on every male
citizen over the age of twenty-one, and the school districts were
allowed to assess local taxes. In 1871 the state legislature formalized
the dual school system, and with the return of Democrats to power in
1874, continued segregation in education was guaranteed.[14] Although
segregated, black schools prospered. As late as 1890, 20 percent of the
state's school districts, black and white, had a black majority on their

school boards and the average per capita expenditure for enrolled students was $6.27 for blacks and $5.87 for whites.[15] However, following the almost complete disfranchisement of blacks by the Democrats in the mid-1890s, funding for black schools steadily declined. By 1920, black students in the state public schools averaged nearly 30 percent of total enrollment, but the state spent only 10 percent of its educational fund on black schools.[16] One missionary in the state commented that the state legislature had placed black schools on a "starvation plan."[17]

Between 1870 and 1920, state funding for black public education steadily declined. This was due, in part, to the state's downward economic spiral. Arkansas was an agricultural state, and cotton fueled its economy. Beginning in the early 1870s the international price of cotton took a sharp downturn and state revenues declined drastically. Subsequently, the state issued scrip to finance public education and pay teachers. Funding for public education became even more chaotic when the state supreme court ruled that scrip could also be used for the payment of taxes. The court ruling led to the near depletion of hard money from the state treasuries. This situation, combined with a decision by the United States Supreme Court in the case of *Cummings vs. the Board of Education,* 1899, made it easy for the state to withhold funding from black schools on economic grounds. In *Cummings,* the court upheld the decision of the Richmond County (Georgia) School Board in maintaining a high school for whites while closing the one for blacks because of financial difficulties.[18]

Armed with the Supreme Court's *Cummings* decision, Arkansas, which was also experiencing serious financial difficulties, almost completely ended funding for black schools. By 1920 there were only six black high schools in Arkansas compared to one hundred sixty for whites. All of the black schools were located in urban areas with significant black populations—Little Rock, Pine Bluff, Hot Springs, Helena, Fort Smith, and Texarkana.[19] In rural areas where 85 percent of the black population lived, only elementary education was available, and in the more remote rural areas there were no schools for blacks, due to stiff resistance from local whites.[20]

Although state funding for black public education was minimal, schools continued to operate in many areas with support from northern philanthropic organizations. The John F. Slater Fund, established in 1882, had contributed $33,780 to the state black schools by 1920.

The John D. Rockefeller–endowed General Education Board (GEB), founded in 1902, paid the salaries for state agents for black schools, constructed buildings and libraries, and paid most of the cost of summer training institutes for black teachers. The Anna T. Jeanes Fund (1908), working through the Arkansas Department of Education and the GEB, provided industrial education teachers for black schools. Perhaps the most active philanthropic organization working to support black education in Arkansas was the Julius Rosenwald Fund (1912). Between 1912 and 1930, the Rosenwald Fund, working through the GEB and the Department of Education, funded the construction of over 320 black schools in rural Arkansas, supplemented the salaries of state-appointed building agents for those schools, and helped pay the salaries of county agents who helped develop agricultural and industrial education programs in those schools.[21]

Even with the support of northern philanthropy, access to public education for blacks still lagged far behind what was available for whites. Reflecting the self-help philosophy which dominated the thinking of black America during the Progressive Era, 1895–1915, independent black educators and religious organizations organized a number of private black schools in an effort to make sure their children were prepared for effective participation in a "democratic society." By 1916 there were over twenty private schools in the state offering elementary and secondary education.[22] Many of these private schools were poorly financed, but they did make education accessible for many black youths who lived in rural Arkansas and who had been neglected by the state.

CHAPTER 2

Black Educators in the Progressive Era

Progress in the Midst of Prejudice, 1895–1920

As the United States entered the twentieth century, there was growing concern about economic and social changes resulting from rapid industrialization, the growth of powerful corporations, the increasing number of European immigrants, and the potential for the economic and social exploitation of the masses. These concerns led to a massive movement for reform, popularly known as the Progressive Movement. The movement, primarily led by middle- and upper-middle-class whites, focused its energies on breaking up business monopolies, political reform, higher moral standards for public servants and the general public, progressive education, and an overall improvement in the quality of life for the American public. Progressive concerns, however, did little to address the educational problems of black Americans, especially those in the South, who were caught in the steel grip of white supremacy, the crop-lien system, and the Jim Crow laws that kept the masses locked in a perpetual state of poverty and illiteracy. In fact, according to the distinguished southern historian C. Vann Woodward, "the typical progressive reformer rode to power in the South on a disfranchising or white supremacy movement."[1] Northern progressive reformers, however, did offer blacks a glimmer of hope for the future when they joined forces in 1909 with leading blacks and established the National Association for the Advancement of Colored People (NAACP) following a devastating race riot (1908) in Springfield, Illinois. During its formative years the NAACP focused its attention on protecting the civil rights of blacks, but it was almost four decades later before the organization turned its attention to the educational needs of blacks.

The social and political climate in Arkansas during the Progressive Era served as a deterrent to the educational goals of its black citizens. This climate, born from the dehumanizing aspects of slavery, the atrocities of Civil War, and the hostilities of the Reconstruction Era, could not, however, squelch the spirit of a people determined not only to survive but also to strive and succeed. Blacks realized that their journey to success would be guided by their educational progress. Foremost in their minds was the knowledge that their "future lay in their children and they wanted their youngsters to have an education,"[2] but to accomplish this goal, they had to struggle against political regimes, agricultural depression, industrial upheaval, and the development of scientific racism that worked to frustrate and deny them access to the Arkansas mainstream.[3]

Economic progress was on the upsurge for some Arkansans during the Progressive Era, that is, for the entrepreneurs connected to the timber industry, railroads, and other business developments. Yet, the masses of Arkansans, black and white, remained poor farmers and day laborers. Arkansas during the Progressive Era was primarily an agrarian state with those living in the cities, "little more than oversized towns," enjoying a better lifestyle. Fortunately, the urban population contained a growing number of successful blacks who constituted the state's black middle class. Included in these were several craftsmen, barbers, plasterers, brick masons, blacksmiths, and carpenters.[4] Also included in the state's black middle class by 1900 were 680 clergymen, 400 teachers, 91 physicians, 27 lawyers, and 101 persons engaged in other professions. But for the majority of black Arkansans, life continued to approximate that of the slavery era since they had exchanged a life of slavery for one of sharecropping and tenantry.

Although blacks participated in state politics during the Reconstruction Era and the early years of the Progressive Era, they were unable to achieve real political power, and the little they were able to achieve was severely damaged as a result of their participation in the Populist Movement. During the Populist Movement of the 1890s, blacks and whites, especially those involved in agriculture, often joined forces to advance common political and social agendas. Realizing the potential of economic and political cooperation between poor blacks and whites, the Democratic party, which controlled state politics during the era, launched a vicious counterattack that promoted disfranchisement and complete segregation. The spirit of state-sanctioned segregation in Arkansas had its legal basis in the school segregation laws of the 1870s and the Arkansas Separate

Coach Law of 1891. The latter became "a first step toward legal black segregation and virtual disfranchisement."[5]

Three Arkansas governors during the Progressive Era expanded or acquiesced in the expansion of segregation laws and policies in the state. The first, Jeff Davis, elected to three terms—1900, 1902, and 1904—often used negative racial epithets when discussing the state's black population. He "knew how to fan the flames of prejudice and distrust" and was considered the single most detrimental factor affecting education for blacks in the state.[6] In 1903 a Davis-sponsored bill passed the legislature which required the segregation of streetcars and jail cells and furnishings. In 1905 he was unsuccessful in an effort to persuade the legislature to pass a statute that would have limited the funding for black schools to property taxes collected on black-owned property. Less overt in their racism were governors George Donaghey and Charles H. Brough. Donaghey, in terms of racial oppression and equal protection of the law, is best known for his failure to end the notorious convict-lease system that closely resembled the "peculiar institution" of the antebellum South.[7] Continued racial oppression was also one of the major accomplishments of the administration of Governor Brough. Brough sided with white planters in Phillips County when they initiated a reign of bloodshed in response to an effort of black farmers and sharecroppers to organize a union to get fair settlements for their crops. In the aftermath of what was called the Elaine Race Riot, which left scores of blacks dead and imprisoned, Brough mobilized the national guard to restore order and to complete the racial oppression initiated by the planters.[8] Therefore, in Arkansas, the Progressive Era was not one that promised expanded opportunities for blacks, but the black community continued to struggle to overcome the obstacles in order to provide a better life for their youth. And the overwhelming majority believed that the future was in a sound educational foundation.

Early Educational Opportunities for Black Arkansans

In an atmosphere of racism, violence, and political and economic suppression, that extended from the Reconstruction Era (1867–1877) into the Progressive Era (1895–1915), approximately one hundred thousand black Arkansans went about the business of establishing their lives and livelihood—finding jobs, raising families, buying property, and organizing schools and churches. As previously noted they were assisted in their desire to educate their children by several northern-based philanthropists and missionary societies and to a lesser degree the state. Although state assistance was minimal, blacks were appreciative as noted by George W. Bell, a black senator elected to represent Desha and Chicot Counties in 1890, who complemented the state legislature for its support of black schools when he said that "you have given us schools and our children are learning and improving their condition."[9]

Two of the shining stars in the educational future of black Arkansans during the Progressive Era were Southland College (Helena, 1864) and Branch Normal College (Pine Bluff, 1875). Southland grew out of an effort by the Quakers to offer basic elementary education to freedmen in the aftermath of the Civil War and matured into an institution that offered high school and college-level classes. Southland's all-white faculty was joined in 1880 by a number of black teachers, who were its own graduates, and continued to grow in terms of enrollment and facilities until it closed in 1935 due to financial problems.[10] Branch Normal College (currently the University of Arkansas at Pine Bluff) was authorized by the 1873 legislature and opened in 1875 as a land-grant institution. In its early years Branch Normal was basically a high school, but it grew to become the only state-supported institution of higher education for blacks. It also became the major teacher-training institution for blacks in the state. In addition to Branch Normal and Southland, there were several other institutions that provided grammar school, high school, and college training for black Arkansans. Among these were Walden Seminary (Little Rock), a Methodist organization founded in 1877 and renamed Philander Smith College in 1882; the Baptist Institute (Little Rock) founded in 1884 and renamed Arkansas Baptist College in 1885; and Bethel in Arkadelphia, Arkansas, which was moved to North Little Rock in 1885, renamed Bethel Institute in 1888 and Shorter College in 1903.[11] These institutions produced the majority of the state's black educational administrators and teachers. In the early history of black education in Arkansas, the principal/administrator of a school was also its head teacher.

African American Schools and Administrators by Region

Reflecting the "philosophy of self-help" that engulfed the black community during the Progressive Era, black Arkansans organized educational institutions throughout the state, but the majority of them were located in the central and southern regions. For the purpose of this study, Arkansas has been divided into five geographical regions (southeast, southwest, northwest, northeast, and central). Schools and administrators will be discussed in each region.

State support for public schools during the Progressive Era was inadequate and black schools received far less public money per pupil enrollment than did white schools. For example, educational appropriations by the Arkansas General Assembly for the 1909–1910 biennial included the following: University of Arkansas, $220,915; the state's four agricultural colleges, $160,000; the University of Arkansas Agricultural Experiment Stations, $39,400; State Normal School, $95,000; Blind School, $62,040; Deaf-Mute School, $130,146; the State Reform School and Branch Normal (the state higher-education institution for blacks at Pine Bluff), $11,600.[12] The funding inequities for black and white educational institutions in Arkansas carried over into the salaries of their staffs. For the 1909–1910 biennium, the legislature appropriated $12.95 for white teacher salaries and $4.59 for black teachers per month.[13] The lack of state support did not dampen the desire of black Arkansans to provide facilities and an education for their children. An example of this desire was reflected by the black community near Marche, Arkansas, which sent its children to dilapidated Round Hill School for blacks that had been established in 1862. In 1921 the black community, after two meetings that focused upon the school's condition, a decision was made to improve the facility and a building committee was formed. According to P. L. Dorman, one of the agents of the Rosenwald Fund for black schools in Arkansas, some blacks "pledged labor, others cut and donated trees to be cut and sawed into lumber. The women and children picked berries and muscadines; these were sold and the proceeds given to the building committee." One eighty-year-old resident of the community who could not provide labor because of poor health, "gave his wagon and team to be used for hauling building [materials] . . . and donated the beef" for a celebratory barbecue when the building was dedicated in 1921.[14] In spite of such heroic efforts, educational facilities remained inadequate with only four high schools for blacks in the state by 1900.

Inadequate funding for black public schools prompted many in the black populace to look to their own communities and to private philanthropy for help. In fact this was a course recommended by some educators at the federal level. In a 1917 study of private and higher education for blacks by the Department of the Interior, private schools were described as the best way for black youths to become educated. Discussing the prevalence of and necessity of private schools, the study reported that

> the private schools now have a property value of $28,496,946, and an annual income of $3,026,460, and an attendance of 83,679, of whom 70,564 are in the elementary grades. These schools have supplied and still supply the large majority of the teachers for the elementary public schools, the religious leaders, and the physicians for the race. With the exception of the state agricultural and mechanical schools, they furnish them the only facilities for industrial and agricultural training. Above all they have been, and still are, the chief agencies for the development of sound ideas of life, physical, mental, and moral. While the ultimate goal of educational effort should be the development of a comprehensive system of public education, the foregoing pressure of public school facilities indicates that private schools are still very much needed.[15]

By the time of the publication of the Department of the Interior's study, blacks in Arkansas had already decided that private schools were needed for the education of their children, and over twenty such schools offering elementary and secondary education had been established.[16] Out of the state's public and private educational institutions, several blacks emerged as outstanding leaders. Notable among these were Edward Craigen, Sarah E. Perry Clark, Joseph Carter Corbin, and Rufus Charles Childress.

Edward Craigen was a native of Newport (Jackson County), Arkansas, a graduate of the black schools in the county and State Normal College (AM&N College/University of Arkansas at Pine Bluff), and a well-respected administrator and teacher in Jackson County between 1888 and 1904.[17] Because of his administrative, teaching, and organizational skills, Craigen was appointed conductor of state institutes for colored people by Arkansas's white superintendent of instructions. His public school educational career in Arkansas, however, was a short one. While serving as a public school administrator in Jackson County, Craigen also studied medicine at Meharry Medical School in Nashville, Tennessee, when the short-term black schools were not in session. In 1905 he graduated from Meharry as the valedictorian of his class. Following his graduation he returned to

Newport and practiced medicine for a few years before moving to Memphis, Tennessee, where he completed his medical career.[18]

Sarah E. Perry Clark (1869–1958) was one of the early black administrators in Arkansas, serving as a teacher/principal in Conway, Pope, and Perry Counties. During her early years, Clark taught public school in Mayflower, Arkansas, where she had the distinction of being one of the few black teachers in the state's public school system to teach white students before desegregation. She was also the principal of a three-room school in Marche, Arkansas, but left Marche to become principal of an elementary school in Morrilton, Arkansas, which was later named the Sarah E. Clark School in her honor. She left behind an educational legacy which was imitated by several of her descendants. Her son, John Clark, taught printing at Arkansas Baptist College in Little Rock. Her niece, Emily Brown, became a principal of the Sarah E. Clark School, and her grandnephew, Dr. Willie James Brown, was a counselor at the Clark School. One of her granddaughters, Joyce Springer Williams, served as the principal of several schools in the Little Rock School District.

When Corbin and Childress became active in the effort to educate black youths, the state's public schools were segregated by the state law and there was little communication between black teachers in the public schools. White teachers in Arkansas were represented by the Arkansas Classroom Teachers Association (ACTA) and black teachers were denied participation in the ACTA because its constitution limited membership to whites only.[19] To provide organization and a voice for Arkansas's black teachers, Corbin and Childress founded the Arkansas Teachers Association (ATA) in Pine Bluff (1898). The goals of the ATA, according to its founders, were "better preparation of teachers, adequate educational facilities, and equitable compensation."[20] Corbin, who was also the chief administrator of Branch Normal, served as the first president of the ATA. Other ATA members who were also public school principals during the Progressive Era and the first twenty years of the twentieth century included William Townsend (ATA president, 1912–1914), Henry Clay Yerger (1914–1916), Paris Joseph Van Pelt (1918–1919), and Rufus Charles Childress (1920–1923). These pioneering leaders of the ATA were also outstanding public school administrators and deserve recognition for their efforts.

Rufus C. Childress was born to former slave parents in Laurens

County, South Carolina, on April 2, 1867. His family moved to Arkansas during the Reconstruction Era and settled near Cotton Plant. The young Childress received his elementary education in an AMA school in Cotton Plant and his high school education in Philander Smith High School in Little Rock. When Philander Smith received college status, Childress was one of its first graduates, receiving his bachelor's degree in 1888.[21] Following his graduation from Philander, he became the first black Arkansan to take and pass the federal civil service exam. He worked as a railway clerk in Little Rock (1889–1893). Childress accredited his success on the civil service exam to the education he had received from dedicated, but poorly paid black teachers in the state underfunded public schools. He left the civil service in 1893 and began a career as a public schoolteacher, rising to the position of principal of a rural Pulaski County school (1909), which was later named the Stephens School in honor of Charlotte A. Stephens, the first black teacher hired by the state of Arkansas. During this period in Childress's educational career, he also worked as an instructor at Philander Smith College until he accepted the position of building agent for the Rosenwald Schools in the state. As the state building agent for the construction of Rosenwald Schools (1921–1932), Childress supervised the construction of approximately four hundred schools for blacks throughout the state.[22] His work on behalf of the Rosenwald Fund earned Childress respect in both the black and white communities, and in 1932 he was offered and accepted the position of assistant supervisor for black public schools, a position he held until 1946. As the assistant supervisor for black public schools, Childress went into the far corners of the most impoverished areas of Arkansas in an effort to provide what was needed to assure that black children had access to public education. At the same time he worked to establish parent-teacher associations, assisted undereducated black teachers in earning college degrees, and supervised Colored Opportunity Schools—a program designed to improve facilities, to provide teacher training, and to provide learning materials for black students. He also supervised Improvement Day in many of the Rosenwald Schools he had helped to construct as the state building agent for the Rosenwald Fund.[23]

While performing his official state duties, Childress also found the time to actively participate in the civic affairs of the black community. He established or helped to establish the ATA (1898) and served as its president (1920–1923), a public library for blacks (1909), the first black Boy Scout troop in Arkansas (1927), the Congress of Colored Parents and Teachers of Arkansas (1928), the Urban League of Greater Little Rock (1937), and the Florence Crittenden Home for Unwed Mothers (1948). Childress's life reflected his concerns for the education and social welfare of his people, and several black schools in the state were named in his honor. When T. E. Patterson wrote his history of the ATA in 1981, he said of Childress, "no other individual did so much for so many Arkansans."[24]

Although access to public education was easier for blacks in Arkansas's cities and towns, the educational needs of those in rural areas, especially the delta, were not neglected. The American Missionary Association and the Society of Friends were especially active in bringing education to the impoverished delta. There, black school attendance varied from 50 percent in 1870, to zero percent in 1876, which officially ended Reconstruction and the temporary closing of black public schools. However, the numbers were up to 8 percent in 1876 and had increased to 50 percent by 1890.[25]

With the establishment of Branch Normal in Pine Bluff, an institution which provided for "the liberal and practical education of the masses of people in the several pursuits and occupations of life," the city emerged as a major center for the education of blacks and for teacher training. During Branch Normal's formative years, the majority of its leaders were either principals or superintendents: Joseph Carter Corbin, principal, 1875–1902; Issac Fisher, principal, 1902–1911; W. S. Harris, superintendent, 1911–1915, and administrative head, 1915–1917; Frederick T. Vinegar, principal, 1911–1917; Jefferson Ish, superintendent, 1915–1921; Charles Smith, superintendent, 1921–1922; and Robert Malone, superintendent, 1922–1928. Later administrators were titled presidents and then chancellors as was befitting the status of a degree-offering four-year institution.[26] The leaders of Branch Normal and the superintendents, principals, and teachers who graduated from the institution spearheaded black public education in Arkansas. Many of these leaders were not, however, native Arkansans.

Black Principals/Educators, Southeast Arkansas

One of the pioneer black educators in southeast Arkansas was Joseph Carter Corbin, a man who carved a wide path across the

Arkansas educational landscape at both the secondary and the higher educational level. Corbin was born to free parents in Chillicothe, Ohio, on March 26, 1833. He enrolled in Ohio University and graduated in 1853 with a bachelor's degree and a master's degree in 1856. While attending college, Corbin worked as a public schoolteacher, but abandoned education for the business world after completing his master's degree program. In 1872, Corbin settled in Arkansas, joined the ranks of the Republican party and moved swiftly up its ranks and was elected to public office the same year. Because of his educational background, he was the party's candidate for the position of state superintendent of public instruction in 1873. He won that election, which automatically made him president of the board of trustees for Arkansas's Industrial University (currently the University of Arkansas at Fayetteville), a position he held until 1875. In 1875, Corbin became the founder and first principal of the Branch Normal School for blacks in Pine Bluff. Many of his first students at Branch Normal were former slaves who had no formal education. He guided many of these students through basic grammar school to teacher training courses and to graduation.[27] Because of the ascendance of the Democratic party in Arkansas in the 1880s, Corbin, a black Republican, was forced out of his leadership role at Branch Normal. He returned to the field of public education, and from 1901 to 1911, he served as principal of Merrill High School in Pine Bluff. It was during his principalship of Merrill that he joined forces with R. C. Childress to found the Arkansas Teachers Association. His goals as a leader of the ATA were the same as those he espoused as an elected public official, public school principal, and teacher: "to foster better conditions for the education of black youth, creating better school buildings, securing better equipment, more adequately prepared teachers, and better health and educational welfare for black people."[28]

Taking advantage of the solid educational foundation that Corbin and Childress had laid, C. P. Coleman shepherded the small rural elementary Hall School in Watson Chapel, Pine Bluff (Jefferson County), Arkansas, into a noted high school for blacks between 1915 and 1955. Under his leadership the Hall School became the Jefferson County Training School and near the end of Coleman's career the school was named the C. P. Coleman High School. The high school graduated its first senior class in 1950 and the majority of students went on to become college graduates. They reflected the philosophy of their principal, who always stressed to students that "hard work and a sincere desire to achieve a positive goal would always bring success." In 1970, the Watson Chapel School District completed the desegregation process, and the C. P. Coleman High School became one of the several elementary schools in the district.

Other pioneering principals from southeast Arkansas were Ashley County's Charles Watkins (1900–1910) and Edward Washington (1910–1919), who served the Wilmot black public school.

Southwest Arkansas

In rural southwest Arkansas, life for black Arkansans was hard. This was timber country where the workday was long and difficult and where little attention was paid to the educational needs of blacks. Sylvester Malone, born in 1910 near the small lumbermill town of Calion (near El Dorado), said this of his youthful days:

> It was hard for me when me and my sister would be left working in the fields and the white children would be passin' on the way to school. They looked so pretty! We colored only went to school for two months in the summer while they went the rest of the year.[29]

The two-month term in Calion provided education only for grades 1–6, which amounted to almost no education. Still, black principals and teachers struggled to provide these remote communities with as much education as possible.

One of the black educational leaders in southwest Arkansas was Samuel P. Nelson, a native of Louisiana who moved to Arkansas in 1905. He was a graduate of Butler College in his native state and had done further study at the University of Chicago and at the Chautauqua Institute in New York. In Arkansas, he served as the principal of the Arkadelphia Baptist Academy from 1905 to 1919 and of the Dermott South East Industrial College from 1919 to 1925 (these were private institutions). He left the private for the public sector and became principal of the Camden Colored School, 1925–1926. Because of his education and administrative talent, he was offered the presidency of Arkansas Baptist College, a position he held until 1934. Due to the deteriorating financial status of the college, Nelson returned to the public schools where he served as principal of Camden's Lincoln High School, 1934–1961. During his long educational career, Nelson served as president of the ATA from 1923 to 1926 and held office in several county teacher associations.[30] In recognition of his outstanding dedication to the education of black students in Arkansas, a school was named for him, the Samuel Paul Nelson Elementary School.

Also laboring in the black educational fields of southwest Arkansas was Henry Clay Yerger. A native Arkansan, Yerger was born in Hempstead County in 1861. He was educated in area public schools and earned a bachelor's degree at Philander Smith College in Little Rock with further studies at Boston University and Hampton Institute. In Hope, Arkansas, his name became synonymous with black education. He is credited with developing the first public school in Hope, the Shover Street School, and with guiding the institution from a one-room building to accredited high school status. With financial assistance from the Jeanes Fund, the Slater Fund, the Smith-Hughes Act, and the Rosenwald Fund, Yerger worked to improve the school so that it could provide a quality education for blacks in the area. From 1886 until his death in 1936, Yerger worked to expand the school's physical plant, taking the school from a one-room building to a two-story structure with annexes for domestic science and arts, a seven-room elementary building, an agricultural department, and a girl's dormitory. As the school's physical plant expanded so did its academic program. Under Yerger's leadership, the Shover Street School, later renamed the H. C. Yerger High School, earned the distinction of being the first training school for blacks west of the Mississippi that offered its students a twelve-grade curriculum that included English, algebra, geometry, Latin, agricultural science, domestic science and art, social science, and choral music. Because of its complete educational program and excellent facilities the state's Department of Education, when it became interested in training black teachers in the 1920s, selected Hope and Yerger High School as one of the sites for its summer teacher training program.[31]

CHAPTER 3

Educating the Mind and the Spirit

The 1920s

In 1914 the nations of Europe hurled themselves into World War One, called the Great War in the United States. The United States entered the conflict in 1917 in order to, in the words of President Woodrow Wilson, "make the world safe for democracy." Many in the white community, aware of the heavy burden of Jim Crow that blacks shouldered, wondered if blacks would be loyal to the nation while it waged a war abroad for what was being denied them at home. Black Arkansans, however, like the great majority of blacks throughout the nation, fully supported the American war effort with the expectation that victory abroad would lead to greater democracy for them on the home front. The Reverend Elias Camp Morris, the most prominent black Baptist minister in Arkansas, and Bishop James M. Conner of the African Methodist Episcopal Church (A.M.E.), Morris's counterpart, aptly summed up their views. Bishop Conner, speaking to state authorities through addresses to A.M.E. members, let it be known that "in this war we are going to do our part . . . In this crisis . . . we should forget our creeds, classes, colors, and conditions, and stand out for Americanism—unsullied, untrammeled, and undismayed." And Morris also let it be known that blacks were supportive of the war effort when he commented: "In all the trials through which we have come we have possessed our souls in peace, and there are no sacrifices which we are not ready to make now for our God and our country, if those sacrifices are to bring the race the same privileges which the law guarantees to all other American citizens."[1]

The Great War came to an end in 1918 and black hopes for greater democracy on the home front quickly vaporized as returning black soldiers were greeted with an outburst of violence and hatred that spawned race riots across the nation, from Washington, D.C., to California. But unlike the riots that characterized the nation at the turn of the century when white mobs invaded the black community with little resistance, this time blacks fought back. The war had produced what Alain Locke, a noted Howard University art critic, author, and professor of literature, defined as the "New Negro." This "New Negro," according to Locke, was no longer passive in the face of racial injustice and was willing to fight in order to defend what he believed were his constitutional rights as a United States citizen. This determination of blacks to defend themselves against white mob violence led James Weldon Johnson, executive secretary of the National Association for the Advancement of Colored People, to describe the riots and bloodshed as the "Red Summer of 1919." Arkansas also experienced this new determination of blacks to seek racial equity, which led to a violent confrontation at Elaine, Arkansas, in the fall of 1919 between the forces of change and those who sought to maintain the pre–WWI status quo. The confrontation, which left scores of black dead or missing, grew out of an attempt by black tenant farmers and sharecroppers to organize a union in order to force local white planters to grant them a fair settlement for their labor and crops. L. S. (Sharpe) Dunaway, a white minister and keen observer of Arkansas culture and politics, said the Elaine incident was "the blackest page in Arkansas history."[2] After the Elaine massacre, black Arkansans readily identified with Emmett Scott, the special assistant for Negro affairs in the War Department during WWI, who expressed his disappointment with the postwar treatment of blacks when he wrote: "as one who recalls the assurances of 1917 and 1918 . . . I personally confess a deep sense of disappointment, of poignant pain that a great country in time of need should promise so much and afterward perform so little."[3]

Although the hopes and dreams of black Arkansans for greater freedom and democracy in the wake of WWI were, for all practical purposes, destroyed in what Leroy Williams described as a "racially hostile society," they were determined to forge a better future for themselves.[4] Some saw their hopes for the future in northern industrial cities and continued the northward migration that had begun during WWI. Many white Arkansans were also concerned about the northward migration of large numbers of blacks, their cheap labor force, during the war. Bishop Conner had an answer to that problem. "If you educate him [the Negro]," he declared, "you will tie him to the South and in return he will give you a law abiding citizen."[5] Better education was indeed a major goal of black Arkansans, and black public school administrators and teachers took the lead in the effort to expand and improve the quality of education available. They were aided in their quest by a new state law that required all teachers to be certified. This statute legally negated a practice by the state Department of Education that allowed high school seniors to teach in black schools. With the adoption of the state teacher certification law, the rallying cry of the Arkansas Teachers Association, the representative body for black teachers in the state, became "A trained teacher in every school in Arkansas."[6] The ATA wanted, at a minimum, all elementary school teachers to be high school graduates and all high school teachers to be college graduates. Responding to the ATAs call and its "Let's Go to Summer School" campaign, more than one hundred teachers, at the urging of their principals and with financial support from the Rosenwald and Jeanes Funds, enrolled in extension and teacher training courses offered by the State Teachers College in Conway and the University of Arkansas at Fayetteville. This was a tremendous step forward because these courses had been limited to whites prior to 1920.

In addition to improving the quality of instruction in black public schools, black leaders also wanted the state to end inequities in funding for black and white schools. The extent of funding disparities between black and white schools is difficult to ascertain because Department of Education records for funding of public schools by race between 1895 and 1928 are incomplete. Records for the 1928–1929 academic year, however, reveal that the state spent an average of $35.05 per white student in its public schools compared to $14.38 per black student.[7] In the 1920s, as blacks became more vocal in their quest for equal educational opportunities, significant improvements were made in black public school facilities as evidenced by the construction of a new vocational education shop at the Conway County Training School in Menifee; the new library at the Pulaski County Training School near McAlmont; the new vocational shop in College Station (Pulaski County); a new teacherage (on-campus home for teachers) and a vocational shop at the Columbia County Training School at Freehope (near Magnolia, Arkansas); a new building at Rowland (Cleveland County); and a new school building in Helena (Phillips County).

Although the number of new facilities constructed for black schools in the early 1920s appeared to be impressive, the state could take little credit and they fell short of the need. Records of the Arkansas Department of Education reveal that the majority of new facilities were constructed in rural areas and financed primarily by the General Education, Rosenwald, and Jeanes Funds and by approximately $30,000 in contributions from the blacks themselves.[8] Crucial to the operations of these new rural facilities were federal funds given to the state through the Smith-Hughes Act, 1917–1927. This legislation focused upon rural America and provided matching funds for the teaching of agriculture in the public schools (teacher training, salaries, agricultural projects). One facet of the legislation required participant schools to enroll young men in state fair competition and to prepare projects for evaluation at their annual state fair. The schools engaged students in four days of intensive training in the handling of agricultural equipment, the growing of field crops, and the raising of livestock and poultry. The Arkansas State Fair, unlike fairs in other southern states, did not separate the projects from black and white schools; all were judged on their own merit. After years of steady progress, projects from black schools won several first-place votes at the 1927 fair.[9] The performance of black students at the Arkansas State Fair was but one example of what black administrators and teachers could accomplish while being denied the funds they needed for their programs. This was significant because black schools in the state were the most needy, but Smith-Hughes funds were distributed by the state's Department of Education not on need but on population percentages. Subsequently, 72 percent of the funds went to white schools and 28 percent to black schools. The percentages represented the black and white population of the state.[10] The inequities in funding, however, did not prevent black administrators from encouraging their teachers and students to strive for excellence.

Black Principals in the 1920s

The records of rural schools in the 1920s have been largely lost, and since there were few black high schools in Arkansas prior to 1926, only twelve, records of the contributions of black administrators to the education of their pupils are at best sketchy. Many of the educators, however, labored in Arkansas's public schools for several decades, and through the few existing records, interviews with those still alive as of this writing, and interviews with families and those who lived in the communities they served, a partial record can be reconstructed.

Central Arkansas

R. C. Barrow and Coy Carr. Barrow, 1923–1925, and Carr, 1925–1931, were two of the legendary principals of Langston High School in Hot Springs (Garland County), Arkansas. Under their leadership Langston was known statewide for its exceptional educational programs and for the success of its graduates.

Southeast Arkansas

William Townsend. Born in Port Gibson, Mississippi (1864), to a financially strapped minister of the gospel, Townsend became one of the early pioneer educators in Arkansas. After graduating from the public schools in Mississippi, his love for learning led him to Alcorn College (Mississippi). Because his parents could not afford to pay for his college education, Townsend worked his way through Alcorn, earning a B.S. degree in 1886. His religious background, his strong desire for knowledge, and his work experiences at Alcorn characterized the remainder of his life. Following his graduation from college, Townsend migrated to the Reed Settlement outside of Monticello, Arkansas, where he began work as a public schoolteacher on July 18, 1886. This job was the beginning of a lifetime career in Arkansas's public schools. In 1893, Townsend began his career as an administrator when he was named principal of the Main Pike School in Pine Bluff (Jefferson County), Arkansas. After one year at Pike, he was named principal (1894) of the Missouri Street School and in 1901 principal of Merrill High School. He remained at Merrill for the next forty years. Townsend was not only an administrator, he was also an effective teacher. He believed that administrators and teachers were required to teach by example and precepts, and he led his staff in that direction.

One of the overriding goals of Townsend was to improve school facilities for black students. To that end he was able to persuade the local all-white school board, in the waning years of his tenure, to construct a new brick building on West Pullen Street for Merrill High. During the same time period he laid the groundwork, at considerable expense, for the purchase of the nearby Longley Park as a playground and athletic field for the school. This project was completed by his successor, R. N. Chanay.[11] In recognition of Townsend's long and outstanding years of service to the city's public schools, a city park and an elementary school were named in his honor.

Lessie V. Davis. Davis was the principal of North Ashlar Street School, grades 1–11, in West Helena (Phillips County), Arkansas, 1922–1924. Documents relative to Davis's accomplishments at North Ashlar have been lost, but elderly residents who remember her recall her strong emphasis on home and school working together to improve student performance and her struggle to get financial support for the school.

O. S. Hammonds. Hammonds was the principal of the Myrtle Street Junior High School in Warren (Bradley County), Arkansas, 1928. He is best remembered for instituting junior high (ninth grade) graduation exercises at the school. Since few black students during the era finished high school, the junior high graduation exercises became one of the social events of the year in the black community.

N. F. Jackson. Mr. Jackson served as principal of Washington High School in El Dorado (Union County), Arkansas, from 1927 to 1954. His strong interest in and support for education resulted in a dramatic increase in graduation rates. Due to his leadership skills, he was elected to two terms as president of the Arkansas Teachers Association, 1930–1933. During his presidency, vocational education in the state's black training schools was emphasized and flourished with the assistance of teachers provided by the Jeanes Fund.

D. W. Jamerson. When Jamerson was named principal of the Chicot County Training School in Dermott (Chicot County), Arkansas, in 1925, the school covered only grades 1–8. By 1929 he had persuaded the local school board to add grades 9–12. He went on to implement a quality curriculum that brought statewide recognition to the school and its graduates.

Southwest Arkansas

Theron Jones. Between 1927 and 1935, Jones was the principal of Washington High School in Texarkana (Miller County), Arkansas. He has been credited with the development of the school's first strong college prep instructional program. This is significant because the vast majority of black schools during the era focused their attention on industrial education.

James Patterson. Patterson was the principal of Southland

School at Lexa (Phillips County), Arkansas, in 1922. Lexa was a poor rural farming community where the black residents realized that education was the escape route from poverty for their children. They remarkably managed to raise enough money to secure a Rosenwald Fund grant for the construction of a school, and Patterson was named principal. Patterson, subsequently, established a strong parent-teacher association, home economic clubs for young women, and 4-H Clubs for young men. He also added to the school's offerings an adult education program, an after-school tutoring program, and a civil defense program. Under Patterson's leadership, the Rosenwald School at Southland became the educational, social, and political hub of the community.

Pearl Franklin Pettis. Pettis was named principal of the combined West Side Elementary and Junior High School in the West Helena (Phillips County), Arkansas, School District, from 1922 to 1924. During her tenure a sound academic program was implemented and a new red brick school was constructed to replace the old dilapidated wood-frame building. Pettis left the principalship of the West Side school to become district supervisor of elementary and junior high education from 1944 to 1949.

CHAPTER 4

The Depression Era

Black Administrators in Arkansas, 1929–1941

The Great Depression of the 1930s struck a materially progressive and socially playful America with the force of an erupting volcano. Businesses, public and social institutions, and the hopes and aspirations of untold millions that were produced by the prosperity of the 1920s faded away like sand castles trying to withstand the force of a tidal wave. Many of the problems faced by Arkansans during the depression years were not new ones; rather, they were old ones aggravated by the sharp economic downturn. One of the areas hardest hit in Arkansas was funding for public education which impacted black schools disproportionately. Prior to the depression, financial support for public education in Arkansas lagged behind other states but improvements were slowly being made. Between 1878 and 1929, the beginning of the depression, state expenditures for public education increased from $276,647 to $14,486,799, respectively. And school enrollments increased from 42,481 to 98,548 for blacks and from 122,296 to 321,558 for whites.[1] The increase in the number of black students attending school and the funding of those schools are somewhat misleading because many blacks in small towns and rural areas had no school to attend. For example, public education for blacks in Sheridan was not available until 1926.[2] And many counties spent less for the operation of black schools than they did for white schools. For the 1927–1928 academic year fifteen counties spent less than they received from the state for funding black schools. Chicot County serves as another example. For the 1927–1928 academic year, the county spent $23,054 on black public schools but received $28,384.88 for black schools from the state.[3]

The failure of local school boards in the state to spend state funds appropriated for black schools reflected the segregationist and white supremacy ideas of many local white school officials. This was clearly reflected in the decisions made by the local superintendent of schools in heavily black populated Jefferson County who declared:

> I started out on the theory that the county superintendent is super-
> intendent of Negro schools as well as white, but being a white man,
> I should first take care of the white schools. This is the only policy
> with which a county superintendent may work in the South.[4]

Subsequently, Jefferson County in 1930 spent $48.37 per white student in its public schools and $16.15 per black student, based upon average daily attendance (ADA). Reflecting this discriminating expenditure pattern in 1930, Chicot County spent $54.11 per white student and $6.35 per black student; Lee County spent $67.67 and $15.10, respectively, on white and black public school students; and Pulaski County, which had the best funded black public schools in the state, spent $61.41 and $32.03, respectively, on its white and black students in the public school system.[5]

Many black schools in Arkansas, due to inequitable state funding, were only able to keep their doors open due to the existence of several out-of-state philanthropic organizations that contributed funds to the state specifically for the support of black public schools. Chief among these were the George F. Peabody Fund (1867), the John F. Slater Fund (1882), the Anna T. Jeanes Fund (1907), and the Julius Rosenwald Fund (1912). Between 1876 and 1932, these funds gave Arkansas thousands of dollars for the construction of black schools, teacher training and salaries, equipment purchases, and transportation. Approximately 45 percent of all black schoolchildren in Arkansas attended schools designed and, to a large extent, paid for by these funds.[6] In his 1930–1932 biennial report on the state of education in Arkansas, C. M. Hurst, state commissioner of education, wrote that "the status of Negro education could not have been reached without the aid of the Funds and to them the state owes a lasting gratitude."[7]

Philanthropic support and state funding for black schools declined during the Great Depression. Between 1930 and 1935, state funding for public education dropped from $18,843,130 to $11,742,388.[8] Public education in the state was in a crisis situation. In 1934 one disgusted educator said of the public schools: "They are dying, Rigor mortis has already begun . . ."[9] Despite the critical state of public education, there was little sentiment for improvement on the part of the state's political leadership. In fact, the governor, J. M. Futrell, believed that a grammar school education was all that was needed to adequately prepare Arkansans to be useful and productive citizens. He was vehemently opposed to state funding for high schools on the grounds that only 10 percent of eligible students attended. High schools, he reasoned, were the responsibility of the counties and the school districts in which they were located.[10]

Fortunately for Arkansas, the philanthropic funds and the federal government, through the Federal Emergency Relief Administration (FERA), continued to support public education in the state during the depression. By 1934, however, continued FERA support had become contingent upon increased state support. In 1934 Harry Hopkins, FERA director, informed Governor Futrell that federal aid would be suspended if the 1935 General Assembly did not pass legislation to support public education.[11] When the 1935 legislature opened, Futrell was faced with the loss of federal educational funds, which would have adversely affected his political career, and urged the legislature to pass appropriate funding for education. He told the legislature that if it did not increase funding for education "it is going to be sorry because we are sitting on a powder keg."[12] The legislature responded with the passage of the Hall Sales Tax Act which levied a 2 percent sales tax on all commodities except food and medicine. Of the $2,250,000 the tax was expected to generate, $1,500,000 was set aside for public education.[13]

The infusion of new monies into Arkansas's public school system benefited black schools little. During the depression era, 1930–1940, black students averaged 24 percent of statewide student enrollments, but black schools received only 10.2 percent of the state school expenditures. During the decade, white schools averaged $32 per white student in the public schools compared to $12 per black student.[14] The growth in black high school attendance during the period was phenomenal, expanding more than 150 percent. The percentage of black high school graduates also increased, and for the first time black schools established a greater percentage in average daily attendance than whites.[15] The increase in black student ADA can be accounted for, in part, by the lack of jobs during the depression and, in part, by the growing emphasis of black parents on education as barriers against unemployment during hard times.

In the midst of growing student enrollments during the depression decade, inadequate state funding for black schools, and poor teacher salaries, $429 per year for white teachers and $290 for blacks, black public school administrators struggled to keep school doors open. The great majority of instruction in those schools, as mandated by the state Department of Education, centered around agricultural, industrial, and vocational training. "It is the firm belief of this division," wrote the state commissioner of education in his 1938–1940 report on black schools, "that more time should be given and greater emphasis should be placed on the vocational interests, needs, and activities of Negro youth and adults in the home, on the farm, and in the shops of the community . . ."[16] While black educational leaders followed the script provided by the education department, they also strove to provide their students with more than basic agricultural and vocational skills.

Southwest Arkansas

While laboring in southwest Arkansas to implement the state Department of Education's plans for black schools and to broaden the horizons of their students, a number of black principals went beyond the call of duty.

Will Vernon Rutherford Sr. This pioneer educator was born in Wilmar, Arkansas, where he received his public school education. In 1931, he earned a B.A. degree at Arkansas Baptist College in Little Rock; he completed additional study at AM&N College at Pine Bluff and later earned a master's degree at the University of Arkansas at Fayetteville. Following several years of teaching in Arkansas public schools, Rutherford was named principal of Yerger High School in Hope, Arkansas, where he served from 1949 to 1969. In 1969, due to the desegregation of the Hope public schools, Yerger High became a Yerger Junior High School, and Rutherford continued as principal until his retirement in 1972. During his tenure as principal of Yerger High, Rutherford engineered the construction of an annex to the school, which featured a new cafeteria and a vocational education building. He also improved the quality of the school curriculum, which led to full accreditation by the North Central Association of Colleges and Schools in 1958.

While leading Yerger High up the ladder of academic excellence, Rutherford was also active in his professional organizations. He was a founding member of the Arkansas Administrators Association, a branch of the Arkansas Teachers Association, and served as the ATA's treasurer prior to its merger with the Arkansas Education Association. He was also the recipient of numerous plaques and certificates for dedicated educational service. When Rutherford retired in 1972, the Hope community came together and paid special tribute to his years of service. He credited his success to the values and education he received while attending Arkansas Baptist College, and he and his wife donated $10,000 to the institution because "Arkansas Baptist College took me in when I had nothing and gave me something back in my life, thus I believe the Lord uses some of us as instruments for His work here on earth and perhaps in this way I am an instrument of His will."

Charles E. Green. Green was the first principal of the Magnolia Colored School in Columbia County, serving from 1915 to 1942. When Green began his principalship in Magnolia, the school covered only the first eight grades and he taught the seventh grade. Under Green's leadership, however, the Magnolia Colored School became the Columbia County Training School for blacks with a twelve-year program and graduated its first class of seven students at the end of the 1939–1940 academic year.

Edward Daniel Robinson. This Arkansas native earned a B.A. degree from Philander Smith College in Little Rock, Arkansas, in 1939 and an M.A. from Fisk University in Nashville, Tennessee, in 1953. He began his career in public education in 1939 at the McCaskill School (Hempstead County) as a social studies teacher where he taught until being named principal of the local Blevins Training School in 1941. After ten years of service at Blevins, Robinson relocated to Stephens (Ouachita County), Arkansas, where he served as principal of Carver High School from 1951 to 1961. He left Stephens at the end of the 1960–1961 academic year and moved to El Dorado (Union County), Arkansas, where he served as the principal of the Washington High School from 1961 to 1963. From El Dorado, Robinson moved to Lewisville (Lafayette County), Arkansas and served as principal of the Foster High School from 1964 to 1968. He left public education in 1968 and accepted a position with the state of Arkansas as manager of the AfterCare Youth Program of Juvenile Services. He held this position until his retirement in 1977.

During his years in public education, Robinson was active in professional organizations. He served as the president of the Hempstead County Teachers Association from 1948 to 1950 and as vice president of the Ouachita County Teachers Association. These associations were affiliates of the Arkansas Teachers Association. As a principal, Robinson was a member of the Southwest School Administrators Association, 1954–1956; the State School Administrators Association, 1956–1958; and the National Association of Secondary School Principals. He also served as one of the first black members of a North Central Association accreditation team visiting schools in Arkansas. Because of his contributions to education in Arkansas, Robinson was the recipient of an award from the National Association of Secondary School Principals and is listed in *Who's Who in American Education*, XXI, 1963–1964.

James Elmer Wallace. Wallace, of Fordyce, Arkansas, served as the principal of the Dallas County Training School for thirty-nine years, from 1923 to 1962. During his tenure the school grew from an enrollment of thirty-three in 1923 to over five hundred in 1962. In virtually all of the reports of the Arkansas Department of Education during the 1920s and 1930s, a critical shortage of black certified teachers was highlighted. Wallace, however, was able to persuade "all" of his teachers to become certified in their disciplines. He was also able to secure for his teachers nine paid sick leave days per year. He also organized the school's first competitive athletic program. Wallace's effective leadership of the Dallas County Training School earned him the respect of his peers across the state, and he was elected president of the Arkansas Teachers Association from 1932 to 1934.

In 1917 Congress passed the Smith-Hughes Act to promote, in part, the teaching of agriculture in rural schools. States who participated in the program were required to match federal funds dollar for dollar. By 1927 there were twenty-three Smith-Hughes agricultural teachers in Arkansas, one of whom was Wallace. He held the dual post of principal and Smith-Hughes teacher until the state legislature passed a statute in 1951 that forbade a person from holding two positions in the same school system. Consequently, Wallace resigned as principal of the Dallas County Training School and his wife, Mrs. Eula B. Wallace, was appointed by the school board as his replacement. She served in that position from 1951 to 1954. In 1954, Mr. Wallace resigned from his job as a Smith-Hughes teacher and assumed the full-time principalship of the Dallas

County Training School and served until his death in 1962. On February 12, 1962, the board of the Dallas County Training School, in recognition of Wallace's long years of dedicated service, changed the name of the school to the J. E. Wallace School.

Benjamin George Williams. Williams was a native of Coldwater, Mississippi, but received his high school education in the high school branch of Arkansas Baptist College in Little Rock, Arkansas. After graduation from the Arkansas Baptist High School, Williams attended Lemoyne College in Memphis, Tennessee, but returned to Arkansas and earned the B.A. degree in sociology at AM&N College in Pine Bluff. He also earned an M.A. degree in school management from Indiana University and completed additional studies at the University of Arkansas and the University of Oklahoma.

Williams began his career in public education in Arkansas at Waldo (Columbia County), Arkansas, where he worked until being named principal of Walker Elementary School in Magnolia (Columbia County), Arkansas, where he served from 1940 to 1946. He was named superintendent of the Walker School District in 1946 and held that position for nine years. During his superintendency, Williams was instrumental in the consolidation of the district's five elementary schools. In 1955, Columbia County began to slowly desegregate its public schools, and Williams left the Walker School District to accept a position with the Department of Education (DOE) as a supervisor of instructions. He remained with the Department of Education for eleven years and traveled throughout the state evaluating academic programs and ranking them for accreditation recommendations. In 1966, Williams moved to the Federal Programs Division of the DOE where he was a supervisor of federal programs (Title 1, Area 3) in eastern Arkansas. In 1969 he became the highest-ranking black in the history of the DOE when he was promoted to the position of associate commissioner for federal programs. He held this position until his retirement in 1979. Upon Williams's retirement his supervisor, Dr. Don Roberts, stated that he always gave a day's work for a day's pay and was a "gentle and humane individual." Following his retirement, Williams was elected to the Little Rock School Board and served until 1985. He officially retired from public life in 1985 and moved to Hot Springs, Arkansas, where he planned to spend his golden years. Although officially retired, he remained active in his fraternity, Omega Psi Phi, and in local civic affairs.

Before leaving the public schools, Williams was active in his local, county, and state educational organizations. He served as president of the Columbia County Teachers Association and as the state director of the American Teachers Association. He was also a member of the Advisory Committee on School Administration, the State Committee on Teacher Education, and a member of the Governor's Advisory Committee on Education. In 1994, Williams was honored at a banquet at the Arlington Hotel in Hot Springs, where he was recognized for fifty years of educational service and the B. G. Williams Scholarship ($500) was established. The scholarship is to be awarded biennially to a third-year Arkansas college student majoring in teacher education. The first scholarship recipient was Nakiea Williams, a graduate of the UAPB School of Education.

J. W. Vines. Vines served as one of the depression era's principals (1932–1935) of the all-black Oak Grove School in Rosston (Nevada County), Arkansas. The district was established in 1920 when J. W. Teeter, the white superintendent of schools for Nevada County, was persuaded by a group of influential blacks to create an all-black school district with its own superintendent and school board.[17] Vines was one of the district's more successful administrators during its formative years. In view of the economic and educational climate of the period, Vines's accomplishments were outstanding. Originally from Jonesboro, Arkansas, he was hired as principal and agricultural teacher of the Oak Grove School in 1932. Many principals in black schools during the period were also agriculture teachers. These "ag-men," as they were called, were paid more than regular teachers, and since they were paid more, it was believed that they should have more responsibility.[18] The night before Vines's first day on the job, the Rosenwald School for blacks burned. Vines immediately went about the business of getting the school rebuilt. During his third day on the job, he and C. C. Bazzelle, president of the school board, went to Little Rock where they were able to secure a grant from the Works Projects Administration (WPA) to build a new school. The WPA grant required the local community to provide all building materials, which it did, while the agency contributed the labor. This was the first WPA project of this kind in southwest Arkansas, and when it was completed it was one of the most impressive schools in the state. The new building had an auditorium in its center, classrooms on each end, an office for the principal, a library, and a covered entrance and covered grades 1–10. The school had only nine grades when Vines was hired. In 1935, Vines was able to secure another WPA grant for the construction of a home economics building. While the new buildings for the Oak Grove School were under construction, Vines often joined in the work. As one of his contemporaries observed: "It was never too early or to late for him to be on the job."[19] When the building projects were completed the Oak Grove School became the Nevada County Training School and accommodated students from throughout the county.

L. W. Johnson. Expanding upon the foundation laid by Oak Grove principal J. W. Vines and school board president C. C. Bazzelle, Johnson, the first black superintendent of the Oak Grove Consolidated School District in Rosston (Nevada County), Arkansas, continued the process of developing the Oak Grove School into a first-rate educational institution. Under his leadership, 1935–1949, the Oak Grove School grew from an institution offering education through the first nine grades to a complete high school (grades 1–12). Prior to Johnson's tenure students desiring a high school education had to go elsewhere at their own expense. When the last two grades were added, Oak Grove attracted students from throughout Nevada County and surrounding areas. To accompany the influx of new students, Johnson was able to persuade blacks and local whites to contribute funds for the purchase of an additional 105 acres of land upon which a new elementary school, teachers' cottages, and dormitories for boys and girls were constructed. The teachers' cottages afforded the rural school district the opportunity to attract and retain quality teachers and the dormitories provided students from outside of Rosston with on-campus housing while completing their high school education.[20]

The instructional program at the Nevada County Training School kept pace with the building program, and the school was renamed the Oak Grove High School and recognized throughout Arkansas and surrounding states. Visitors often referred to Oak Grove High School as "a little Tuskegee," because of its resemblance to the educational program offered at Tuskegee Institute under the leadership of Booker T. Washington.[21]

In addition to its excellent educational program, Oak Grove High School was also known for its fearsome basketball teams, which defeated almost all of its competitors. The success of the basketball program is notable, considering that the team had no gym in which to practice or play games. The local white high school in nearby Prescott occasionally and reluctantly allowed Oak Grove to use its gym for home games if nothing else was scheduled. To rectify this situation, Johnson spearheaded a drive for the construction of a gym on the Oak Grove campus. With the assistance of Basil Munn, the county superintendent for white schools, Johnson contacted representatives of the Works Projects Administration, one of Franklin D. Roosevelt's New Deal depression recovery agencies, and requested funds for the construction of a gymnasium for Oak Grove because "the school does not have any building for recreational activities." The WPA granted Johnson's request, and the construction of the gym began in May 1938 and was completed in 1939. The new facility was named the Wortham Gymnasium in honor of Roger Q. Wortham, the county judge for Nevada County and supporter of Oak Grove's educational program. The Wortham Gymnasium was the first high school gym for blacks in Arkansas, a fact that Johnson never tired of boasting about. The facility not only provided a home for Oak Grove's basketball teams, it was also a multipurpose building that served as a community center. Because of its architectural design and importance to the black community in Nevada County, the Wortham Gymnasium was listed on the National Register of Historic Places on April 19, 1990.[22]

Johnson's success won him the respect and admiration of his peers throughout the state, and he was elected as president of the Arkansas State Summer School Teachers Association, registrar of the Arkansas Teachers Association, and vice president of the Arkansas Principals and Head Teachers Alliance. He also served as president of the AM&N College Alumni Association, the Arkansas Teachers Association, and the Jefferson County Retired Teachers Association.

Mattie Bazzelle. Mrs. Bazzelle was one of several principals who served the all-black, including the school board, public school system in Rosston (Nevada County), Arkansas. The local Oak Grove High School was one of the few schools for blacks in southwest Arkansas and, consequently, attracted students from throughout the region. In addition to an array of educational buildings, Oak Grove also had one of the largest gymnasiums in southwest Arkansas and often hosted the state basketball championship games for black schools.

Bazzelle was the principal of the Oak Grove High School from 1940 to 1961. Under her leadership the school experienced steady growth in facilities and educational programs. In 1961, Mrs. Bazzelle was named superintendent of the Oak Grove School District, a position she held for one year, 1961–1962. During her superintendency, Mrs. Bazzelle added adult education to Oak Grove's academic programs. The programs, of which she was especially proud, provided many of the adults in this rural agricultural community the opportunity to earn the equivalency of a high school diploma by earning a GED.

In 1962, Mrs. Bazzelle left the superintendency of the Oak Grove School District and returned to her position as the principal of the Oak Grove High School. During her second tour of duty, 1962–1976, the name of the Oak Grove High School was changed to the Oak Grove/Nevada County Training School. This change occurred because the school served not only the black population in the city of Rosston where it was located, but all of Nevada County. Several of the school's graduates during Mrs. Bazzelle tenure went on to graduate from college and earn graduate degrees in law, theology, medicine, and higher education. Their success was a reflection of Mrs. Bazzelle's philosophy which stressed "educating the whole child for a full life dedicated to educational enrichment."[23]

C. E. Smith. Smith was a pioneer educator in Emerson (Columbia County), where he served as principal of the Doss Academy Community School from 1930 to 1940. Doss Academy was a junior high school, and Smith added a grade until the school graduated its first students in 1937. The land upon which the academy was built was donated by Anthony Doss, a local black supporter of education.

Emma Peyton. Mrs. Peyton was one of the leaders of the struggle to bring quality education to the black community in Malvern (Hot Spring County) during the waning years of the Great Depression. She served as principal of the black school in Malvern from 1939 to 1941. When she came to Malvern, the black school covered only the first nine grades. Students desiring a high school education had to move to Little Rock or other cities that had black high schools. One of the goals of Peyton was to provide a quality education for her students. A second goal was to garner community support for the school. Her first move was to reorganize the defunct Parent Teacher Association (PTA). Her slogan was: "It's not my school, it's not your school, it's our school." Community response was overwhelming. The community contributed cooking utensils to the school, and volunteers from the reorganized PTA cooked and served food to approximately 250 students per day. To broaden the educational horizon of students, Peyton added music education and dramatic arts into the school's curriculum. She also established, for the first time, a competitive junior high athletic program (boys' and girls' basketball). When Peyton was forced to resign in 1941 due to illness, the Malvern Junior High School was recognized as one of the best in the region.[24]

Southeast Arkansas

Southeast Arkansas contained some of the most fertile farmland in the state. The region was controlled by large plantation owners whose first priority was not the education of the black populace, most of whom were poor sharecroppers or tenant farmers. Often the sharecroppers were forced by the white planters to keep their children out of school in order to work the cotton fields. The majority of Arkansas's black population was located in the delta, and few of the children attended school. According to the 1938–1940 report of the state commissioner of education, only 5 percent of black youth attended high school and less than one-half of 1 percent graduated.[25] Several black school principals and educators, however, fought to overcome the odds and improve the education and quality of life for the region's impoverished black population.

Edith Stewart. Stewart was one of the many educators who worked to expand the intellectual and cultural environment of blacks beyond the traditional agricultural and vocational domains. She served as the principal of St. Mary Rosenwald School in Phillips County from 1936 until 1950. Stewart is best known for the introduction of art education classes at St. Mary's.

Samuel L. Minor. Minor served as principal of the Mount Holly Elementary and Junior High School at Mount Holly (Union

County) from 1930 to 1949. Union County had a large black population consisting of sharecroppers, day laborers, and domestics.
Minor worked hard to show his students that there were nonagricultural jobs available if they acquired a good education.
Subsequently, while at Mount Holly, he initiated an after-school
stay-in-school program. One night per month, Minor met with students and parents in the community and distributed and discussed
literature relative to nonagricultural careers.[26]

Albert M. Williams. Williams's career as a public school administrator began in 1940 when he was named principal of the Selma
Junior High School in Monticello (Drew County), where he served
from 1940 to 1943. He apparently worked out of state before returning to Monticello as the principal of Drew County High School
from 1969 to 1970. He only served one year as principal of Drew
County High, but it was a productive year. Under his leadership the
school experienced notable improvements in its academic programs,
its faculty qualifications, and its physical plant.

Northeast Arkansas

Northeast Arkansas, like its southeastern neighbor, is an integral
part of the rich (farmland) Arkansas delta. And, like its neighbor,
there was little emphasis placed upon the education of blacks by the
ruling planter elite. During the depression, for example, Lee County
spent, on the average, only $15.10 per black student in the public
schools compared to $67.67 per white student.[27] The inequities in
educational funding, however, did not prevent black principals and
educators from trying to improve the education and self-sufficiency
of the black community.

Elmyra M. Brown. Born on a farm near Proctor (Crittenden
County), Arkansas, Brown began her career in public education as
a classroom teacher. In the late 1940s she was named principal of
the McCrory (Woodruff County) "Colored School" where she
served until her retirement in the 1950s.[28] Woodruff County, like
the majority of the counties in the Arkansas delta, was cotton country, and the black school received little financial support from the
school board, which was comprised of local white planters. Brown,
however, was able to persuade the board to improve the school's
physical plant. She also encouraged her teaching staff to return to
college to complete their degrees and improve their teaching skills

and spent countless hours working with black parents in an effort to expand their education and get them involved in the academic programs of her school. The community demonstrated its support for her efforts by naming the school where she worked Brown Elementary. Others also recognized the value of her contributions to the education of the black community in McCrory, and she is listed in *Who's Who for American Black Women*. Mrs. Brown, who is over ninety years of age, currently (2001) lives in Hot Springs, Arkansas.

Hyman King. This depression-era/World War II educator began his administrative career in public education at J. S. Phelix High School in Marion (Crittenden County), Arkansas, where he served from 1939 until 1947. He was the school's first full-time principal. At the end of the 1947 academic year, King left Phelix High to accept the principalship of the Morrilton Colored School (named L. W. Sullivan High during his administration) in Morrilton, Arkansas. He was the principal of the black school in Morrilton from 1947 until its closure in 1965 due to desegregation. Under King's leadership, Sullivan High School earned a State Department of Education rating of "A" and was in the process of being evaluated for membership in the North Central Association of Colleges and Schools when it was closed. During King's principalship, Sullivan High was noted for the academic achievements of its students and the 100 percent membership in state and national professional education associations. Following his retirement from public education, King devoted the majority of his time to the religious programs of his church, St. Paul A.M.E., where he served as a steward and trustee.

Frederick C. Turner. This talented and dedicated educator began his administrative career in public education as the principal of the Nevada County Training School, 1925–1932, in the Oak Grove School District. During these years Turner and Mrs. Ila D. Upchurch, the Jeanes Fund supervisor for the district, secured funds from the Rosenwald Foundation for the construction of the district's first modern school building. The Oak Grove School District was located in a rural farming area, and it was difficult for students to get to and from school. To solve this problem, Turner and Upchurch also worked together to secure the district's first bus for student transportation. The bus was actually a truck which was fitted with benches and covered. Turner also expanded the school's curriculum to include music and home economics.

Turner left Nevada County in 1932 and moved to Jonesboro (Craighead County), Arkansas, where he served as the principal of Booker T. Washington High School, 1932–1946. As the principal of Booker T. Washington, Turner was both an educator and social worker. He not only stressed academic excellence, but also worked with parents to make sure that students had what they needed to learn, including food and clothing. He often purchased supplies for students out of his own pocket.[29] Turner believed, according to Mrs. Frances Cole Johnson, one of his former students, that "a child could not learn when he was hungry and cold."

During his administration at Booker T. Washington, Turner strengthened the school curriculum, added a music department, and organized a competitive debate team that competed throughout northeast Arkansas. The debate team often doubled as a choral group specializing in spirituals. The choral group practiced after school hours. Turner, an accomplished vocalist, worked with the young men, and his music teachers, who taught music and English during school hours, worked with the young women. Turner's willingness to spend long hours with the students of Booker T. Washington in order to develop them educationally and socially won him the support and respect of the black community. According to one of his former students, Mrs. Izora McKinney Prentice, "Professor Turner's major accomplishment (at Booker T. Washington and in the black community) was to raise the Negro students understanding of the importance of education. He worked not only with the students but also with their parents. Economic background nor social standing had absolutely no bearing on his work in the community. He established and institutionalized programs that enhanced students ability to speak publicly and to promote the concept of self-reliance and service. Although during Mr. Turner's principalship, Arkansas had an agricultural economy, he prepared us for the Industrial Age."

In 1946, Turner resigned from his principalship of Booker T. Washington and joined the nation's armed forces and traveled throughout Europe as a member of the American Red Cross. Following his tour of military service, he became a federal employee and worked for the government until he retired. Turner died in 1993, but his contributions to the Jonesboro community live on. His son, Frederick Turner Jr., was one of the first black students to be admitted to and graduated from Arkansas State University, the local white university in Jonesboro. He later returned to the university as the first black member of its Department of Military Science (Reserve Officers Training Corps). He and his wife, the late Gussie Turner, are the parents of former Miss America Debbie Turner, who is also a graduate of Arkansas State University.

Stanley McIntosh. From 1933 to 1940, McIntosh served as principal of the Armorel schools for blacks near Osceola (Mississippi County). Like most of the black communities in the Arkansas delta, the great majority of the black population in Mississippi County were poverty-stricken sharecroppers. In this bleak atmosphere, McIntosh sought to prepare black students and their parents for a better life. He regularly met with parents after school hours and taught them how to read, write, fill out business papers, and do basic mathematics so they could weigh their own cotton and calculate what they were owed.

William R. Golden. From 1931 to 1937, Golden served as the principal of the black grade school, grades 1–9, in Turrell (Crittenden County). Under his leadership the small school grew from approximately 150 students into a high school with more than 350 students. In honor of his dedication to the education of the black community, the Turrell school was renamed the Golden High School in his honor.

Zelmon Emerson Barr. From 1928 to 1969, Barr served as the principal of the Birdeye Elementary School in the Coldwater School District in Cross County. Like most black principals during the depression years, Barr was responsible not only for the education of his pupils, but also for the maintenance of school facilities. While he made sure that all school facilities were properly maintained, he did not neglect the education of his students. Barr developed teaching materials for his small faculty and planned educational programs to enhance teaching and learning. His implementation of a learning program for all grades is considered to be one of his major accomplishments.

LeRoy McNeil. This well-known Arkansas educator was a native of Curtis, Arkansas, and one of the seven children of Nathan and Carrie McNeil. He received his elementary education in the black public school in Curtis and his high school diploma from the high school branch of Arkansas Baptist College in Little Rock. He went on to earn a B.A. degree from AM&N College at Pine Bluff, an M.A. in public school administration from the University of Arkansas, and forty-five hours above the M.A. from Arkansas State University at Jonesboro.

McNeil's service to public education in Arkansas covered more than four decades. Following a few years as a public schoolteacher, he was named principal of the Immanual Industrial Training School for blacks in Elmyra, Arkansas. From there he moved to the Tyronza School District in Earle (Crittenden County), where he served as principal of the black training school. From 1932 until his retirement in 1972, McNeil was the principal of the black high school in Crawsfordville (Crittenden County), Arkansas. As a result of his effective leadership the Crawsfordville School Board honored McNeil by naming the black school the NcNeil High School. To have an institution named after its leader during his tenure is a rare and most noteworthy achievement.

During his tenure as principal of the school named in his honor, McNeil compiled an outstanding record of accomplishments. He expanded and improved the school's physical plant, established separate music and drama departments and a home economics department, and helped establish 4-H Clubs, New Farmers of America, and New Homemakers of America. Students in these clubs competed against other students from the state's black schools in annual statewide events and often won the first-place prize. In addition to sound academic programs, McNeil also established competitive athletic programs: football, and girls' and boys' basketball, and track. He was also instrumental in getting a new gymnasium constructed for the basketball program.

McNeil High School was located in rural Crittenden County and was surrounded by large white-owned plantations, and many of the students and their parents lived in poverty. To brighten the future for his students, McNeil encouraged them to strive for academic excellence. He also realized that hungry students were poor learners and, consequently, played a major role in getting a hot lunch program established in the school. McNeil and his wife demonstrated their concern for the future of McNeil High graduates by taking several of them to Arkansas Baptist College and to Philander Smith College, both in Little Rock, and paying the tuition out of their own pockets. Some of these students went on to graduate from college and earn positions in business and education throughout the nation. The McNeils were interested not only in the future of the graduates of McNeil High School, but they were also interested in the education and welfare of their parents. They regularly worked with the adult population, teaching them how to read, do mathematics, and keep accurate records of debts and income.

With the advent of public school desegregation, McNeil High School was renamed the Crawsfordville High School and the former all-white high school became a junior high. This was unusual because in the vast majority of cases the physical plants of black high schools were inferior when compared to white schools and were either abandoned or converted into junior highs when the school system desegregated. The fact that McNeil High School was converted into Crawsfordville High School is, in itself, a testimony to McNeil's leadership and to the type of facility he built during his tenure as principal.

Anna M. P. Strong. Strong served as the principal of the Robert R. Moton High School in Marianna (Lee County) from 1926 to 1957. Lee County, like most counties in the delta, was dominated by elite white planters whose major concern was not the education of their cheap labor force. Strong, however, was determined to improve the quality of life for her students and their families. When she became principal of Robert R. Moton, the facility was a three-room training school located in the middle of a cotton field. Under Strong's leadership, however, the school grew into a nine-room structure with thirteen teachers, and before her tenure ended, the school boasted a two-story brick building with fourteen classrooms, a 625-seat auditorium, and a separate vocational agricultural building. Her labors to educate and improve the quality of life for blacks extended beyond Lee County and reached throughout the Arkansas delta and to the state and national level. She was a child of the delta, born and reared in Phillips County, where she was educated by Quakers at the highly regarded Southland School at Lexa, Arkansas. In 1914, Leo M. Favrot, supervisor of rural schools for the Department of Education, in a report to the directors of the Jeanes Fund, described Southland "as the best Negro school that I have seen."[30] Strong excelled in the classroom and was hired as a teacher at age thirteen and quickly developed a reputation as an excellent communicator, teacher, and leader. While teaching as a teenager, she earned a degree from Tuskegee Institute and later attended Columbia University. It was because of her education and reputation as a leader that she was named principal of Robert R. Moton in 1926. Three years later, in 1929, her leadership skills were recognized by her peers, and she was elected president of the Arkansas Teachers Association. In her initial address to the ATA, she urged teachers to continue their own education and to educate the whole child.[31]

In 1932 the organizational and leadership skills of Strong were recognized by the Arkansas Department of Education, and she was appointed assistant supervisor of education for rural Negro schools in the state. In this position, while still serving as principal of the Robert R. Moton High School, she established an educational program for rural schools known as the Key Schools Program (KSP), a program designed to develop rural life through a coordinated effort of the home, school, and church. Teachers in the KSP attended a ten-week summer workshop at AM&N College where they were given special training in rural education. These poorly paid teachers were able to attend the workshops on scholarships paid for by the General Education Board. The KSP began with twenty schools in 1934 and grew to over one hundred by 1940 and was recognized by the DOE as one of the most successful and innovative educational programs in the state.[32]

While serving as principal of Robert R. Moton and directing the Key Schools Program, Strong found time to actively participate in state, regional, and national professional organizations where her communication and leadership skills were also recognized. In addition to serving as president of the ATA from 1929 to 1930, she represented Arkansas in 1934 in Washington, D.C., where Harold Ickes, secretary of the interior, had organized the first National Conference on Fundamental Problems in the Education of Negroes. She also served as president of the American Teachers Association, which she helped to establish.[33] At the 1942 meeting of the

American Teachers Association, Strong shared the stage with Mrs. Franklin Delano (Eleanor) Roosevelt, one of its chief supporters.[34] During the closing years of her long and distinguished career, Strong was the recipient of an honorary doctorate from AM&N College, and in the early 1970s, following the consolidation of black and white schools in Lee County, the Robert R. Moton High School was renamed the Strong High School in her honor.

Northwest Arkansas

The black population of northwest Arkansas was extremely small when compared to that of the delta regions of northeast and southeast Arkansas. The few blacks in the region who went to school attended scattered grade schools in Washington County (Fayetteville).[35] Grade school education for blacks in Fayetteville began in 1866 with the establishment of the Henderson School by the American Missionary Association. This school served the black community in Washington County until it was demolished in 1936 and replaced by the Lincoln School, grades 1–9, which served the black community until the desegregation of Fayetteville's public schools in 1965. Beginning in 1947, black students who wanted an education beyond grade nine were bussed to either Fort Smith or Hot Springs at the expense of the Fayetteville School District.[36]

Edith Talley. Mrs. Talley was one of the principals of historic Douglas High School in Van Buren, Arkansas, and her legacy is part of the school's rich heritage. Erected in 1872, Douglas was the first black school in Van Buren and was designed to serve the local black community and that of nearby Alma. Initially Douglas was a combination elementary and junior high school. During Talley's administration, which began in 1938, four brick rooms were added to Douglas and the institution became a high school.

Charles L. Williams. Williams served from 1927 until 1942 as the principal of Lincoln High School in Fort Smith (Sebastian County), Arkansas, during the Great Depression and the early years of World War II. Lincoln was the first school constructed for blacks in Fort Smith (1891), and when Williams became principal in 1927, it was in the process of being renovated.[37] He oversaw the remodeling process, which included the addition of new classrooms, an auditorium, a gymnasium, and an office for the principal. Due to the small black population of northwest Arkansas, Lincoln served as one of the few high schools for blacks for many years. It was well known for the ability of its administrators and teachers and for the quality of its instructional programs. There were several black grade schools in northwest Arkansas, such as the ones in Alma and Fayetteville, but blacks desiring a high school education had to commute to Fort Smith. In Fayetteville, which was located high in the Ozark mountains, blacks referred to the trip to Fort Smith as "going down the mountain."

Under Williams's leadership, Lincoln's students competed in and won several statewide academic contests sponsored by the Arkansas Teachers Association. The ATA was the official voice of Arkansas's black administrators and teachers, and Williams served as its president from 1934 to 1936. Williams's presidency of the ATA reflected the respect that he had earned among his professional peers. He was respected not only by his peers, but also by the Fort Smith black community, which he introduced to musical reviews, Sunday Vespers, and the Boy Scouts of America.[38]

Other principals who served Lincoln High School included E. O. Trent, 1886–1911 and 1915–1917; L. M. McCoy, 1911–1915; F. D. Johnson, 1917–1925; and J. Harris, 1925–1927.

E. P. Roland. Roland was the first principal, 1938–1945, of Douglas High School in Van Buren (Crawford County), Arkansas. Little is known about his educational program, but he is remembered for establishing the first competitive boys' and girls' basketball teams.

Jesse W. Mason Sr. This native of Elliot, Arkansas, a small community near Camden (Ouachita County), received his basic education in the local public school and his high school diploma from the high school branch of Arkansas Baptist College in Little Rock. He went on to earn a B.A. degree in agriculture from Tuskegee Institute in Alabama and did further study at the University of Oklahoma at Norman. Following his own personal motto, "It's not where you come from, but where you are going," Mason went on to become a member of a small cadre of black educators who served northwest, south, southwest, and central Arkansas.

Mason began his career in public education as the combination principal/teacher in Fayetteville (Washington County) in the Lincoln School, which was simply called "the colored school" by the local population. The black population of Fayetteville was too small to sustain a full-time teacher at a living wage, and Mason was forced to relocate. He moved to Almyra (Arkansas County), where he served as principal of the Immanual School. In both Fayetteville and Almyra, Mason stressed the importance of a good education and high moral character to his students, some of whom took his mentoring to heart. Theressa Hoover, one of his students at Fayetteville, became the secretary for the National Organization of United Methodist Women, and Oliver B. Elders of Almyra went on to graduate from college and become a nationally recognized basketball coach at Hall High School in Little Rock. Competing in the state's largest-school classification, Elders's teams won several conference and state championships and his players were recruited by major colleges and universities throughout the nation. In 1999, Elders was inducted into the Arkansas Basketball Hall of Fame. His success was due, in part, to the solid educational background and character building he received under Mason's tutelage.

Although Mason was fully devoted to the education of his students at Almyra, his salary was only thirty-five dollars per month and was often paid with a school voucher that local merchants would not cash unless he accepted a discounted rate. Consequently, Mason left the public schools in 1942 to accept a more lucrative and challenging position with the United States Department of Agriculture (USDA) where he worked as an assistant county supervisor for the Farm Security Administration (FSA). The FSA, an agency of the USDA, operated several agriculture resettlement projects that assisted low-income farmers in purchasing their own small farms with long-term low-interest-rate government loans. The agency also provided the farmers with instructions in farm management, including the building of houses and barns and the growing of crops. Mason, who was stationed in Murfreesboro, Arkansas, taught those skills to farmers in his service area. After a year with the USDA, Mason left to accept a position with the Arkansas Cooperative Extension Service, operated by the University of Arkansas as an assistant county agent for Negro work. He was assigned to Crittenden County in eastern Arkansas with Marion as his headquarters.

Initially, Mason was not well received by the white plantation owners in Crittenden County who had developed hostile attitudes toward the FSA because it had caused them to lose some of their best black sharecroppers to the agency and its home-ownership program. Mason, however, was able to win their respect when he assured them that he was not there to recruit for the FAS, but to work with black farmers who rented or owned their own land. As the assistant county agent, Mason taught black farmers how to keep accurate records, how to vaccinate and care for livestock, and how to preserve fruits, vegetables, and fresh meat. He organized a Ham & Egg Show for black farmers, which allowed them to enter their cured hams in the competition at the annual Crittenden County Fair. Some of his clients won first-place prizes in their division. He also worked with 4-H Clubs in the local public schools. His motto in working with youths was "training hands, heads, hearts and health." The 4-H Club members were taught how to prepare agricultural projects for competition and judging at the annual state 4-H Club meeting and competition held on the campus of AM&N College at Pine Bluff. Every year during Mason's tenure in Crittenden County, 1942–1947, the county 4-H Clubs won the state 4-H Loving Cup, the highest possible award.

Mason left the Arkansas Extension Service in 1947 and returned to the USDA where he became an assistant county Farmers Home Administration supervisor, 1947–1959, with the responsibility of supervising black farmers enrolled in the agency's home-ownership program in Crittenden County. His duties, however, were very similar to those he had while working for the Extension Service. Mason's clients had exemplary records in terms of payments on their homes and agricultural productivity. Because of his success in Crittenden County, he was transferred to Phillips County where the USDA had a similar home-ownership project in Lakeview. Again his record was outstanding. Mason's success in Crittenden and Phillips Counties led to him being named program specialist for the USDA Farmers Home Administration Program. As a program specialist, he was responsible for the hiring, training, and supervision of all black assistant county supervisors in Arkansas. In 1976, Mason retired from the USDA and accepted a position as a student recruiter for Philander Smith College, 1976–1978. He was more than a student recruiter, though; on more than one occasion, he personally delivered students to Philander Smith, at his own expense, and then helped them to find off-campus jobs to pay tuition costs. Mason, however, missed working for the federal government and left Philander in 1978 to become a supervisor of the Green Thumb Program in Arkansas and Mississippi for the United States Department of Labor. The program employed low-income senior citizens on projects to remove trash and debris from parks and other government properties. Mason's motto for the program was "Jobs Are Ageless."

Just as "Jobs Are Ageless," so too is the legacy of Jesse W. Mason, which is reflected in the many awards and commendations he received for human service. In 1954, he was recognized as the Arkansas County Agent of the Year and as Employee of the Year by the Farmers Home Administration Program in 1967. Also in 1967, he was awarded a Doctorate of Humane Letters by Arkansas Baptist College in recognition of his unselfish service to his state and community. The honors continued: Mason was awarded a Certificate of Commendation from President Richard M. Nixon for exceptional service to others in the finest American tradition in 1971 and a Tuskegee Professional Rural Leadership Award in 1972; in 1998 he was inducted, posthumously, into the Arkansas Agriculture Hall of Fame. In recognition of his long years of unselfish service, the Rural Development Agency of the USDA presents the Jesse W. Mason Award to an outstanding Rural Development Agency during its Black History Month program each year. And a scholarship named in his honor is awarded to students who attend UAPB, Philander Smith College, Arkansas Baptist College, or Tuskegee Institute and major in consumer and family living and other disciplines. In addition to his professional activities, Mason was also very active in his church, Greater Archview Missionary Baptist. Although heavily involved in his church and professional duties, Mason did not avoid becoming involved in civic projects, some of which included serving as an advisor to the Boy Scouts of America, organizing the Arkansas Baptist College Alumni Association (president), and playing an instrumental role in organizing the Arkansas Leadership Roundtable Conference and the Rural Life Conference.

Central Arkansas

Both formal and informal education for black Arkansans probably began in Pulaski County. Formal education dates back to 1863 when Wallace Andrews, a former slave, opened a school for blacks in Little Rock. After a few months of operations, Wallace turned his school over to Quaker missionaries, who ran the institution until the city organized its own public school system in 1868. There were a number of schools for blacks in Little Rock and central Arkansas, but the best-known black school in the area was the Paul Laurence Dunbar High School. When Dunbar opened in 1929, the onset of the Great Depression, it was rated as one of the best black high schools in the South.[39]

John H. Lewis. Lewis was the first principal of the Paul Laurence Dunbar High School, 1929–1943. From 1929 until 1931, Dunbar became a combination high school and junior college, and under Lewis's direction a $7,500 state-of-the-art library was constructed with $5,000 contributed by the local Parent Teacher Association and supporters in the community and $2,500 from the Rosenwald Fund. Lewis also persuaded the black community to contribute $500 for campus beautification. Also added to Dunbar during Lewis's tenure was a comprehensive program that served not only Dunbar students, but all black schools in the city. Dunbar received North Central accreditation before Lewis left to become the full-time president of Dunbar Junior College.[40]

CHAPTER 5

Winds of Change and Educational Progress, 1941–1954

In 1941 as a result of the surprise Japanese attack on the United States Naval Base at Pearl Harbor, Hawaii, America joined the European democracies in the World War II battle against German Nazism and Japanese Imperialism. It was a war to preserve freedom, democracy, and equality around the world. While war raged in Europe and Asia, another battle was being fought on the American home-front as black Americans fought for the same principles that were being fought for abroad. The internal battles were fought on many fronts, but in Arkansas the first major confrontation took place on the field of public education where black educational leaders fought for equal salaries and educational facilities for black public schoolteachers and students. Even before the war, public education in Arkansas in general was in a state of crisis. The crisis was deepened by the outbreak of war and the movement of war industries into the state. In 1940 there were 13,173 employed public schoolteachers in Arkansas, but many of these abandoned their jobs in the public school for better-paying ones in the rapidly growing war industries.[1] The average teacher salary for the 1939–1940 academic year was $570 with wide variations across the state. In Clark County (Arkadelphia) the average monthly salary for white teachers was $57.83 per month and $31.12 per month for black teachers. Teachers could make as much, or more, per week working in the war industries, which desperately needed an educated labor force.[2] The war adversely impacted public education in general. And public education for blacks, which was grotesquely underfunded, was hit especially hard, and black administrators struggled to keep teachers, to keep school doors opened, and to improve facilities and curriculums.

Arkansas was basically a rural agricultural state when the nation entered WWII and the majority of its public schools, especially those for blacks, were located in rural areas. These schools were dependent on the state for most of their funding and were especially hard hit by the war. Enrollments declined and teachers left for jobs in the war industries. No relief came from the state. Before the end of the 1940–1941 academic year, rural schools were told not to expect any state aid for the next year because the state's school equalization fund was already operating at a $350,000 deficit, and if schools wanted to continue operating, they would have to do so on a student tuition basis.[3] The passage of the Community Facilities Act by Congress in 1940, commonly known as the Lanham Act, provided some relief for schools in defense centers (urban areas) by appropriating federal funds for child-care centers and for the expansion of elementary and secondary schools.[4] The legislation had little impact on Arkansas's public school systems because the majority of them were rural and did not qualify for federal assistance. Consequently, educational leaders in Arkansas, and in similar states, began to lobby their congressmen for additional federal aid.

In 1943, Congress, responding to urgent requests from the states for federal aid for public education, began consideration on Senate Bill 637 (S.B. 637) sponsored by Senators Lister Hill (Alabama) and John E. Thomas (Oklahoma). The Hill-Thomas bill called for the annual appropriation of $200,000,000 during the war and other national emergencies to the states to supplement teacher salaries and for the establishment of a permanent annual appropriation of $100,000,000 to equalize educational opportunities in the states. The $200,000,000 was to be distributed to the states based on pupil enrollment and the $100,000,000 on the basis of financial need. This was just what Arkansas needed and Forrest Rozzell, field representative of the "all-white" Arkansas Education Association (AEA), strongly supported the measure and urged AEA members to write their congressmen in support of S.B. 637. Rozzell told the AEA to support the measure because "by next year we will be going on all fours if we don't get federal aid."[5] Arkansas's congressional delegation also supported S.B. 637 until Senator William Langer (N. Dakota) succeeded in attaching an amendment to the proposal which prohibited discrimination in "its benefits or in state funds supplemented thereby on account of race, creed, or color."[6] The Langer amendment would have forced Arkansas, which was spending twenty-five dollars for each white student in the state's public school system compared to ten dollars for each black student, to equalize its educational expenditures, which it was not inclined to do. The amendment led to the defeat of

S.B. 637. The state's Department of Education and the AEA still wanted federal aid but, according to Rozzell, "we want federal aid in a form that will allocate money to the states on the basis of an objective formula without discretionary powers allocated to any federal office."[7] There was also the fear that the Langer amendment could possibly lead to the desegregation of public education. This was clearly expressed by Arkansas's senior senator, John L. McClellan, who, commenting on his vote against S.B. 637, said that "I could not vote for the bill without voting to sacrifice our dual (system of) education in the South, segregating white and Negro races."[8]

While the nation was engaged in a war abroad against Japanese Imperialism and Nazi Germany's ideas of racial supremacy, Arkansas's white educational and political leaders continued to seek ways to preserve the state's wretched system of racial segregation and discrimination even if it meant denying white public school students the federal aid that they desperately needed. Black educational leaders, however, during the war and the years that followed, focused their attention on overcoming the barriers to equality. In 1940, a group of leading black educators, meeting at Arkansas Baptist College in Little Rock, formed the Committee for Consideration of Educational Problems of Negroes (CCEPN) and adopted a proposal calling for the equalization of teacher salaries and educational opportunities, improved high school facilities for blacks, more financial support for AM&N College at Pine Bluff (the only state-supported institution of higher education for blacks), adequate funds for black graduate study, and greater employment opportunities for blacks.[9] The proposal was forwarded to Governor Homer Adkins's Advisory Committee on Public Education, which was, at the time, studying the state's educational needs. There was no official response to the CCEPN's proposal, but the position of the governor and educational officials was revealed during the 1940 interracial conference, in Little Rock, on the employment problems of Negroes. During the meeting Eli W. Collins, director of the Division of Unemployment of the State Department of Labor, told the conferees that "Negroes need training not in the field of competition but in those areas where he is traditionally accepted — domestic, custodial, and agricultural work."[10] Collins's views coincided with those of the state Department of Education, which stated in its 1938–1940 report on black schools that "it is the firm belief of this division that greater emphasis should be placed on the vocational interests of Negro youths and adults on the farm, and in the shops of the community."[11] These views were a direct rejection of the position of the CCEPN and of Laurence Oxley of Washington, D.C., supervisor of the Negro Placement Service of the United States Bureau of Employment Security, who told the conference that what blacks in Arkansas needed was more training in the fields of competition.[12]

Undeterred by the segregationist and white supremacy views of Arkansas's educational and political leaders, black educators, reflecting the views of a nation at war against Nazi Germany's ideas of racial supremacy, aggressively launched themselves on a course of action designed to equalize teacher salaries and educational opportunities for blacks. The inequities were great. In 1941 salaries for white teachers averaged $625 per year compared to $370 for blacks, and black schools received only 11 percent of state expenditures for public education while counting for 24 percent of state enrollments based upon average daily attendance.[13] The road to educational equality for black educators proved to be a challenging and costly one, but they willingly rose to meet the challenge.

Inspired by the United States Supreme Court ruling in *Alston vs. School Board of the City of Norfolk* (Virginia), 1940, which ruled that wage differentials between black and white teachers were discriminatory and violated the due process clause of the Fourteenth Amendment, black teachers throughout Arkansas began to petition their local school boards for salary equalization.[14] The first petition, and perhaps the most important one, was filed by the all-black City Teachers Association of Little Rock (CTA). In the spring of 1941 the CTA, which represented all of the black teachers in Little Rock's public schools, petitioned the all-white Little Rock School Board (LRSB) for salary equalization. After waiting a year without a response from the LRSB, the CTA unanimously voted in February of 1942 to file a class action suit with the United States District Court at Little Rock against the LRSB in the name of Susie Morris (Sue Cowan Williams). Morris was an English teacher at Dunbar High School in Little Rock and chair of the English department. The CTA was represented by Scipio A. Jones, a local black attorney, who argued that the LRSB was guilty of violating the due process clause of the Fourteenth Amendment and asked the court to issue a permanent injunction restricting the LRSB from making any distinction in the fixing of salaries in the Little Rock schools based upon race.[15]

The initial reaction of state and local officials was one of severe criticism. Ralph Jones, the state commissioner of education, accused the CTA of "using strong-arm methods" and of "trying to take advantage of a national emergency" (WWII) in their quest for salary equalization.[16] In its official reply to the CTA's suit in U.S. District Court, presided over by Judge T. C. Trimble, the LRSB denied that the Fourteenth Amendment rights of black teachers had been violated. In a tone that reeked with insinuations of white racial supremacy, the LRSB admitted that black and white teachers were required to meet the same qualifications for a teacher's license, but that black teachers were paid less than whites because "Negro teachers differ as compared to white teachers in degrees of special training, ability, character, experience, duties, service, and accomplishments."[17] Ignoring the constitutional issue involved in the suit and the Supreme Court's ruling in *Alston vs. School Board of the City of Norfolk,* Judge Trimble dismissed the CTA's suit against the LRSB on the grounds that the CTA was an unincorporated body and could not sue or be sued in federal court. On motion by the plaintiffs' attorney, Judge Trimble did agree to hear Morris's salary discrimination suit on its own merits.[18]

In Morris's individual salary discrimination suit against the LRSB, *Susie Morris vs. Little Rock School Board,* her attorney, Scipio A. Jones, was joined by the attorneys J. R. Booker of Little Rock and Thurgood Marshall of New York, who represented the National Association for the Advancement of Colored People (NAACP). The attorneys argued that Morris, who was a graduate of Talladega College in Alabama, had earned grades of "A" in graduate English courses at the University of Chicago, with seven years of teaching experience, and was the victim of racial discrimination because whites with lesser qualifications were paid more.[19] To support Morris's charge of salary discrimination, John H. Gipson, a mathematics instructor at Dunbar and president of the CTA, who was also a college graduate and had completed graduate work at the University of Kansas, testified that his salary had only increased seventy-nine dollars over a seventeen-year teaching career in Little Rock's public schools.[20] Expanding the racial argument it used in the original CTA suit, the LRSB argued that white teachers were paid more than blacks because of "better training, experience, and other qualifications including cultural background, personality, cooperative spirit, and additional intangibles."[21]

The thinly veiled white supremacy argument of the LRSB was laid bare in the testimony of Annie Griffey, a white supervisor of elementary teachers in Little Rock for thirty years. Testifying on behalf of the LRSB, Griffey said that "regardless of college degrees and teaching experience, no white teacher in Little Rock is inferior to the best Negro teacher."[22]

The views of the LRSB and Griffey were clearly reflected in the system the board used to evaluate teachers. Black teachers were evaluated by white supervisors who visited black schools for that purpose. This ensured that they would not be rated as high as white teachers. The Morris case was a perfect example. Morris, who held a B.A. degree and grades of "A" in graduate English courses from the University of Chicago where she was required to present papers describing the methods she used to teach English to her students, was evaluated by Charles B. Hamilton, the principal of a local white school who served as the supervisor of instructions over Dunbar's black teachers. He rated Morris between 3 and 4 on a 5-point scale. Her principal, John H. Lewis, who believed that she deserved an "A" rating, was not allowed to participate in her evaluation.[23] Judge Trimble, however, ruled against Morris on the grounds that "proof that Negro teachers over a period of time were paid less than white teachers was not sufficient within itself to show discrimination because of race" and that the LRSB had "the right to fix the salary of each teacher in the school system and is not required to follow an arbitrary standard of college degrees or a mechanical method of determining salaries."[24] Morris's attorneys informed Judge Trimble that his decision would be appealed to the federal Circuit Court of Appeals in St. Louis, Missouri.

While the Morris case was making its way through the federal courts, state education officials continued to seek ways to practice salary discrimination. This was clearly revealed in their response to the requirements of the teacher salary law passed by the state legislature in 1941. The statute required that 75 percent of all revenue in excess of that received in the base academic year of 1939–1940 be allocated for teacher salaries. When the all-white Little Rock Classroom Teachers Association requested that a state formula be established for the distribution of the funds because some of it was going to principals and supervisors, rather than classroom teachers, the commissioner of education, Ralph Jones, and AEA field representative F. Rozzell told

the teachers not to complain because the establishment of a state formula would permit black teachers to demand as much of the excess as
whites.[25] This desire to continue to discriminate against black teachers, however, was prohibited in 1945 when the United States Circuit
Court of Appeals at St. Louis reversed Judge Trimble's decision in the
Morris salary equalization suit and ordered the LRSB to equalize the
salaries of black and white teachers.[26]

The salary equalization battle was a costly one for Little Rock's
black teachers and principals. Susie Morris and John H. Gipson were
fired at the end of the 1942–1943 academic year, and John H. Lewis,
the eminent principal of Dunbar High School, was forced to resign.[27]
Although Morris was vindicated by the U.S. Court of Appeals in
1945, she was not reinstated as a teacher in the Little Rock School
District until 1952 and only then after constant pressure on the LRSB
from L. M. Christophe, the new principal of Dunbar. The Morris
salary equalization suit also affected black teachers in the separate
North Little Rock School District. In 1942 the North Little Rock
School Board, which monitored the Morris case from the beginning,
sought to avoid a similar suit by voluntarily increasing the salaries of
black teachers by five dollars per month, but one-third of the teachers were advised to seek employment elsewhere for the 1942–1943
academic year.[28]

The Morris salary equalization suit was only the first battle in the
war to equalize black teacher salaries and educational facilities for
black public school students. In 1949 a second battle erupted when
black parents in Fort Smith and DeWitt, with the strong support of
the NAACP and black principals, filed suit in federal court seeking
equalization of black and white school facilities and state and local
expenditures for student enrollments. Reacting to the lawsuits, Ed
McCuistion, director of the Division of Negro Education for the
Arkansas Department of Education, admitted that inequities existed
and told a reporter for the *Arkansas Gazette*, the state's largest circu-
lating newspaper, that "I have never visited a Negro school, of any
size, where facilities and programs for the races are equal."[29] Inequities
between black and white schools were dramatically emphasized in a
1949 *Time Magazine* article that focused on the West Memphis
(Crittenden County), Arkansas, public school system. In 1948 the
black school in West Memphis burned and little was being done by
state and local authorities to replace the structure. *Time Magazine*

became interested after the northern-born and -raised editors of the local paper printed several stories critical of local school officials. Both the stories in the local paper and *Time* revealed how black students were forced, as a result of the fire, into makeshift, overcrowded, and unsanitary classrooms. The stories also pointed out that state and local authorities only spent $19.51 for the education of each black student in the public school system compared to $144.51 for each white student.[30] In a follow-up story the *Arkansas Gazette* pointed out similar inequities across the state.[31] The battle to equalize facilities, salaries, and educational opportunities for Arkansas's black administrators, teachers, and students legally came to an end in 1954 when the U.S. Supreme Court in its landmark *Brown vs. Board of Education* ruled that segregated public schools were a violation of the Fourteenth Amendment and therefore unconstitutional. Throughout the educational battles of the 1940s and early 1950s, black principals across the state risked their careers seeking equality for their teachers and students.

Southwest Arkansas

Dr. Llewellyn William Williamson. He was one of the more progressive public school principals from 1941 to 1954, although his career was much longer, 1930–1971. Dr. Williamson began his career as the principal of the Walnut Grove and Redland High School in Hempstead County, 1930–1938. From 1938 to 1971, he was the principal of Lincoln High School in Washington, Arkansas, the sight of his most impressive accomplishments. While at Lincoln, Williamson led the school from a state rating of "C" to "A" and to the highly prized accreditation by the North Central Association of Colleges and Schools. He was also successful in getting a modern home economics building constructed for the school, the addition of a commercial department to the school's curriculum, and the construction of a gymnasium, which included additional classrooms and a cafeteria. During his tenure as principal of Lincoln, Williamson also improved his own qualifications as an educational leader. He earned a B.A. degree from Philander Smith College in Little Rock (1941), an M.S. degree from the University of Arkansas at Fayetteville (1953), a doctorate in education from Minerva University of Italy (1960), and a second doctorate in school administration from the Free Protestant Episcopal Church University of

London, England (1968). In 1979 Dr. Williamson published *Footprints around Arkansas*, which discussed his educational and life experiences.

Sanford Bernard Tollette. The administrative career of this native of Tollette, Arkansas, covered almost two decades. He was the principal of the Gurnsey High School (Hempstead County), 1951–1953; Union Grove High School, Harmony Grove School District, 1953–1956; Townsend Park High School (Jefferson County), 1956–1957; the Smackover Training School in Smackover (Union County), 1957–1961; and the Wilson High School (Mississippi County), 1961–1962. During his career, Tollette served as president of the Ouachita County Teachers Association, an affiliate of the Arkansas Teachers Association and as secretary of the Southwest Administrators Association, and he was a candidate for the presidency of the ATA.

In an effort to improve learning and educational achievement, Tollette initiated and supervised a specialized reading program for grades 1–12 and had his students participate in a nationwide testing and survey program sponsored by the United States Department of Education and the Bureau of Naval Personnel. He also established a hands-on vocational educational program, in which students learned how to construct homes, and an exemplary training program for Pulaski County public schools.

Rucker E. Clayton. This veteran administrator spent the majority of his career in the black schools of Magnolia (Columbia County), Arkansas: Free Hope Public School, 1945–1961; Calhoun Heights Elementary School, 1963–1965; Columbia County Elementary School, 1966–1967; and Eastside Elementary School, 1968–1992. During each administrative stop, Clayton stressed the importance of regular school attendance, academic excellence, and school and community pride.

Hovey A. Henderson. During his forty-one years of service to public education in Arkansas, Henderson spent twenty-seven of those years as principal of Langston High School in Hot Springs (Garland County), 1941–1968. As principal of Langston, Henderson became well known for his strong leadership skills and his cordial, but firm, relationship with students and parents. In 1968, as Hot Springs was completing the desegregation of its public schools, Henderson was "promoted" from his principalship to the position of director of Title I federal funds for the Hot Springs School District and served in this position until his retirement in 1976. He was the first black to serve in the administrative offices of the district.

Eula B. Wallace. Mrs. Wallace began her career in public education in 1939 as a social studies teacher at the Dallas County Training School in Fordyce, Arkansas, where her husband, James E. Wallace, was the principal and agricultural teacher. She was named principal of the school in 1951 when her husband was forced to resign the principalship because of a new state law that prohibited one person from holding two paid positions in the same school. He resigned because his salary as a Smith-Hughes agricultural teacher was more than that of a principal. In 1954, the salary of the principal was increased; a new agricultural teacher was hired; and Mrs. Wallace resigned as principal and her husband resumed the principalship of the school. During her brief principalship of the Dallas County Training School, Mrs. Wallace continued the academic programs established by her husband and proved to be a capable administrator.

Robert L. White. White was the principal of the New Hope High School in Mount Holly (Union County), Arkansas, in 1946. He is credited with persuading the local school board to construct a new high school for black students. The new school featured a modern science laboratory and a separate wing for elementary students. An accomplished musician, White also taught piano to students and others in the community after school. He said that the accomplishment of which he was most proud was being able "to witness an increase in the number of New Hope graduates each year and the high percentage that went on to attend and graduate from college."

George S. Ivory. Like many of the Arkansas public school administrators, Ivory's career was a long one. He began as the principal of the Harrison Chapel School, 1935–1939, at Rosston. From there he moved on to the principalship of the Sweet Home Elementary School at Willisville, 1939–1949, and from 1949 to 1961 he served as the principal/superintendent of the Oak Grove High School and the Oak Grove Consolidated School District, all in Nevada County. From 1961 to 1971, he served as principal of Lincoln High School in Camden (Ouachita County), but his most impressive work was done while he served as principal/superintendent of the Oak Grove High School and Consolidated School District. During his leadership of the Oak Grove High School and School District, Ivory was instrumental in the consolidation of the six separate schools in Nevada County that finally comprised the consolidated school district. The new district featured one black high school for the county, two junior high schools, and seven elementary departments. Not only was Ivory a builder, he also stressed quality education. His emphasis upon quality education led to the certification of all Oak Grove teachers in their teaching areas and state accreditation for the Oak Grove High School.

James Roy McBeth. From 1940 to 1953, McBeth was the principal of Childress Junior High School at Emmett (Nevada County), Arkansas. A musician by training, McBeth taught his students how to properly render old Negro spirituals. His students performed throughout Arkansas, and their performances became one of the trademarks of Childress Junior High. From 1953 to 1969, McBeth was the principal of Biscoe High School in Prairie County, but he is best known for the musical and voice training of his students at Childress.

Oscar Hamilton. After serving in the navy during WWII, Hamilton began his educational career in 1953 as the principal of the Unity Public School in Foreman (Little River County), Arkansas, where he served for seventeen years. When the public schools in Little River County were desegregated, Hamilton was promoted to the assistant superintendent's position for the district and served in that position until his retirement in 1967. On the surface it appeared that Hamilton's promotion was a step up the administrative ladder in the district, but in fact it was a loss for black students because the promotion removed him from daily contact with the students who needed him most.

Seth Porchia. A native of Ouachita County, Porchia served as principal of a Rosston Junior High School (Nevada County), 1949–1950, and of Chidester High School (Ouachita County), 1950–1955. During his tenure at the Chidester High School, he led the school from a state rating of "C" to "A." He also improved the school through the addition of a library and a music department. Due to desegregation, Porchia lost his job as a public school principal and ended his career in 1984 as a teacher in the Booker Magnet School in Little Rock.

Fairbanks Buffington. A graduate of Arkansas Baptist College (Little Rock) and Fisk University (Nashville, Tennessee), Buffington was the principal of the Magnolia (Columbia County) Colored High School from 1942 to 1969. When he took over leadership of the school it had five hundred students. Under his leadership the faculty was expanded, and an administration building, a home economic wing, and a vocational/agricultural building were added to the school. The Magnolia Colored High School went through several name changes before being named the Columbia High School.

F. L. Curry. "Asking nothing else but the satisfaction of knowing that some have benefited because of my labor" was one of the favorite quotes of Curry, who was the principal of McMittress High School (Columbia County) from 1941 until 1969. He lived his favorite quote and was known throughout the community for his keen judgment, for an unfailing sympathy for the less fortunate, and for his unselfish service to his school and community. In 1953, the McMittress senior class dedicated *The Raven*, the school's yearbook, to Curry in recognition of his leadership and dedication to their school and community.

Northwest Arkansas

The black population of northwest Arkansas has historically been small and that did not significantly change during the 1940s and early 1950s. There were, however, a few black educators in the region who made their presence known during the fight for equal salaries and educational facilities.[32]

Ava Vann Williams. Williams was the principal of Booker Elementary School at Alma (Crawford County), Arkansas, 1954–1964. This small school closed in 1964 as a result of desegregation and a declining black student population. The vast majority of blacks in the Alma area moved to nearby Fort Smith during World War II in search of better jobs, and the population continued to decline during the postwar years. Mrs. Williams, who is retired, currently (2000) resides in Fort Smith where she is active in community affairs.

C. M. Green. Green was the principal of Lincoln High School in Fort Smith (Sebastian County) from 1943 to 1956. Under his leadership, Lincoln became one of the two black high schools in Arkansas to be accredited by the North Central Association of Colleges and Schools; the other was Dunbar High School in Little Rock. Because of its high academic standards it was also the focus school in one of the 1948 issues of the *Bulletin of the Arkansas Teachers Association.* During Green's tenure, Lincoln also enjoyed the distinction of being one of the few schools in Arkansas where black and white teacher salaries had been equalized following the Supreme Court's 1940 ruling in *Alston vs. School Board of the City of Norfolk (Virginia)* that prohibited school districts from discrimination in teacher salaries.[33]

Southeast Arkansas

Carl Emmett Jones. Jones spent his entire administrative career in Jefferson County where he served as principal of the Springhill Elementary School, 1948–1950; Wabaseka High School (currently the J. S. Walker High School), 1950–1957; and Tucker High School, 1957–1963. During his long career, he focused most of his time on improving school curriculums and the overall learning environment of his students.

Chester A. White. White was the principal of the Calhoun County High School in Thornton (Calhoun County), Arkansas, from 1947 to 1969. During his tenure, he developed a mandatory curriculum that exceeded state requirements for graduation. He also established a comprehensive program for elementary and high school students in band and choral music. Student attendance, however, was sporadic. To facilitate student attendance in this rural school district, White was instrumental in establishing the first bussing system in 1950. Between 1953 and 1957, the black schools in the nearby Harrell community were consolidated with the Calhoun County High School, and White spearheaded the construction of a new school in 1957 and the school's first gymnasium.

Reuben Napoleon Chanay. Poverty and racism, according to Chanay, were the products of ignorance and one could overcome poverty through hard work and education. A product of his own belief, Chanay began his long educational career as a teacher at Merrill High School in Pine Bluff (Jefferson County) in 1912. Through continuous education and hard work, he became principal of the school in 1941 and led the school's development through the turbulent war years. As principal of Merrill, Chanay pushed his faculty to complete their college degrees and emphasized high scholastic achievements for students. This combination led to Merrill being accredited by the prestigious North Central Association of Colleges and Schools. In addition to demanding quality performance from faculty and students, Chanay also worked to expand the cultural experiences of his students and, to a degree, the black community at large. In this regard he brought to Merrill many outstanding public figures to address the faculty, students, and community. Included in these personalities were Mary McLeod Bethune, president and founder of Bethune-Cookman College in Florida; Freda DeKnight, the food editor of *Ebony Magazine;* and a traveling Nigerian (Africa) performing group. As part of his service to the community, Chanay also played a major role in establishing the first Boy Scouts Troop in Pine Bluff. His activities, however, were not limited to his local school and community. From 1944 to 1946, he served as president of the Arkansas Teachers Association. As president of the ATA, Chanay increased membership in the organization and supported Susie Morris (Sue Cowan Williams) in her salary equalization suit against the Little Rock School Board.[34]

Lillian Cannon Booker. From 1950 to 1965, Booker served as principal of the St. Mary Rosenwald Elementary School in Helena (Phillips County), Arkansas. During her principalship she not only stressed basic education, she also became well known throughout the local community through her sponsorship of school plays and other social activities that were designed to enhance the educational and cultural development of her students.

Roland Leon Buchanan. From 1944 to 1968, Buchanan was the principal of the West Side Elementary School, West Helena (Phillips County), Arkansas. During his leadership an auditorium and a cafeteria were added to the school and, for the first time, poor children in this delta were served free school lunches. Consolidation of the Helena and West Helena School Districts occurred during

Buchanan's principalship, and for the first time students were bussed to elementary schools. When desegregation came to the Helena-West Helena School District, Buchanan was reassigned to the position of supervisor for elementary schools in the district.

Dr. Albert Sidney Baxter. This well-known educator served as the principal of Holman High School in Stuttgart (Arkansas County), Arkansas, 1950–1958. When Baxter took over the leadership of Holman, students were attending school in a dilapidated and overcrowded facility. He successfully lobbied the all-white school board for a new building, which included modern classrooms, cafeteria, and gymnasium. He also added home economics and industrial arts to the new school's curriculum and organized the school's first marching band. Under Baxter's leadership, Holman rose from a state class "C" school to "A." Baxter left Holman in 1958 for a position on the mathematics faculty at AM&N College at Pine Bluff where he completed his career. While at AM&N, he earned a doctorate from the University of Arkansas at Fayetteville. His often quoted doctoral dissertation was a study of the impact of desegregation on black public school administrators and teachers.[35]

R. C. Caesar. This outstanding educator and advocate of educational equality for black students and teachers began his career as principal of the McRae High School in Prescott, Arkansas, and ended it as the principal of the Lake Village High School in Chicot County. Throughout his career in public education, Caesar worked for the implementation of a consecutive nine-month school year for black students. In Arkansas's rural districts, which covered most of the state, black students attended schools with split sessions. Typically they began school in late July and continued through August. Schools were then dismissed and opened again in late October or early November. Schools were closed so that students could work in the fields to gather the cotton crops of white planters. Caesar believed that such an interrupted educational system was ineffective because much of what was learned was forgotten during the harvest season, and he fought to terminate the system wherever he worked. Many of these rural school districts only had junior high schools for blacks, and Caesar wanted to make high schools available to every black student in the state.

In 1940, while serving as principal of the Lake Village High

School, Caesar was elected president of the Arkansas Teachers Association. The high points of his ATA presidency were the establishment of financial stability for the organization and the 1940 hosting, in Little Rock, of the annual meeting of the American Teachers Association, the national organization of black teachers.

It was during the Caesar administration, 1940–1942, that the ATA began to consider taking legal action to equalize the salaries of black and white teachers (the ATA supported the Morris salary equalization suit against the Little Rock School District), to improve educational facilities for black students, and to gain access to the state's white graduate schools for black teachers who wanted to pursue graduate study. In order to make in-state graduate study accessible for black teachers, Caesar appointed an ATA committee to study the issue and make appropriate recommendations. As a result of the committee's study, the Arkansas Legislature in 1943, unwilling to desegregate higher education in the state, passed legislation authorizing the payment of tuition of black teachers who attended northern graduate schools.[36]

Irvin R. Phillips. A native of Grady (Lincoln County), Arkansas, Phillips began his career as a public school principal during the changing and controversial 1950s. From 1950 to 1956, he was the principal of the Grady Colored Public School. During his principalship, he worked tirelessly for new textbooks for his students to replace the books, which were often outdated and in poor condition passed on from the white school, to expand the curriculum of this rural school, and to establish high academic standards. He also established the school's first competitive athletic program, boys' and girls' basketball. In 1956, Phillips left Grady for Merrill High School in Pine Bluff where he served as a coach, director of athletics, and chair of the physical education department until his retirement in 1970.

Jeanette S. Buckner. Mrs. Buckner was the principal of the Upper Elementary School in the Lakeside School District in Lake Village (Chicot County), Arkansas, 1986–1998. She is remembered not only for her dedication to her school, but also for her community service.

Dr. Clifton Maurice Claye. This innovative educator served as the principal of the M. M. Tate High School in Marvell (Phillips

County), Arkansas. While at M. M. Tate, Claye spent most of his time lobbying the local school board for the construction of a modern physical plant for the school. He wanted to departmentalize elementary education and construct a new three-wing elementary school. When the local school board refused to support Claye's progressive educational ideas, he left Marvell and worked in Arkansas's black public schools at Fordyce, Stamps, and Wilmar before leaving the state to accept a position on the educational faculty at Texas Southern University (TSU) in Houston. During his career at TSU, Claye became a noted scholar, researcher, and grant writer. He excelled in grant writing, receiving seven federal grants from the Department of Health Education and Welfare, four research grants from TSU, and two from the local school district.

M. D. Jordan. Living his motto, "there is no end to what you can do if you don't care who gets the credit," Jordan, who served as the principal of Merrill High School in Pine Bluff, 1951–1975, worked tirelessly to improve the school's curriculum and enrich the lives of students. Under his leadership a fine arts building was constructed at Merrill and a student guidance program, complete with full-time counselors, was added to better help students select careers. True to his motto, Jordan refused to take any personal credit for his accomplishments.

John Henry White Sr. After serving as the principal of black schools in Eudora and Jonesboro, White found his way to Eliza Miller High School in Helena (Phillips County), where he spent the remainder of his career, 1939–1973, and made his most impressive contributions to the education of black students. White strongly encouraged the teachers at Eliza Miller to complete their college undergraduate degree programs and pursue graduate work. He also encouraged students to strive for academic excellence and to attend college so that they could escape the poverty that engulfed their delta community. He was known for transporting students to college at his own expense. His emphasis on quality education led to the accreditation of Eliza Miller by the North Central Association of Colleges and Schools.

White's accomplishments at Eliza Miller earned him the respect and admiration of his peers, and he was elected to two consecutive terms, 1946–1948, as president of the ATA. White's presidency of the ATA occurred during the period that the organization was aggressively fighting to equalize teacher salaries and improve educational facilities for black students and he did not hesitate in speaking out about the injustices. When he was told by his superintendent that there was not enough money to equalize teacher salaries and educational facilities, he replied that there was "if you divide everything by two." White was an outspoken advocate of educational equality and human dignity. The following excerpt from one of his addresses to the ATA clearly revealed his philosophy.

> I was asked upon one occasion if the Negro wants social equality. My answer was that the Negro wants working equality, eating equality, sleeping equality, riding equality, walking equality, educational equality, talking equality, housing equality, social equality, and all other kinds of equality; but we have never asked for social intermingling.[37]

Although not an advocate of desegregation, the first discussions of a merger between the ATA and the all-white Arkansas Education Association took place during White's ATA presidency, and he supported the idea but only if blacks were assured of complete equality in the organization.

Mattye Mae Woodridge. This remarkable woman's principalship was a short one, North End Elementary School, West Helena-Helena School District (Phillips County), 1950–1954, and she is best remembered as an English teacher at Eliza Miller High School, 1954–1974, who was responsible for the establishment of National Teachers (recognition) Day by Congress in 1953. Mattye Mae Whyte Woodridge was born in Kosciusico, Mississippi, on February 25, 1909. Her parents moved to Arkansas when she was an infant and settled in Helena where their daughter was educated in the public schools, graduating from Eliza Miller High School in 1927. She graduated from Fisk University in Nashville, Tennessee, in 1934 with a bachelor's degree in English. Following her graduation from Fisk, she returned to Helena where she taught the second and third grades at the North End Elementary School while waiting for a position to become open in English at Eliza Miller. The desired position at Eliza Miller became open in 1940. During her tenure at Eliza Miller, Woodridge developed a reputation as an excellent teacher and for two consecutive years, 1941–1942, she won the prestigious Eliza Miller Award which was given to the school's outstanding faculty member.[38] Inspired by the award, Woodridge believed that all teachers should be recognized for their efforts, and with the support of her principal, John H. White, she began planning a Teachers Day that would recognize all black teachers in the West Helena-Helena School District.

In January 1944, the first Teachers Day was celebrated in the Helena-West Helena School District. The program for the celebration, which was open to the public, included guest speakers, songs, and student-written poems honoring teachers. The event was held in a local church because the auditorium at Eliza Miller did not have any chairs for public seating. The program and following ones were so successful that in 1947 Woodridge, unsuccessfully, tried to get the white superintendent of schools to endorse the program and urge white teachers to participate. Undeterred by the superintendent's rejection of her invitation, Woodridge personally invited active and retired white teachers to take part in the celebration and several accepted the invitation. By 1947 she had also expanded the Teachers Day celebration by organizing a local radio broadcast of the activities and by soliciting gifts and commemorative letters for teachers from local merchants, school supply companies, and book sellers. The first Tuesday in March of each year became the established day of celebration. Until 1947, Teachers Day was a local celebration, but beginning in that year, Woodridge began lobbying for the establishment of a national teacher recognition day and wrote all of the nation's state governors seeking their support. She also wrote Eleanor Roosevelt in 1949 seeking her support. Mrs. Roosevelt, who supported the idea, advised Woodridge to share her idea with the United States commissioner of education.

In 1950, Woodridge left Eliza Miller to accept the principalship of the local North End Elementary School, but she continued to work on the establishment of a national teacher recognition day. She also continued to expand the local celebration program. An annual student lyrics contest was added. By 1950 more local white teachers had begun participating in the celebration, and black and white students competed in the lyrics contest, with the winning composition being printed on the annual Teachers Day greeting card. Woodridge also continued to correspond with Mrs. Roosevelt soliciting her support. Her determination was rewarded in 1953 when the Eighty-first United States Congress, influenced by Woodridge, Mrs. Roosevelt, the commissioner of education, and several state governors, passed legislation establishing a National Teachers Day and set the first Tuesday in March of each year for its celebration.

Although Congress had set the date for the celebration of National Teachers Day, conflict arose in Arkansas when Sid Johnson, president of the Arkansas Education Association, requested that the state legislature change the date of the celebration to the second Tuesday in March to coincide with the date for Arkansas school board elections. In 1977, responding to Johnson's request, the legislature passed Act 372 changing the date, and Governor David Pryor signed the legislation into law and recognized Johnson as the founder of National Teachers Day. When Woodridge learned of Johnson's actions, she informed him that the proper date had already been established by Congress and requested that he accept that date, but he refused. Consequently, Woodridge went on statewide television and pointed out to the public that National Teachers Day and the day for its celebration had already been set by Congress and that she was the founder. Once informed of his mistake, Governor Pryor also went on television and acknowledged his error. The issue was put to rest in 1979 when Governor Bill Clinton signed into law new legislation, Act 385, which recognized the original date for the celebration of National Teachers Day. He also recognized Woodridge, who was present for the signing, as its founder and gave her the pen with which he signed the document.

For her years of service to educators in Arkansas and throughout the nation, Woodridge has been recognized and honored by the *Memphis (Tennessee) Press Scimitar*, the *Arkansas Gazette*, and her hometown paper the *Helena World*. She has also been honored by numerous civic and social organizations including the Eta Sigma Omega chapter of the Alpha Kappa Alpha Sorority, of which she was a member (Outstanding Educator of the Year, 1974), the Parent Teacher Association of the North End Elementary School, and the Helena Chamber of Commerce. She has also been recognized by the National Biographical Institute and is listed in the 1980 edition, volumes 2 and 3, of the *International Who's Who of Intellectuals*.

Northeast Arkansas

Dr. Charles A. Hicks. Serving as the principal, 1938–1940, of the Rosenwald School for blacks in Osceola (Mississippi County), Arkansas, taught Hicks "an appreciation for the challenges of Negro leadership in rural Arkansas" and increased his desire "to make a positive impact on the life of those served." He wanted to make sure that black students in the public schools received a quality education and found the opportunity to pursue that goal in 1945 when he accepted the position of supervisor of instruction for Negro schools with the state Department of Education, a position he held for twenty years. In this position he was able to visit black schools throughout Arkansas and make sure that their curricular included not only basic education courses, but also courses that prepared students for effective participation in an increasingly competitive society. This was also a challenging position for Hicks because he often had to meet with white superintendents of schools who were not really interested in quality education for black youth and convince them to approve of college preparatory classes for black students instead of the traditional agricultural and vocational courses.

Perhaps one of the greatest challenges Hicks faced came in 1948 when he was called upon by Governor Ben Laney to support a plan to send black teachers to regionally desegregated graduate schools in order to avoid the desegregation of the state's white graduate institutions. In 1941 the state legislature passed a statute (Senate Bill 270), authorizing the payment of tuition for black teachers who attended northern graduate schools. By the end of World War II there were over one hundred applicants for out-of-state graduate tuition fees and the program was costing the state approximately $20,000 per year. Seeking a cheaper alternative Laney, in 1948, called a meeting of leading black educators in Pine Bluff at AM&N College and requested that they support his plan. As a state employee, Hicks felt pressured to support the governor's proposal, but since the University of Arkansas School of Law at Fayetteville had admitted its first black student (Silas Hunt) that same year, he rejected the governor's proposal and suggested in a letter to the governor that blacks be allowed to attend the University of Arkansas.[39] Hicks, like many of his contemporaries, was willing to put his career on the line in the battle for educational equality and equal opportunity.

Dr. McKinley Newton. A graduate of AM&N College at Pine Bluff (University of Arkansas at Pine Bluff), Newton was the principal of the black high school in Tuckerman (Jackson County), Arkansas, from 1949 until 1967. When Newton accepted the principalship of the black school in this rural farming community it was a junior high, but Newton was able to persuade the planter-controlled school board to add a grade each year until the school became a complete high school. Since the black community in Tuckerman was extremely small, Newton's ability to persuade the school board to provide a full high school education for blacks was no small accomplishment. While Newton was working to expand the educational opportunities for blacks in the Tuckerman community, he was also improving his own educational credentials, earning a master's degree from the University of Arkansas at Fayetteville and a doctorate from Xavier University in New Orleans, Louisiana.

In 1968, Newton left Tuckerman for Little Rock to accept a position as a vice president at Philander Smith College. During his tenure at Philander Smith, where he is currently (2001) employed, Newton has served as director of the institution's Cooperative Science Program and as the coordinator of Title III federal funds. He has used these positions to secure millions of dollars in grants for the strengthening of Philander's academic programs.

H. O. Williams. From 1943 to 1957, Williams was the principal of the Woodruff County Junior High School. He also coached basketball and won a state championship. He is best remembered as an outspoken, but dedicated servant to his school and community.

Willis C. Williams. This native of Forrest City, Arkansas, began his administrative career in Arkansas's public schools as principal of Brown High School in McCrory (Woodruff County), 1953–1961. During his tenure at Brown, Williams expanded the school's curriculum and its physical plant and built strong community support. Because of Williams's strong leadership and community support, Brown High was renamed Williams High School in 1961. The renaming of Brown High was an extraordinary tribute to Williams because rarely is a building named for an administrator during his active tenure. Williams continued as principal of Williams High School until he accepted the principalship of the Southside

Elementary School in the Helena-West Helena School District (Phillips County) in 1969.

When Williams arrived in Helena, the school district was in the process of desegregation, and "he was one of the individuals who helped make possible a smooth transition from 'separate but equal' facilities to fully integrated facilities."[40] Because of his leadership and communication skills, Williams was transferred from Southside Elementary to the principalship of the West Helena Junior High School in 1975 and served in that position until being named deputy superintendent in 1990. He retired in 1993. Commenting to a newspaper reporter on his years in the Helena-West Helena School District, Williams said, "I don't regret a minute of it. I've seen hundreds of instances where education made a difference, I know it works, it helps provide a better way of life for a lot of people." To make sure that education continued to improve the lives of students in the Helena-West Helena School District, Williams established an annual scholarship to be awarded to a deserving Central High School student.[41]

Leo D. Jeffers. This well-known and respected educator's career as a public school principal began in Emerson (Columbia County), Arkansas, where he was the principal of the Emerson Elementary School from 1932 to 1938. He is best known, however, for his work as principal of Harrison High School in Blytheville (Mississippi County), Arkansas, 1938–1978, and for his role in the establishment of the Southwest Arkansas School Administrators Association (1952). During his tenure at Harrison, he was known as a superb motivator of faculty and students. Not only was he concerned about the education of his faculty and students, he was also interested in the long-term economic welfare of his faculty and school employees, and in 1952 he organized the Chickasaevila Federal Credit Union (CFCU), the first of its kind for black teachers and staff in the state. After the desegregation of Blytheville's public schools, the CFCU served black and white teachers until it was incorporated into the privately owned and operated Northeast Arkansas Federal Credit Union.

In the 1940s as black principals became more aggressive in their pursuit of across-the-board educational equality, Jeffers believed that they would be more effective if they were organized. Subsequently, he began discussing his ideas with other black school administrators, and in the spring of 1949 they extended an invitation to all black administrators in southwest Arkansas to meet at the Howard County Training School in Tollette to discuss common goals and objectives and to get better acquainted with one another. Approximately thirty principals attended the meeting, which led to the formation of the Southwest Arkansas School Administrators Association (SASAA). The first official meeting of the new organization was held in 1952 at AM&N College in Pine Bluff where a constitution was adopted and Jeffers was elected president. The SASAA became so successful and powerful that the Arkansas Teachers Association, the statewide association of black teachers that initially opposed the formation of a new group, was forced to reorganize into three divisions: a division of higher education, a division of classroom teachers, and a division of school administrators.[42]

James Madison Smith Jr. For thirty-five years, 1936–1971, Smith was the principal of Carver High School in Augusta (Woodruff County), Arkansas. During his tenure at Carver High, Smith negotiated with local property owners to obtain land for the school's expansion, which led to the construction of an elementary school, an agricultural shop, a cafeteria, and a gymnasium. Under his leadership Carver's students excelled in academic achievements, music, debate, oratory, and competitive athletics. Following the merger of the all-black Arkansas Teachers Association and the all-white Arkansas Education Association in 1969, one of Smith's students, Cora Duffy McHenry, excelled to the executive directorship of the all-inclusive Arkansas Education Association. She was the first black to hold that position.

Coy E. Draper. Draper began his principalship in Earle (Crittenden County), Arkansas, in the late 1940s at Dunbar High School. He was one of the first black principals to serve in this agricultural community. During his tenure, however, there were few high school graduates. Because of the split school sessions, teenagers and younger children were often kept out of school to harvest the local cotton crops.

Iredell Golden. Mrs. Golden succeeded her husband (William R.) as principal of the school named in honor of her husband, Golden High School at Turrell (Crittenden County), Arkansas. She was principal from 1947 to 1970. Under her leadership this predominantly black school in rural Arkansas expanded its student services. She was responsible for the purchase of a piano for the music department and for the purchase of three "new" sewing machines for the home economics department. Mrs. Golden, who was trained as a home economist, also taught sewing for several years during her principalship.

Walter C. Potts. Known throughout northeast and southeast Arkansas as an excellent athletic official, Potts was also an effective educational administrator. From 1942 to 1967 he was the principal of J. S. Phelix High School in Marion (Crittenden County), Arkansas. This delta school of 362 students and 8 overworked teachers in 1944 had little support from the white planter aristocracy that controlled the county, but under Potts's progressive leadership an industrial arts building and a gymnasium were added to Phelix High School.[43]

George Monroe Kimbell. Kimbell spent his entire career as a school principal in northeast Arkansas. He served as principal of the Clarendon High School (Monroe County) for blacks, 1946–1952; the Rosenwald School at Osceola (Mississippi County), 1952–1955; Holly Grove High School (Monroe County), 1955–1956; and the Booker T. Washington High School in Jonesboro (Craighead County), 1956–1960. He is best known for leading Booker T. Washington to full accreditation by the North Central Association of Colleges and Schools.

Sandy A. Robinson. For thirty-five years, 1952–1987, Robinson was the principal of the Kaiser Elementary School at Kaiser (Mississippi County), Arkansas. He saw his job as one of preparing students for junior high school academics. Following the desegregation of the Mississippi County public schools, Robinson played a major role in helping students and parents adjust to the new educational environment.

W. L. Richardson. From 1948 to 1955, Richardson was the principal of Central High School in Parkin (Cross County), Arkansas. Not only was he the principal of the high school, which he was largely responsible for getting constructed in this rural agricultural community, he was also active in the local community where he stressed the importance of a good education.

Emanuel N. Jones. Jones was the principal of the Marion Anderson High School in Brinkley (Monroe County), Arkansas, from 1950 to 1968. Emphasizing academic excellence, Jones led Marion Anderson High School from a state rating of "C" to "A." By the time of his resignation in 1968, all of the school's teachers had earned degrees in their academic discipline.

J. C. Mabins. This native of Luxora (Mississippi County), Arkansas, began his career as a public school principal in his hometown. From 1944 to 1951, he was the principal of the local Carver High School. During his tenure, and at his consistent urging, the all-white school board terminated the practice of passing along to the black school poorly conditioned and outdated textbooks that had been previously used by the local white school. Mabins also instituted a system of accurate record keeping at Carver that was later adopted by neighboring school districts.

Mabins was also a community political activist. Responding to the United States Supreme Court decision in the case of *Smith vs. Allwright* (1944), which outlawed "all-white" Democratic primary elections, Mabins urged local blacks and blacks throughout Mississippi County to pay their poll taxes and vote in the state's Democratic primary elections so they could influence those public officials who made laws regulating their daily lives. These elections were extremely important because the Republican party in Arkansas during the era was so weak that whoever won the summer Democratic primaries was almost guaranteed victory in the coming fall elections. In 1955, perhaps due to political pressure, Mabins left Arkansas to accept a principalship of a high school in Missouri, where he served until his retirement in 1965.

Robert Wiley. A native of Mississippi County, this outstanding educator and community activist began his career in education as a teacher at the Flat Lake Elementary School (Mississippi County) in 1929. From Flat Lake, he moved to the Promised Land School, near Blytheville, where he served until the United States entered World War II. During the war, Wiley was a staff sergeant in the U.S. Army Medical Corp. After the war he returned to Arkansas where he used his GI benefits to complete college (B.A., Philander Smith College in Little Rock) and resume his career in education. From 1946 to 1950, he taught mathematics and history at Harrison High

School in Blytheville and also organized and coached the school's first competitive football team. In 1950 he served in the dual position of head teacher and principal of the Elm Street Elementary School in Blytheville. The Elm Street school burned shortly after Wiley began his tenure and was replaced with the Robinson Elementary School, and Wiley continued as principal of that institution until his retirement in 1972.

During his career in Blytheville, Wiley accumulated a number of firsts. He helped organize Mississippi County's first Head Start Program and the first Adult Education Program. During this period he also taught classes for the Veterans Administration at the Blytheville Air Force Base. Currently in his nineties, Wiley continues to be active in local community affairs.

Central Arkansas

Central Arkansas, especially Little Rock, had the highest-rated black public schools in the state and some of the state's more progressive black educational leaders. The activities of black principals and teachers in Little Rock between 1941 and 1954, in pushing for equal pay and educational facilities, played a major role in bringing about the Supreme Court's landmark decision in *Brown vs. Board of Education* (1954).

J. K. I. Blakley. Blakley's career as a public school principal began in Hope (Hempstead County), Arkansas, where he was the principal of Yerger High School from 1939 until 1944. He left Yerger in 1944 to become principal of the Conway County Training School at Menifee, Arkansas. He was the first black principal of the Conway County Training School and fought for more funding for his school and the right to spend the allocation as he saw fit, rather than be dictated to by the white superintendent of schools. He was determined not to be principal of his school in name only. His battle for administrative independence foreshadowed the battle black administrators fought throughout the 1940s and early 1950s.

Sylvia Tallier Caruth. This history-making native of Peoria, Illinois, was raised in Little Rock, Arkansas, where she graduated from the city's black public schools, Philander Smith College (B.A.) in the city, and the Teachers College of Columbia University in New York (M.A.). In 1938, she began what evolved into a forty-three-year career with the Little Rock School District, where she

worked as a teacher of music and physical education at South End
Elementary School (later named Washington Elementary School)
and at Gibbs Elementary School, and as a principal at Rightsell
Elementary from 1961 to 1963. In the 1960s, as the LRSD was going
through the desegregation process, leaders in the black community
aggressively complained to the school board about the lack of blacks
in administrative positions. Responding to these complaints the
board, led by the superintendent Floyd W. Parsons, began to
actively seek qualified blacks for administrative positions in the
LRSD, and Caruth was viewed as one of the most qualified. In 1964,
she was appointed to the position of supervisor of elementary
schools in the LRSD, thus becoming the district's first black
administrator.[44]

During her long career in the LRSD, Caruth was active in her
professional organizations, in community affairs, and in her church.
She was a member of the Arkansas Education Association and
served as president of the Little Rock Classroom Teachers
Association. Following her retirement, she served as secretary of the
AEA's Retired Teachers Association. Her community involvement
included membership in the Greater Little Rock Federation of
Women's Clubs and in the Arkansas Association of Women's Clubs
where she served as chair of the Arts Committee. She was also a
member of the Arkansas Association of University Women and
served as treasurer of the Little Rock chapter. Caruth was also a
member of the Delta Sigma Theta Sorority and served several years
as the president of the Little Rock alumnae chapter. Although
Caruth took pride in her community service organizations, she took
special pride in the religious programs of her church—Mount Zion
Baptist—where she was a member of the Outreach Sunday School
Class and chair of the Board of Christian Education.[45]

Dr. Leroy M. Christophe. This Arkansas native was a graduate of Gibbs High School in Little Rock, Talladega College in
Alabama (B.A.), the University of Chicago (M.A.), and New York
University (Ed.D.). Christophe began his career in public education as a science teacher at the Paul Laurence Dunbar High School
in Little Rock in the early 1930s. During the late 1930s he became
principal of the city's Stephens and Bush Elementary Schools.
When the United States entered World War II in 1941, Christophe
joined the U.S. Navy. After the war he returned to the Little Rock

public school system and served as the principal of Dunbar High School from 1946 until 1955. In 1955 he was named principal of the city's newly opened Horace Mann High School where he served until June 1959. He left Little Rock after nineteen years of service to assume principalship of Howard High School and Brown Technical High in Wilmington, Delaware. He retired from active service in 1975.

The 1940s and early 1950s were challenging years for black principals because of their leadership in the struggle for equal teacher salaries and equal educational opportunities for black students. Christophe did not shy away from the challenge. He was an outspoken supporter of Susie Morris (Sue Cowan Williams), who had been fired in 1943 as a result of her salary discrimination suit against the Little Rock School District. Although the federal courts ruled in her favor in 1945, she was not reinstated until 1952 and then only after Christophe pressured the district to do so. His courage and leadership skills led to his election to the presidency of the Arkansas Teachers Association, 1953–1954, and he threw the support of the organization behind the 1954 salary discrimination suit of James L. Wise against the Gould, Arkansas, School District. Although the U.S. Supreme Court had ruled that salary discrimination was unconstitutional in *Alston vs. School Board of the City of Norfolk* (1940), and the U.S. Circuit Court of Appeals at St. Louis had done the same in *Morris vs. Little Rock School District* (1945), schools in Arkansas were slow to obey the law, which explains, in part, Christophe's support of the Wise case. Before the Wise case could be settled (the federal district court was awaiting a ruling by the Supreme Court which was hearing the case of *Brown vs. Oklahoma* when Wise's suit was filed), Christophe left the Little Rock School District for a public school principalship in Delaware.[46] After he left Arkansas, Christophe maintained close contact with the ATA and friends in the state, and in 1985 he was inducted into the Arkansas African-American Hall of Fame. He was elected president of the National Dunbar Alumni Association, 1985–1989.

Elza Harris Hunter. This native of Little Rock, Arkansas, was born to Eliza and Turutha Hunter on July 14, 1908. He was a graduate of the city's black public schools, Langston College in Oklahoma (B.A.), and the University of Arkansas at Fayetteville (M.S.). He began his career in public education as a teacher of Industrial Arts at Scipio A. Jones High School in North Little Rock (Pulaski County) in 1935. He proved to be an enthusiastic, congenial, talented, and dedicated teacher. Subsequently, in 1942 when the North Little Rock School Board initiated a search for a new principal for Jones High, Hunter was selected as the school's new leader and held that position until 1970. His personal philosophy for students and teachers was "Regardless of how you treat me, I'm going to treat you right," and under his leadership, Jones High became the celebrated "Great Jones High."

A strong advocate of educational equality and excellence, Hunter led Jones High to the prized accreditation of the North Central Association of Colleges and Secondary Schools. He also served two terms, 1950 and 1951, as president of the Arkansas Teachers Association. The early 1950s were challenging years for the ATA as it considered a proposed merger with the all-white Arkansas Education Association. Hunter supported the merger only if the ATA was granted unrestricted membership in the new organization. In his 1951 address to the annual ATA meeting, he told the organization that any merger between the ATA and the AEA had to guarantee blacks the right to attend all meetings, the right to hold any elective office, and the right to serve on all committees and vote on all issues considered. Because of the insistence for equality of ATA leaders like Hunter, the AEA and the ATA were unable to consolidate as a united voice for teachers until 1969.

Jones High School was not the only beneficiary of Hunter's talents and leadership skills. He was also an influential member of the North Little Rock Administrators Association, the National Education Association, the Arkansas Education Association, the National Association of Secondary School Principals, the National Association for Public and Continuing Education, and the Board of Trustees of Shorter College (North Little Rock). Hunter served as state membership secretary of the Arkansas School Commission and as treasurer of the Little Rock Urban League. In addition to his busy professional schedule, Hunter also found time to actively participate in the religious activities of his church—Miles Memorial C.M.E.—where he was a class leader and a member of the stewards board, the trustee board, and the missionary society. He was also quite active in the civic affairs of his community where he was a member of the Board of Management of the A. W. Young YMCA;

a member of the board of the Metropolitan YMCA; president of the Apollo Terrace Housing Project; secretary of the Shorter College Housing Project; and a member of the I.P.B. of Elks. Hunter was also a 33rd Degree member of the Prince Hall Masons and a Shriner, Mohammed Temple #34. During his long and distinguished career, he received numerous commendations and awards for his unselfish service, including being named Man of the Year by the Omega Psi Phi Fraternity and Ninth District Family Man of the Year by the Urban League of Little Rock.

Gwendolyn McConico Floyd. Mrs. Floyd was the elder daughter of the late J. H. McConico, who was a pioneer in the establishment of a black fraternal, health, and burial organization in Arkansas during the 1910–1920 era. She is a graduate of Fisk University (Nashville, Tennessee) and the University of Wisconsin. The forty-one-year career of Floyd as an educator in the Little Rock public schools began in the 1930s as a teacher at Dunbar High School. From 1942 to 1945, she was the principal of the Stephens Elementary School. When Floyd was named the principal of Stephens, the school was still on the drawing board. She participated in the planning of the new facility and presided over its dedication when it was completed. In 1945 Mrs. Floyd was assigned the principalship of Washington Elementary School. This facility was poorly supplied, and Floyd immediately launched a successful campaign to stock the school's library with badly needed books and other educational materials. In 1973 the library was named in her honor.

During her career, Floyd was active in professional organizations and in civic and religious affairs. In addition to her active membership in the Arkansas Education Association and the National Education Association, she was also a member of the American Association of University Women and served as chairman emeritus of the Little Rock Urban League.

CHAPTER 6

From "Separate but Equal" to "All Deliberate Speed"

Almost eleven decades before the United States Supreme Court's landmark ruling outlawing public school segregation in *Brown vs. Board of Education* (1954), on the grounds that segregated public schools were "intrinsically inconsistent," the Supreme Court of Arkansas in *Maddox vs. Neal* (1885) declared:

> It is the duty of the directors of a school district to provide equal School facilities for the blacks and whites. . . . It is the clear intention of the constitution (Arkansas) and statutes alike, to place the means of education within the reach of every youth. Education at the public expense has thus become a legal right extended by law to all people alike.[1]

The Court's ruling in *Maddox vs. Neal* was not taken seriously by Arkansas's political and educational leaders, nor were federal court rulings in *Missouri ex. rel. Gaines vs. Canada* (1938) and *Alston vs. School Board of the City of Norfolk, Virginia* (1941). In *Missouri ex. rel. Gaines vs. Canada*, the United States Supreme Court ruled that the states were required to provide, within their borders, the same quality of education (graduate) for blacks that they provided for whites. And in *Alston vs. School Board*, the Court ruled that salary differentials between black and white (public school) teachers were unconstitutional. Since Arkansas had no graduate institutions for blacks, no law school, no medical school, and no graduate degree programs, it sought to circumvent the Court's ruling through the passage of Senate Bill 270, which was designed to keep the state's universities "all white." The statute authorized the payment of tuition for black teachers who enrolled in graduate courses at northern universities. The funds to pay for the out-of-state tuition program, however, were to be taken from the budget of the only state-supported black institution of higher education, AM&N College at Pine Bluff, which was already disgracefully underfunded.[2] While state education and political leaders sought ways to keep its institutions of higher education segregated, they simply ignored the Court's *Alston* decision because it would have cost the state $1,000,000 to equalize black and white teacher salaries.[3]

Arkansas was not the only southern state that refused to comply with the federal court ruling relative to equal educational access and equal teacher salaries. The latter, because of the cost involved and the general belief that black teachers were inferior to white teachers, became a very controversial issue in Arkansas during and after World War II when black teachers began to actively seek salary equalization. In 1949, black teachers in Fort Smith and DeWitt filed salary equalization suits in federal court against their respective school districts. The Fort Smith suit charged discrimination in facilities and asked the court for equalization, while the DeWitt suit made the charge, but asked the court to grant blacks the right to attend the better funded and equipped local white school.[4] Once the suits were filed in federal court, Ed McCuistion, director of the Division of Negro Education for the State Department of Education, admitted that there were gross inequities in educational facilities (approximately $7,000,000 to $10,000,000, for black and white schools), and said that it would take approximately $4,158,000 just to equalize per pupil expenditures, exclusive of building costs. And A. B. Bonds, commissioner of education for Arkansas, also admitted that discrepancies existed, but charged that they were due to the fact that local education officials had diverted funds to white schools that had been appropriated for black schools. Responding to the news of funding inequities and to Bonds's comments, Governor Sid McMath threatened to sue local school districts if the diversions continued.[5] Reacting to the governor's threat, a few local school districts in Arkansas made an effort to improve educational facilities for blacks and teacher salaries. In Lawrence County, for example, expenditures on black schools increased from $20 per pupil to $59, while expenditures for whites only increased from $74 to $78. This was clearly an example of an effort to gradually equalize expenditures, but other counties took no action or moved in the opposite direction. The latter was the case in Faulkner County where per pupil expenditures dropped from $71 to $64 for blacks and increased from $76 to $82 for whites.[6]

Although a few Arkansas school districts moved toward equalizing facilities and salaries for black schools and their teachers, the majority continued to discriminate. In 1949, due to the diversion of state appropriated funds for black schools to white schools, the cost of equalization was $11,000,000; by 1952 that had grown to an estimated $21,000,000.[7] Due to the failure of the Arkansas Department of Education to force local school districts to disburse funds for their appropriated purposes, many black educators, as early as 1949, began to reluctantly consider the desegregation of public education as the only solution to the problem.[8] While a few blacks began to look at desegregation as a solution to the inequities between black school buildings and teacher salaries, others sought to seek full implementation of "Separate but Equal" through the federal courts. In 1953 James L. Wise, a black social studies teacher, coach, and bus driver in the Gould (Arkansas) Special School District, who only earned $175 per month, filed a salary equalization suit in federal court against his district on behalf of himself and other black teachers. He was immediately fired by the district, and other black teachers identified in the suit were fired at the end of the 1952–1953 school year.[9] The federal circuit court did not render a decision in the Wise case because it was awaiting a ruling from the U.S. Supreme Court which was considering the case of *Brown vs. Board of Education of Topeka* which covered many of the issues in the Wise suit and those filed by blacks in Fort Smith and DeWitt. On May 17, 1954, the Court handed down its decision in *Brown* which, in part, declared that "We conclude that in the field of public education that the doctrine of 'separate but equal' has no place. Separate educational facilities are inherently unequal."

The *Brown* decision ushered in a new and controversial era for public education in Arkansas. The Court had ruled segregated public education unconstitutional and ordered its end. In response, a few school districts in the state began to comply. The first was the Fayetteville School District in Arkansas. Within days of the Court's decision (May 21, 1954), the Fayetteville school board voted unanimously to desegregate its senior high school, grades 10–12. Prior to 1947, black students in Fayetteville did not have access to a complete high school education, but in that year the Fayetteville School District voted to pay the expense of sending black students who qualified for a high school education to either Fort Smith or Hot Springs, Arkansas.[10] The speed of the desegregation process in Fayetteville led Daisy Bates, leader of the movement to desegregate Central High School in Little Rock, to comment, "that all the brains and law-abiding white people of Arkansas live in Fayetteville."[11] There was little opposition when the district desegregated, but a crisis developed when Hoxie (Lawrence County) moved toward desegregation in 1955. White supremacists, led by Amos Guthridge, a segregationist attorney from Little Rock, and James D. Johnson of Crossett, Arkansas, converged on Hoxie and urged massive local resistance. Desegregation was achieved, however, after the Hoxie School Board obtained a federal court injunction that restrained the troublemakers. The Hoxie situation was a preview, in miniature, of what was to come when Central High School in Little Rock faced the challenge of desegregation.[12]

While Little Rock engaged in a heated desegregation battle, other school districts in the state attempted to circumvent the *Brown* decision by equalizing black and white teacher salaries, by improving the physical facilities of black schools, and by adopting "freedom of choice" programs. By 1963, Arkansas ranked first in the nation in the percentage of funds spent on black schools. The circumvention strategy, however, did not work because, in spite of the improvements in the physical structure of black schools, few black students chose to attend white schools and no whites chose to attend black schools. Thus, Arkansas's public schools remained basically segregated. In 1963, nine years after the *Brown* decision, only .21 percent of black public school students in the state were attending predominantly white schools.[13] Not only did the schools remain segregated, so did their faculties. Although the Southern Education Reporting Service did not keep statistics on faculty desegregation in Arkansas for the 1954–1964 decade, it did issue the following statement relative to faculty desegregation in the state:

> Little Rock had four white and four Negro teachers in desegregated situations in 1965–66, but segregation generally was maintained at this level in the state until 1966–1967.[14]

In its 1954 *Brown* decision and its 1955 "All Deliberate Speed" decree, which called for an immediate end to segregated public schools, the Supreme Court did not specifically address the issue of public school faculty desegregation. Subsequently, as desegregation slowly progressed in Arkansas, many black teachers lost their jobs and black administrators were either demoted to faculty positions or "promoted" into created positions with impressive sounding titles (assistant principal, assistant superintendent, assistant supervisor for instructions, etc.), but with no real authority or badly needed contact

with black students. White school superintendents attempted to jus-
tify the dismissals and demotions on the grounds that many of those
who lost their positions were incompetent or inadequately trained.[15]
The insinuation of black racial inferiority was a reflection of the
inherent racism of many white public school superintendents, and
black educators strongly resented the racial slur.[16] Educational statistics revealed that there was little difference between the qualifications of black and white teachers and administrators. By 1963, 90
percent of all black teachers held college degrees in their speciality
areas, the same as whites, and only two percentage points separated
black and white master's degree holders—13 and 15 percent—
respectively.[17] Race, not college degrees, was the issue when it came
to faculty desegregation. As Dr. Albert S. Baxter, an associate professor of education at AM&N College, commented in 1970: "If I had
a degree from the Sorbonne (in France), my education would still be
inferior because I am black."[18]

Unfair dismissals and demotions during the first two decades of
desegregation in Arkansas forced black administrators and teachers
to turn to the federal courts for protection. In 1966, Terry Humble,
the white superintendent of the Morrilton (Arkansas) School
District, informed the black principal of the all-black Sullivan High
School that he was being retired because he had reached age sixty-
five and, due to desegregation, the school would be closed and all of
its black teachers dismissed. In an effort to keep his job, Clement S.
Smith, a science teacher at Sullivan, filed suit against the district in
the U.S. Eighth Circuit Court. In *Smith vs. Board of Education,
Morrilton School District No. 32*, the Court ordered the district to
retain Smith and awarded damages to the six dismissed teachers. The
Court in granting Smith relief said:

> It is our firm conclusion that the reach of the *Brown* decisions,
> although they specified only pupil discrimination, clearly extends
> to the proscription of the employment and assignment of public
> school teachers on a racial basis.[19]

The Court reaffirmed its decision in several other similar cases filed
against Arkansas public school districts.[20]

In the 1960s, the federal courts in case after case ruled in favor of
black principals and teachers who had lost their jobs due to desegregation, but the discriminatory behavior of white school boards and
superintendents continued. From 1966 to 1968, two hundred and

twelve black administrators and teachers lost their jobs due to the racism that accompanied desegregation.[21] Many of those who were able to keep their jobs owed their continued employment to the protective efforts of the Arkansas Teachers Association, the Legal Defense Fund of the National Association for the Advancement of Colored People, and the hard work of a group of courageous attorneys in Little Rock led by J. R. Booker and John W. Walker, who spoke for them before the United States Eighth Circuit Court.[22] Not only did black administrators and teachers go to federal court in an effort to keep their jobs, many of them met the challenge of desegregation by increasing their educational credentials, by creative teaching, and by instituting innovative educational programs in their schools. Several of those who were able to survive during the early years of desegregation went on to play influential roles in the transition from segregated to desegregated public schools. The following pages tell, in part, the stories of black administrators, primarily experienced black high school principals, who both suffered from and sometimes triumphed over the odds against them in the desegregation battle.[23]

Southwest Arkansas

Wilmar Moss. This native of Magnolia (Columbia County), Arkansas, was the principal of Holman Elementary School in Stuttgart (Arkansas County), Arkansas, from 1960 to 1972. In 1972, due to the desegregation of Stuttgart's public schools, Moss returned to Magnolia where he was principal of the predominantly black Walker Elementary School, 1972–1980, and superintendent of the Walker School District, 1980–1988.

X. L. Jones. Jones, principal of the Rockport Elementary School, 1960–1965, was an experienced educator who spent his entire professional career in Malvern (Hot Spring County), Arkansas. At the end of the 1964–1965 school year, Jones was transferred to the local Tuggle Elementary School where he served as principal from 1965 to 1975. By 1975, Malvern had completed the desegregation of its public schools, and Jones lost his principalship and was forced to return to the classroom. He returned to the administrative level in the Malvern schools in 1987 as the director of federal programs and served in that position until retirement in 1992.

Johnnie Belle Henderson. For more than thirty years Mrs. Henderson was an outstanding mathematics teacher at Langston High School in Hot Springs (Garland County), Arkansas. During her teaching career, Langston received several grants from major American corporations to support her mathematics education program, and a number of her students received mathematics scholarships from major universities. In 1969, Henderson was pulled out of the classroom and appointed principal of Langston. She was the last principal of Langston High School because by the end of the 1969–1970 academic year the Hot Springs School District had completed its desegregation process and Langston became a junior high school.

Peter G. Faison. Faison's career as a public school principal in Arkansas spanned almost three decades. His first principalship was at the Wynn High School in Garland (Miller County), Arkansas, 1959–1960. Following his brief stop in Garland, Faison moved on to become principal of the Immanuel High School at Almyra (Arkansas County), Arkansas, 1960–1963, and of Central High School (Chicot County), 1963–1968. In the fall of 1968, Faison moved to Little Rock and served as principal of the predominantly black Pine Elementary School in North Little Rock (Pulaski County) from 1968 to 1972. During his tenure at Pine Elementary, the school's faculty was desegregated. Faison was able to retain his principalship, but according to Faison, the superintendent of schools took his best teachers and replaced them with white teachers of a lower caliber, which severely hurt the quality education program he was trying to establish.

Clifford L. Bradford. Bradford was the superintendent of the rural Oak Grove School District in Rosston (Nevada County), Arkansas, 1966–1967. Although he only served one year as superintendent, it was a productive one. During that year, Bradford was able to secure Title I federal funds for the implementation of a needed reading program and for the purchase of the district's first Xerox machines.

Reverend Jeff F. Carr. Carr began his tenure in public school administration at the J. E. Wallace High School in Fordyce (Dallas County), Arkansas, where he served from 1982 to 1985. He left the public schools in 1985 and accepted a position with the Arkansas

Department of Education as a supervisor of migrant education. This position took Carr from his first love, public school administration/teaching, and he resigned his position with the state education department and accepted a teaching position in the Little Rock public schools where he is currently (2001) employed.

Hyacinth Dean. From 1983 to 1986, Dean was a principal in the Oak Grove School District at Rosston (Nevada County), Arkansas. During her administration, an effective program for dealing with students with discipline problems was established.

Reverend Marvin T. Easter. Reverend Easter was the principal of the poor and overwhelmingly black New Harrison Grove Elementary School in Rosston (Nevada County), Arkansas, 1958–1961, and of the local Oak Grove High School, 1961–1966. Because this was a financially strapped district, Easter spent most of his time raising funds in order to make sure his teachers and students had the necessary teaching and learning materials.

Hugh Perry Watson. Watson was a native of Texarkana, Arkansas, but grew up in El Dorado (Union County), where he graduated from high school. He went on to earn a B.A. degree at Tuskegee Institute in Alabama and did further study at Lemoyne Owens College (Memphis, Tennessee), Henderson State University (Arkadelphia, Arkansas), and the University of Arkansas at Fayetteville. Following a short teaching career in Alabama, Watson returned to Arkansas where he taught in several public schools before being named principal of Washington High School in El Dorado in 1964, becoming the only graduate of Washington High School to become principal of his alma mater. Watson was one of the few black principals who was able to maintain his position as a principal during the first turbulent decade of desegregation. This was due to his administrative skills and his ability to effectively communicate with black and white leaders of the community. In fact, his white superintendent credited him for the smooth nonconfrontational way the El Dorado School District was desegregated.

Darlene Shepherd. Following a brief career as a classroom teacher, Shepherd was named superintendent of the Walker School District at Magnolia (Columbia County), Arkansas, in 1962. After three years in this position, 1962–1965, she left the superintendency to become the principal of the local Walker High School, 1965–1967. She eventually left the Walker School District, but returned in 1992 and served another five years as superintendent, 1992–1997. Among her many accomplishments and the one she took the most pride in was the construction of a one-thousand-seat gymnasium in her poor district. The gym also served as a multipurpose building for the community.

Dr. Luther H. Black. Dr. Black, one of seventeen children, was born in Kilbourne, Louisiana. Since there were no black public schools in Kilbourne, Black received his elementary education in a local church school and at a private religious school in Dermott, Arkansas. He later attended the Dunbar High School in Little Rock and completed his secondary education at Arkansas Baptist College in Little Rock, where he graduated from its high school division. He remained at Baptist and earned an associate of arts degree before transferring to Philander Smith College where he earned the B.A. degree in education and social science. Thirsting for knowledge, Black went on to earn an M.A. and a diploma of advanced study in administration and supervision at Columbia University in New York. He also held honorary doctorates from Shorter College and Arkansas Baptist College. While earning his advanced degrees, Black worked as a public schoolteacher and principal and devoted forty years of his life to public education in Arkansas. The last two decades of his career were spent educating Arkansas's adult population, and when he retired in 1987 he had become known as the "Father of Adult Education in Arkansas."

Black began his administrative career as the principal of Unity High School in Foreman (Little River County), Arkansas, 1947–1953. He left Unity High in 1953 to become principal of the Foster High School in Lewisville (Lafayette County), Arkansas, where he served from 1953 to 1965. During Black's tenure at Foster High, Lafayette County desegregated its public schools, and Black is credited with making the desegregation process a smooth one. In 1965, Dr. Black left public school education to accept a position with the Arkansas Department of Education as a supervisor of adult education. He later became the first black to be named director and manager of the program. Under his leadership the Adult Education Program expanded from one small office in the DOE to cover almost all of the state. During his tenure as the director of DOE's Adult

Education Program, Black authored *Prescriptions for Adult Education and Secondary Education* (Detroit: Harlo Press, 1974), which was adopted by several colleges and universities and used as a guide for the establishment of education programs. During his retirement dinner in 1987, speaker after speaker recognized and praised Dr. Black for his dedication and contributions to the education of Arkansans. Larry Young, an adult education administrator, described him "as a persistent man who never set a goal he did not reach." Effie Parham, an instructor at Mississippi County Community College, said he was a man with "an unconditional regard for our fellow man." And W. F. "Bill" Foster, a state legislator from England, Arkansas, said that "he was our guide in providing education for adults." Black's contribution to adult education was also recognized by several cities in the state. The adult learning center in Benton, Arkansas, was named the Luther H. Black Learning Center, and a day-care center in Dermott, Arkansas, was named the Luther H. Black Day Care Center.

As a public school and adult education administrator, Black was quite active in his professional organizations. He served on the Board of Directors of the Arkansas Teachers Association, was one of the founders of the Arkansas School Administrators Association and its treasurer for many years, a member of the Advisory Council on Community Service and Continuing Education, and a life member of the National Education Association. Also on the national level, he was the first black to be elected chairman of the board of directors for the National Association for Public and Continuing Education. Dr. Black was also an avid reader with a special love for reading and writing poetry. In 1967, he wrote a book of poems, *This Life*, which was published by Vantage Press in New York. Black was a man of ordinary beginning, but one who made a unique and lasting impact on the education of the people of Arkansas.

Mattie L. Collier. From 1949 to 1971, Mrs. Collier was the principal of Goldstein Elementary School in Hot Springs (Garland County), Arkansas. Goldstein was one of the first schools in the Hot Springs School District to desegregate its faculty and student body. During the process, Collier earned a reputation as a good and fair administrator. Her success can be attributed to her high visibility and to her administrative and communication skills. Those characteristics also helped her and Mrs. Lillie Peters, of Jonesboro, serve as co-presidents of the newly integrated Arkansas Association of Elementary School Principals.

Everett Edward Taylor. This educator and Baptist minister spent thirty-eight years, 1933–1971, as the principal of the Little River County Training School in Ashdown, Arkansas. Taylor was a native Arkansan who graduated from the state's public schools, AM&N College at Pine Bluff (B.A.), and Henderson State University at Arkadelphia (M.A.). During his thirty-eight years as principal of the Little River County Training School, Taylor also served, simultaneously, seventeen years as the moderator of the Little River District Missionary Baptist Association and for thirty years as the pastor of the Honey Creek Baptist Church. In 1988, because of his success as an educator and public servant, Governor Bill Clinton appointed Taylor to a seven-year term on the Board of Trustees of Henderson State University.

Thomas E. Patterson. Patterson, a native Texan, moved to Arkansas following World War II and became one of the most influential educational leaders in the state. He was a graduate of the public elementary schools in Texas, Polytechnic High School in Los Angeles, California, Wiley College in Texas (B.A.), and Indiana University (M.A.), and he also did further study at the University of California and the University of Texas. After serving the U.S. Army as a master sergeant during the war, he settled in Arkansas where he had accepted a position as a teacher in the Ozan High School in Howard County where he organized and served as secretary of the Howard County Teachers Association. In 1947, he was named principal of Ozan High. Just as he had organized the Howard County Teachers Association, Patterson, as a principal, played an influential role in the founding of the Southwestern Administrators Association.[24] He was the principal of Ozan High until he was hired as the superintendent of the Childress School District in Nashville (Howard County), Arkansas, in 1962, becoming one of four black public school superintendents in the state. While serving as a teacher and a principal, Patterson was a strong supporter of the Arkansas Teachers Association, the professional organization for black educators in the state.

In 1962, Patterson became the first full-time executive secretary of the ATA, served under four presidents of the organization, and became one of its pillars of stability and progress. The 1960s were challenging times for Patterson and the ATA as the pace of desegregation increased, threatening the careers of black administrators and teachers. As the ATA's executive secretary, Patterson devoted much of his time to preparing black principals, teachers, and parents for desegregation, and defending their legal rights under law. He was the principal organizer of the ATA's Citizen Education Program, a program designed to help blacks qualify to vote, to encourage family support for public schools, and to promote the general welfare of educators and students. As desegregation progressed in Arkansas, it was inevitable that there would be a merger of the two separate organizations for teachers in the state, the Arkansas Teachers Association and the all-white Arkansas Education Association. Merger talks between the two organizations had begun as early as 1948, and Patterson, as executive secretary of the ATA, played a major role in outlining the terms of the merger, which finally occurred in 1969. Under the merger agreement, the ATA was absorbed by the larger AEA and Patterson became the assistant executive secretary of the AEA, 1969–1977, and associate executive secretary, 1977–1981. In the "new" AEA, Patterson also served as chair of the organization's Commission on Human Relations. As chair of the human relations commission, Patterson was responsible for defining and evaluating policies relevant to equal educational opportunities, salaries, race relations, intergroup relationships, and for developing appropriate programs to address those issues.[25]

During his tenure as executive secretary of the ATA, before the merger, Patterson helped to complete a thirty-year goal of the organization—the construction of a headquarters building for the organization. He not only helped design the building and develop plans for its use, he also presided over its dedication ceremony on April 11, 1965. The facility served not only as the headquarters for the ATA, but also as Patterson's headquarters when he became the first black to successfully run for a position on the Little Rock School Board where he served five three-year terms. During the closing years of his outstanding career, Patterson was commissioned by the National Education Association to write a history of the ATA. His history of the organization, entitled *History of the Arkansas Teachers Association*, was completed and published in 1981.

Much of the information in this chronicle on black public school administrators has been taken from Patterson's work.

Mitchell Roland. This progressive administrator held the dual positions of principal at Carver High School in Rosston (Nevada County), Arkansas, and superintendent of the Oak Grove School District, 1961–1969. During his superintendency of the Oak Grove School District, a new elementary school was constructed. Roland also secured Title III and Title VI federal funds to expand the library and implement a special program in mathematics to improve student math skills.

Southeast Arkansas

In terms of numbers, northeast and southeast Arkansas, commonly referred to as Arkansas's "Black Belt," contained the majority of the state's black population. These areas were dominated by white planters, poor black sharecroppers, and day laborers who had to be taught the value of a good education. The black public school administrators who labored in these areas, in this case, southeast Arkansas, performed yeomen duty.

Fred Martin Jr. Martin spent his entire professional career in Altheimer (Jefferson County), Arkansas, and left an outstanding legacy of achievements. He began his career in 1949 as a mathematics teacher in the Altheimer Training School and became its principal in 1955. From 1955 to 1961, Martin worked to expand the school's curriculum and physical plant. In 1961 the school board, in recognition of Martin's dedication, changed the name of the Altheimer Training School to the Martin High School, and Martin continued to serve as principal of the school. In 1969 the name of Martin High was changed to Altheimer High School, and Martin was again retained as principal. After ten years of existence as the Altheimer High School, the institution underwent another name change as a result of desegregation and became the Altheimer-Sherrill High School. Martin continued to serve as principal of the school until he was hired as the superintendent of the Altheimer School District in 1982. He served in this capacity until his retirement in 1988. During Martin's tenure as principal of Altheimer High School, a new red-brick school was constructed, a new gymnasium was built, the school's first band and competitive athletic program were organized, and, more importantly, the school was accredited by the North Central Association of Colleges and Schools. Not only was the school accredited by North Central, Martin became the first black Arkansan to serve on a North Central accrediting team.

During Martin's superintendency, the Altheimer School District continued to grow in terms of educational programs. With assistance from the Ben J. Altheimer Foundation, Martin was able to secure, over a twelve-year period, two million dollars for the implementation at the Altheimer-Sherrill High School programs in vocational arts and business administration.[26] Classes in these programs were open to everyone in the community, student and adults, and were taught during the summer months by selected faculty from the high school. Martin left the public schools in 1988 and entered politics and currently (1999) serves as mayor of the city of Altheimer, Arkansas.

Homer L. Watkins. Watkins was the principal of the C. P. Coleman High School in Pine Bluff (Jefferson County), Arkansas, 1955–1970. Under Watkins's leadership the all-black school improved from a state class "C" rating to "A" and was fully accredited by the North Central Association of Colleges and Schools. In 1970 Coleman High, due to desegregation, was merged with the all-white Watson Chapel High School, and Watkins became another experienced black administrator victimized by the desegregation process. Following the merger of Coleman and Watson Chapel, Watkins was "promoted" to the position of assistant superintendent of schools for the Watson Chapel School District. One of Watkins's outstanding achievements as principal of Coleman, and as the assistant superintendent for the Watson Chapel School District, was his success in getting students to read. Here are three of his favorite quotes were: "The journey of a thousand miles begins with one step forward"; "Keep your eyes focused in the right direction"; and "Watch your evaluation as you progress."

S. E. Bullock. Bullock was the principal of the Bradley County High School in Warren (Bradley County), Arkansas, from 1950 until 1956. During his administration, Bullock was able to persuade the school board to build a new high school for blacks. The new structure included a library and a gymnasium, but no funds were included in the building project for stocking the library. Bullock, subsequently, launched a library fund drive in the local community and raised the money needed to stock the library. He also expanded the curriculum of the new school to include typing and shorthand. The new physical plant, well-equipped library, and expanded curriculum led to the full accreditation of Bradley High by the North Central Association of Colleges and Schools. In 1956, perhaps due to his proven record as an educator and a builder, Bullock was hired as principal of Lincoln High School in Fort Smith (Sebastian County), where he served until 1966 both as principal of Lincoln and as the supervisor for three elementary schools. If the Fort Smith School District was looking for an educational leader and builder when Bullock was hired, they were not disappointed. During his tenure at Lincoln, Bullock expanded the school's curriculum to include a counseling program and music (band). Although Bullock had an outstanding record as a public school administrator, he was not retained when Fort Smith desegregated its public schools. In 1966, he, like several other former black administrators, accepted a job with the state Department of Education where he worked as a supervisor of secondary and adult education until his retirement in 1982.

Dr. John L. Phillips. An accomplished educator, Dr. Phillips served as principal of three Arkansas schools: Pastoria Elementary in Sherrill (Jefferson County), 1957–1960; Fields High School in Gould (Lincoln County), 1960–1962; and the Immanuel High School in Almyra (Arkansas County), 1962–1964. Everywhere Phillips served, he made significant improvements in curriculums and student services. While at Pastoria Elementary, Phillips established a nutritional food program (milk and other refreshments) for low-income students. At Fields High School he substantially improved communications between the local school board and the black community. And during his two years at Immanuel, he designed and implemented an educational program that departmentalized grades 3–6. The program allowed students to rotate through language arts, reading, mathematics, and science classes. This system allowed students to benefit from instructions from teachers who had special training in the subject areas and was cited by one of the state supervisors of elementary education as an excellent model for elementary schools. In 1964 Phillips was hired as superintendent of Arkansas School District No. 73. He was the first and only black to hold this position. During his superintendency, Dr. Phillips helped the Stuttgart and DeWitt public schools make a smooth transition from segregation to desegregation.

Juanita Leverett. Mrs. Leverett spent her entire career as a principal in the public schools of Dumas (Desha County), Arkansas. From 1965 to 1970, she was the principal of Reed Elementary, and from 1970 to 1986 she was principal of Central Elementary. While at Reed, Leverett led the school from a state rating of "C" to "A." When she assumed the leadership of Central, the school already had a state "A" rating, but was not a North Central accredited institution. Under Leverett's leadership, Central received the long-sought and important North Central accreditation.

Dr. Levenis Penix. A native of Thornton (Calhoun County), Arkansas, Penix was a graduate of the local public schools, Shorter College in North Little Rock (B.A.), Henderson State University in Arkadelphia (M.A.), and East Texas State University (Ed.D.). He also completed further studies at the University of Wisconsin (Madison), Indiana University (Bloomington), and George Peabody College for Teachers in Nashville, Tennessee. He began his career in public education as a mathematics and science teacher and his principalship in 1969 when he was named principal of the Calhoun County High School in his hometown. He served only one year as principal of Calhoun because Thornton desegregated its public schools in 1970 and the students at Calhoun were sent to the formerly all-white Thornton High School. Unlike many black administrators during the early desegregation years, Penix was retained as principal of Thornton where he served until 1985. He was the first and last black principal of the school. During his administration at Thornton High, Penix expanded the school curriculum through the introduction of ethnic/multicultural studies, a comprehensive music program, choral music, and a competitive band program. Many of Thornton's students received music scholarships at major universities. Penix's style of leadership earned him the respect and support of the school board and black and white community leaders. Unfortunately for Penix, the patrons of the Bearden School District did not hold the same respect for Penix as those in Thornton, and when the larger Bearden and Thornton School Districts consolidated in 1985, he lost his principalship.

Penix, however, was a proven administrator and was not to be kept out of administration permanently, and in 1987 he was named principal of the Bearden Junior High School where he served until 1991. When the district reorganized in 1991 the Bearden Junior High School, at Penix's suggestion, was abolished and replaced with a middle school, and Penix was named principal of the new Bearden Middle School. Under Penix's leadership, the new middle school was fully accredited by the North Central Association of Colleges and Schools. He also expanded the middle-school curriculum through the establishment of special courses that allowed students to earn high school credits while still in the eighth grade.

Although no longer in public education, Dr. Penix continues to be active in civic and professional affairs. Currently (1999), he is a licensed and practicing professional counselor in Thornton and serves as secretary of the Board of Directors of the South Arkansas Regional Health Center and the Arkansas Board of Examiners in Counseling. He also holds a seat on the Thornton City Council and on the Board of Trustees of Shorter College in North Little Rock.

Waymon T. Cheney. Like the overwhelmingly majority of black administrators, Cheney began his career as a public schoolteacher before becoming a principal. He began his principalship at the Indiana Street Elementary School in Pine Bluff (Jefferson County), where he served from 1942 to 1958. After sixteen years at the Indiana Street Elementary School, Cheney was assigned to the local Southeast High School where he served until 1970. Under his leadership, Southeast progressed to an "A" state rating and full accreditation by the North Central Association of Colleges and Schools. When Pine Bluff completed the desegregation of its public schools in 1970, Cheney was "promoted" to the assistant principalship of Pine Bluff High School where he served until retirement in 1979. The Cheney Elementary School in Pine Bluff was named for this outstanding educator.

Louis Thomas Black. One of three brothers (Luther H. and Lloyd W. Black), to simultaneously serves as public school principals in Arkansas, Black was the principal of the Onedia Elementary and Junior High School at Onedia (Phillips County), Arkansas, 1960–1961. Black set out to build a quality educational program at Onedia by hiring only teachers who had completed degrees in their speciality areas. Unfortunately, Black was not able to complete his plans because of his untimely death after only eight months on the job.

Cota Theophilus Cobb. Cobb (1907–1988) was one of five children born to William and Ola Cobb in Madison (St. Francis County), Arkansas. He was educated in the local black public schools of Madison and Forrest City, Arkansas, and went on to earn a B.A. in mathematics at Rust College in Holly Springs, Mississippi, and an M.S.E. at the University of Arkansas-Fayetteville. He also studied at Fisk University in Nashville, Tennessee.[27]

Cobb began his career as a public school educator at the Robert R. Moton High School in Marianna (Lee County), Arkansas, where he taught mathematics and served as the school's principal from 1930 until 1932. He resigned from his position at R. R. Moton in order to return to his hometown of Madison where he served as the principal of the Madison Training School from 1932 to 1941. According to those who remembered him, Cobb did an outstanding job at Madison and in recognition of his accomplishments, the nearby Forrest City School District offered him the principalship of the much larger Lincoln High School in that city. He accepted, and served from 1941 to 1965.

When Cobb was named principal of Lincoln, the school served as a junior high and high school. In 1958, the junior high became a separate academic unit with its own principal and staff, and Cobb proceeded to transform Lincoln into a modern educational complex which featured departments of home economics, music, art, trades and industry (for those who lived in Forrest City), agriculture (for students who were bussed into the city from rural areas), business education, and physical education. Cobb also successfully lobbied the all-white Forrest City School Board to build a gymnasium for Lincoln's developing basketball program. This was an important addition to Lincoln because prior to the gym's completion in 1954, the school's basketball team practiced on an outdoor packed-dirt court and played all of their games on the road.[28] Cobb also played a significant role in persuading the school board to construct a football field for Lincoln so that the school would not have to share a field with the all-white Forrest City High School, which often caused scheduling conflicts. The new athletic field, with adequate seating, lighting, and a security fence, was dedicated in 1965 and named Cobb Field.[29] When asked about his accomplishments at Lincoln, Cobb, always modest, gave all the credit to others and said that "my success is due largely to the cooperation of all parties concerned—our school board, superintendents [he served under four], patrons, teachers, and students."[30] Because of his outstanding leadership at Lincoln, Cobb earned a listing in *Who's Who in Education in the South and Southwest*.

The Forrest City School Board began the desegregation process in 1965, and Cobb was "promoted" to the position of assistant superintendent of the Forrest City School District. He served in this position until his retirement in 1971. He is remembered by many of Lincoln's graduates for his famous annual spring speech to them about the "birds and bees," and for the many conversations he held with them during Lincoln High School reunions, 1981, 1984, and 1987.

During his long career in public education, Cobb was an active member of the all-black Arkansas Teachers Association and of the Arkansas Education Association after the merger of the two organizations in 1969. He also held a lifetime membership in the National Education Association. His retirement from the Forrest City school system, however, did not lead to inactivity. He was an active member of the St. Francis County Retired Teachers Association until his death, and he devoted much of his time to the community service programs of his fraternity (Omega Psi Phi, XI Rho Chapter, Keeper of Finance for twenty years), and the Charles Summer Masonic Lodge #185, the Marion and Gold National Alumni Association of Lincoln High School, and the Forrest City Public Housing Authority. Cobb was also a deeply religious man and did not allow his busy professional or retirement schedule to interfere with his service to the Madison Light Missionary Baptist Church where he served in several capacities including church clerk, Sunday School teacher, and deacon/trustee.

Clyde W. Thompson. In 1964, Thompson was named principal of the Desha County High School in McGhee, Arkansas. With the support of a reorganized and effective Parent Teacher Association, for which he was responsible, Thompson made school an important part of the recently desegregated public school system. His administration was characterized by a personal touch as he often paid encouraging visits to the homes of students and parents who were experiencing difficulty in adjusting to a desegregated school environment. Thompson's undergraduate training was in music, and he was an accomplished pianist and organist. Consequently, the music department at McGhee High School won regional and state recognition for its excellence.

Alice B. Banks. Mrs. Banks began her educational career as a teacher in the Desha County Elementary Training School in McGhee, Arkansas. When the McGhee public schools were desegregated, the county training school for blacks became the Desha County Elementary School, and Banks served as its principal from 1965 to 1984. Although there was an initial decline in enrollment due to desegregation and the appointment of a black as principal of the elementary school, Banks quickly developed a reputation as a caring and professional administrator. Under her leadership the curriculum of Desha Elementary expanded and the school regained many of the students it had lost due to desegregation.

Leon A. Phillips Jr. This educational fixture in Phillips County began his administrative career as principal of the Lake View Elementary School, 1960–1968. From 1968 to 1977 he served as principal of the local C. V. White High School, and in 1977 he was hired as superintendent of the Lake View School District and currently (1999) serves in this position. During his tenure as superintendent of the Lake View School District, he managed to secure funds for the construction of a new elementary school, a home economics building, and a gymnasium. To encourage unity and to help solve discipline problems, Phillips, in 1995, persuaded parents in the district to adopt uniforms for grades K-6. In 1999 the uniforms became a district requirement for all grades.

The Lake View School District is located in a section of Phillips County that was once controlled by white planters, and support for local black public education was almost nonexistent. The district was and continues to be poorly funded, and teacher salaries are still among the lowest in the state. Therefore, Phillips's accomplishments within this almost barren environment looms large. In 1998, Phillips, seeking to improve funding for his district so that salaries and facilities could be improved, successfully sued the Arkansas Department of Education on the grounds that its formula for funding public schools discriminated against poor districts. The state courts ordered the DOE to recalculate its funding distribution formula to ensure equity. As of this writing (2000), the DOE and the Arkansas Legislature are trying to develop a more equitable funding formula that will meet court requirements. While the state legislature and the DOE work on a solution to the funding problem, Phillips continues to serve as superintendent of the Lake View School District and as mayor of the city of Lake View.

Fulton J. Walker. For thirty-six years Walker labored as a public school administrator in Arkansas. From 1954 to 1965 he was the principal of the Lincoln Elementary and High School in Star City (Lincoln County); Carver Elementary in Pine Bluff (Jefferson County), 1965–1968; and Forrest Park Elementary School, also in Pine Bluff, 1968–1972. While at Carver, Walker organized a thirty-piece concert and marching band, one of two elementary bands in the area. In 1968, Walker left Carver to become the first black principal of the local and formerly all-white Forrest Park Elementary School. Following a familiar pattern relative to the positioning of black administrators during the first two decades of desegregation in Arkansas, Walker lost his principalship in 1972 and was demoted to an assistant principal's position and placed in charge of federal programs. He remained in this position until his retirement in 1986.

Clyde N. Toney. For one year, 1951–1952, Toney was the principal of the Spring Hill Elementary School in Pine Bluff (Jefferson County), Arkansas. Toney worked in other school systems for a decade, but returned to Pine Bluff in 1962, during the early desegregation years, and served as principal of the all-black Townsend Park Elementary School, 1962–1966, and the local junior high school, 1966–1975. In 1975 Toney left Pine Bluff for Rosston (Nevada County), Arkansas, where he served as the superintendent of the predominantly black Oak Grove School District, 1975–1983. During his superintendency of the Oak Grove School District, Toney consolidated and computerized the five small schools that comprised the district and stabilized its finances. When Toney became superintendent, the district was struggling and operating with a deficit; when he left it had a $65,000 surplus.

Dessie Perkins Kennedy. From 1965 until 1987, Mrs. Kennedy was the innovative principal of two elementary schools in the desegregated (1970) Helena-West Helena School District in Phillips

County: Helena Crossing Elementary, 1965–1980, and the Jefferson Kindergarten and North End Elementary School, 1980–1987. Although the Helena schools were desegregated by 1970, the legacy of neglect that characterized black schools prior to desegregation continued, and Kennedy was determined to overcome that legacy. While at the Helena Crossing School, Kennedy accomplished a number of firsts. She implemented the school's first individualized reading program, the first nongraded classes, and the first remedial reading program. Outside of the elementary school setting, Kennedy also organized an Adult Education and Homeowner Program in Phillips County. In 1980, Kennedy took her skills and abundant energy to the principalship of the Jefferson Kindergarten and North End Elementary School where she served from 1980 to 1987 and continued to be an innovative administrator.

John M. Lewellen. From 1959 to 1962, Lewellen was the principal of the West Side High School in Hermitage (Bradley County), Arkansas. When Lewellen began his principalship at West Side, the high school also included the elementary grades. Lewellen, however, was able to persuade the school board to separate the elementary grades from the high school and construct a new elementary school building. As principal of the high school, Lewellen focused much of his attention on improving teacher salaries and on student academic achievement, major issues during the 1950s and early 1960s. Because of the emphasis on academic excellence, over 50 percent of each graduating class of the West Side High School during Lewellen's administration attended college. This was a remarkable accomplishment since few black students from rural areas attended college during the period.

George Alvin Meekins. Meekins's career as a principal began in Ouachita County as the principal of the all-black Ouachita County High School in Bearden, 1948–1958, but his most notable administrative accomplishments took place during his principalship of Holman High School in Stuttgart (Arkansas County), 1958–1970. Under his leadership, Holman's curriculum was expanded to include advanced study courses in mathematics and science and a counseling program with a full-time counselor. He also persuaded the school board to construct a new middle school for the district. In 1970 all of Stuttgart's public schools were desegregated and, following the familiar desegregation pattern, Meekins was demoted to an assistant principal's position in the Stuttgart School District.

Earl Nelson Chanay. Recognized by parents, students, and community leaders as a fair, thoughtful, considerate, and accommodating leader, Chanay served as the principal of three different schools in Pine Bluff (Jefferson County), Arkansas: Indiana Street School, 1958–1965; Greenville Elementary School, 1965–1970; and Broadmoor Elementary, 1970–1991. His twenty-six years in public school administration is a testimony to his effectiveness as an administrator.

Patricia Dean. Dean has served as the principal of three schools in the Helena-West Helena (Phillips County) School District: North End Elementary, 1984–1986, where she was instrumental in implementing a Direct Instruction Reading Program; Jefferson Elementary School, 1986–1992, where she reestablished an effective Parent Teacher Association; and the Woodruff Kindergarten Center, 1992–1997, where she persuaded the local community to purchase and install playground equipment for the facility.

Joyce Cowan Owens. This teacher, coach, and administrator began her career in public education as a teacher/coach in Conway, Arkansas. She taught and coached at Solgahachia, Wonderview, and Pine Street Elementary Schools. During her coaching career, Owens's teams won over twenty trophies. In 1952, Owens left the coaching ranks for full-time administration and served as principal of two schools: Center Junior High School, 1952–1966, and the Jerusalem School, 1966–1967.

Earnest Simpson Jr. Simpson is a modern educator who emphasizes the team concept and student incentive approach to learning. Since 1996 he has been the principal of the Eliza Miller Junior High School in the Helena-West Helena (Phillips County) School District. His educational philosophy has decreased discipline problems and increased student daily attendance, performance on standardized tests, and participation in extracurricular activities.

Earnest Sims. Sims is a native of Helena (Phillips County), Arkansas, who returned home after graduating from college to give something back to the school district where he received his elementary and high school education. After a brief tenure as an elementary teacher, Sims was named principal of the West Side Elementary School in the Helena-West Helena School District where he served from 1986 until 1993. Under his leadership the school was remodeled and computers were placed in all classrooms. In 1993, he was transferred to the principalship of the Wahl Elementary School where he currently (2001) serves.

Northeast Arkansas

Located in the rich farmlands of the Arkansas delta, northeast Arkansas, like its southeastern neighbor, was an area controlled by large white planters and populated by poor black sharecroppers and tenant farmers. Several of the counties in the area had near black majority populations, but the huge numbers did not translate into increased state and local support for black public schools. Black administrators and teachers in the area, therefore, were often forced to purchase needed school supplies out of their meager pay in order to provide the poor children of tenant farmers and sharecroppers with the materials they needed if they were to break the circle of poverty that bound them to the land. Black administrators in these delta schools did not accept the status quo and they consistently, sometimes successfully, lobbied the local planter-controlled school boards to improve the salaries of black teachers and upgrade school facilities.

Eddie Shaw. Shaw was the principal of Central High School in Parkin (Cross County), Arkansas, 1955–1970. Central was located in an area dominated by large white planters who viewed the local black population as a source of cheap labor for their agricultural operations. To them the planting and harvesting of crops was much more valuable than the education of their work force. Thus, when Shaw was named principal of Central, the school had little support from the planters and little support from the majority of the local black parents who, because of decades of deprivation, placed more emphasis on day-to-day survival than they did on the education of their children. Central High, therefore, presented an immense challenge to the administrative skills of Shaw. He met the challenge by stressing the value of education and academic achievement, and he led the school from a Department of Education ranking of "C" to "A." From Central, Shaw took his administrative skills to the local Parkin Middle School where he was principal from 1971 to 1987.

At the middle school, Shaw found a faculty that was well qualified and dedicated to the education of their students, but their morale was low due to extremely low salaries. Although the state legislature had ordered school districts to equalize black and white teacher salaries in the aftermath of the successful 1945 Susie Morris salary equalization suit against the Little Rock School Board, the white superintendent of schools in Parkin and the local school board did not comply with the law. Therefore Shaw, displaying the courage that characterized numerous black administrators and teachers during the period, filed and won a salary equalization suit against the Parkin School Board.

Frederick D. Carroll. Carroll, a graduate of AM&N College at Pine Bluff, Arkansas, was the principal of the Spear Lake Elementary School in Lepanto (Poinsett County), Arkansas, 1959–1967. The black population of Poinsett County was small during the period and the Spear Lake School, located in Lepanto, served black students from the nearby communities of Wilbeth and Alto. When Spear Lake students completed the sixth grade, they were bussed to Marked Tree, Arkansas, where they attended the Carver High School for blacks. While at Spear Lake, Carroll and his wife, Lillie Paschal, comprised the school's teaching staff. She taught grades 1–3, and he taught grades 4–6 and handled the day-to-day operations of the school. During his tenure, he instituted sixth-grade graduation exercises which became one of the major highlights of black life in this rural agricultural community.

Harold L. Wilson. The Arkansas educator Harold Wilson was a native Texan who was educated in the public schools of that state, at Texas College (B.A.) in Tyler and at Prairie View University (M.A.). He began his teaching career in Arkansas as a mathematics and science instructor in the Howard County Training School at Tollette in 1948. He taught those same subjects at the W. F. Branch High School in Newport (Jackson County) from 1955 to 1964. Wilson's administrative career began at the White County Training School in Searcy, Arkansas, where he served as principal from 1964 until 1966. Due to desegregation, the White County Training School was closed at the end of the 1965–1966 school year, and Wilson became the assistant principal and media specialist for the newly desegregated Searcy Junior High School where he served from 1966 to 1973.[31] Because the local school board recognized that Wilson was a competent administrator, in 1973 he was again given the responsibility for operating a school and was named principal of the Southwest Middle School in the Searcy School District where he served until his death in 1987.

Samuel L. Whiting. This native of Marion (Crittenden County), Arkansas, graduated from the local black public schools in Marion. He received a B.A. at Philander Smith College (Little Rock) and an M.A. in counseling from Arkansas State University (Jonesboro). After graduating from Philander Smith, Whiting returned to his hometown of Marion where he taught science at the J. S. Phelix High School, 1948–1965. Phelix High was located in the all-black Sunset Community in the Marion School District, and like most teachers in black delta schools, Whiting had little to work with in terms of educational equipment and materials and subsequently worked a second job in order to purchase materials and supplies for his science students. After earning a degree in counseling at Arkansas State University during the summer months, Whiting was named counselor at Phelix High. Upon completion of his degree in counseling, Whiting began working on a degree in educational administration and, in 1967, he was named principal of J. S. Phelix, his alma mater. During his tenure as principal of Phelix, Whiting stressed academic achievement to his students, and their academic performance and college attendance rate more than doubled. The Marion School District completed its desegregation process in 1970, and Whiting was named principal of the newly desegregated Marion Junior High School where he served until retirement in the early 1990s. Whiting's alma mater, J. S. Phelix High School, was closed by the Marion School District as a result of desegregation and was eventually purchased by the J. S. Phelix High School Alumni Association and currently serves as a community center for the black population of the Sunset Community.

Dr. Charles J. Latimer. Dr. Latimer, principal of the DeRossitt (St. Francis County) Elementary in the Madison community near Forrest City, Arkansas, 1954–1965, was a scientist by training, not a college-trained educator. He settled in Forrest City sometime during the late 1930s where he planned to organize a branch of his company, Bondal Laboratories. Latimer's company manufactured and sold chemicals throughout the United States. He began his career as a public school administrator when he was asked to serve a few weeks as the substitute principal of DeRossitt due to the untimely death of the school's regular principal. That substitute appointment matured into an eleven-year career.

Dr. Lloyd G. Nichols. Nichols was the principal of the George Washington Carver High School in Clarendon (Monroe County), Arkansas, 1957–1960. Monroe County was cotton country, and like most black schools in the Arkansas delta, George Washington Carver had little local support. The school was in such poor condition when Nichols was named principal that he had to struggle just to keep its lowly "C" rating by the state Department of Education. Nichols remained there until he took a sabbatical leave to work on his doctorate at the University of Arkansas-Fayetteville.

Clarence Chambers Jr. This graduate of AM&N College in Pine Bluff, Arkansas (B.A.) and the University of Arkansas at Fayetteville (M.A., educational administration), worked in several schools in the Forrest City (St. Francis County) School District between 1958 and 1976. He served as a teacher, as dean of boys, and as an assistant principal before becoming the first black principal of the Forrest City Middle School in 1976 where he worked until retirement in 1995. He counts among his major accomplishments the accreditation of the middle school by the North Central Association of Colleges and Schools during his administration.

L. R. Jackson. Often referred to by local residents as "Mr Wonder High School," Jackson was the principal of Wonder High School in West Memphis (Crittenden County), Arkansas, from 1951 until 1965. He was the first "certified" principal of the troubled school with a history of local and state neglect. In late 1947 the black public school in West Memphis, which served approximately one thousand students, caught fire and "burned like kindling." Local planters who controlled the school board were in no hurry to replace the structure that tried to educate the children of their poverty-stricken sharecroppers and day laborers, but in September of 1948, ten months after the fire, they opened a new $300,000 school for whites in the West Memphis School District. Blacks, in the meantime, were forced to attend school in local black churches and in other buildings that were filthy and overcrowded.

Upset by the lack of action on the part of the West Memphis School Board toward rebuilding the black school, Jack Coughlin, the northern-born thirty-three-year-old editor of the *West Memphis News*, wrote several blistering editorials criticizing the school board and describing the conditions under which blacks were being "educated." One of those editorials, reprinted by *Time Magazine*, more than adequately described the situation and read, in part:

> Many West Memphis school age Negro children have never been to school at all, but some 800 of them are being "educated" under conditions which defy description. Words, nor even pictures, can describe the crowding, utter lack of modern facilities or the filth and squalor which abound in the miserable shack of a school and the tiny little church to which colored children trudge through slimy gumbo mud in an alarming and vain quest for learning.[32]

Time's story on the West Memphis schools shocked the nation and embarrassed state and local educational officials. Work was begun almost immediately on a new black school in West Memphis. The new Wonder High School was an ultra modern facility, and under Jackson's leadership it became known throughout the state and the nation for its academic programs. He added to the school's curriculum a science department, a music department, a separate choral music department, and an athletic department. Wonder High also received full North Central accreditation. As the principal of Wonder High, Jackson won the respect and support of leaders in both the black and white communities. Out of respect for Jackson's contributions to the education of black youths and to the community at large, in 1963 the city of West Memphis named its new elementary school the L. R. Jackson Elementary School, and in 1966 a community center was constructed in West Memphis and named the L. R. Jackson Community Center.

Vernard Metcalf. From 1961 to 1970, Metcalf was principal of the Cleveland Street School in DeValls Bluff (Prairie County), Arkansas, his hometown. Under Metcalf's leadership, the Cleveland Street School grew from an institution with only eight grades into a complete high school with an expanded faculty and two additional permanent classrooms and, because of growth, several portable classrooms were added. At the end of the 1969–1970 academic year, Metcalf left the Cleveland Street School to become principal of the black school in nearby Hazen, Arkansas. His plans to improve and expand the black school in Hazen never materialized because of desegregation. Metcalf was in Hazen only one year, 1970–1971, before the Hazen schools were desegregated, and he was not retained as principal. Subsequently, he returned to DeValls Bluff and accepted a position as a mathematics teacher in the junior high school. As of this writing (1999), he still works in DeValls Bluff, Arkansas.

Cartheau Jordan Jr. Jordan was a longtime educator in Marianna (Lee County), Arkansas, who succeeded Mrs. Anna M. P. Strong as principal of the local Robert R. Moton High School in 1958. Mrs. Strong had become an educational legend in Marianna and throughout the state and region and, to a lesser extent, nationally. Since Robert R. Moton already had a well-balanced educational program when Jordan became principal, one of his first administrative challenges was dealing with the Strong legacy and establishing his own identity and administration. He met the challenge by dealing fairly with his faculty and continuing the tradition of academic excellence stressed by his predecessor. Not only did Jordan stress student academic achievement, he also emphasized the moral and social responsibilities of his students. "To the Motonites," he regularly told students during school assemblies, "our entire educational program is centered around you. May you remember, it is not who is right, but what is right that is important." The "Motonites" appreciated Jordan's concern about their educational and social welfare and paid a special tribute to him in the 1965 Robert R. Moton yearbook. The students wrote:

> We pay a special tribute to our beloved principal, Mr. Jordan, whose leadership, guidance, and sincerity are highly esteemed. An energetic educator, Mr. Jordan always exemplifies the following toward the faculty, student body, and the community: He is a good leader and is always cooperative; he is sincere about his work and always shows humane interest in the child's welfare. . . . Needless to say, Mr. Jordan, those are only a few of the exemplifications we admire you for, and for those and many others we pay special tribute.

In 1963 the name of the Robert R. Moton High School was changed to the Anna M. P. Strong High School, but Jordan was retained as principal and retired at the end of the 1965–1966 academic year.

Acie L. Johnson. This native of Helena (Phillips County), Arkansas, and educator extraordinaire was a product of the Helena public schools and a graduate of AM&N College (B.S.) and Michigan State University (M.A., educational administration). He did further study at Michigan State, Columbia University in New York, the University of Arkansas at Fayetteville, and Brigham Young University at Provo, Utah. During his administrative career, Johnson was the principal, assistant principal, or assistant superintendent of several different schools in the state before his retirement in 1991. He served in an administrative capacity at W. O. Field High School in Gould (Lincoln County), 1954–1960; Chicot County Training School in Dermott, 1960–1966; and Robert R. Moton High School in Marianna (Lee County), 1966–1971; as the first black assistant superintendent of the Lee County School District, 1971–1972; and as the assistant principal of the Dunbar Junior High International Studies/Gifted and Talented Magnet School in Little Rock, 1972–1991. At each stop he left an enduring educational and community service legacy.

When Johnson accepted the principalship of the W. O. Field High School in Gould, the thirty-year-old wood-frame building was in a sad state of disrepair. To improve this dismal educational environment, Johnson and his wife, Frances, organized the school's first Parent Teacher Association, and with their support the building's interior and exterior were repaired and painted. Johnson then turned his attention to the education of Field's students. He realized that student learning suffered as a result of the split school session and, using his excellent communication skills, persuaded the local school board to adopt a regular nine-month school year. He also persuaded the board to add to the school new elementary classrooms and a gymnasium. The gym was later named the A. L. Johnson Gymnasium in his honor. Gould was located in a rural agricultural area, and few of Field's students lived within walking distance of the school. Johnson, therefore, persuaded the school board to purchase the school's first "new" school bus. The bus was used not only to transport students to and from school, but also to take them to meetings and conferences in other areas. The out-of-town engagements were exciting for Field's students because many of them had never traveled outside the boundary of their own community. Although the school board had authorized the construction of new elementary classrooms and a gym, it did not provide funds for necessary school supplies. Consequently, Johnson, with the support of the PTA, devised a plan for the purchase of the needed learning materials and supplies. The PTA, assisted by the New Homemakers of America (organized by Johnson's wife, who was the home economics teacher at Field's), and parents enrolled in adult education classes, sold plate lunches, and donated one day's earnings from working in the fields to the school for the purchase of supplies. Johnson's hard work at Field's was revealed in the number of graduates who attended college and in the respect for his leadership. When he became principal of the W. O. Field High School in 1954, only three of its students met graduation requirements; by 1960 there were thirty-one graduates, and eighteen went on to earn a college degree. The class of 1960 showed its appreciation for Johnson by inviting him and his wife, at its expense, to a five-day school reunion held at the MGM Hotel in Las Vegas, Nevada.

In the fall of 1960, Johnson took his administrative ability to Dermott, Arkansas, where he served as principal of the Chicot County Training School, 1960–1966. This too was a productive stop. The black population in Dermott, not unlike their counterparts in Gould, was waiting for someone to provide effective leadership for their school and, to a lesser degree, the local community. They were not disappointed by Johnson. During his tenure as principal of the Chicot County Training School, Johnson reorganized an effective PTA, expanded the school curriculum, improved its physical plant, and increased student enrollment by 35 percent. He also organized the school's first marching band (sixty-five members), and with the assistance of the PTA paid for its instruments and uniforms in two years. When Johnson took over the leadership of the Chicot County Training School, it was a financially strapped institution, when he resigned to accept the challenge of another school district in 1966, he left the school with a bank balance of $2,500.

From Dermott, Johnson moved on to become principal of the Anna M. P. Strong High School in Marianna (Lee County), Arkansas, 1966–1971. Although Strong was a good school when compared to others Johnson had led, he still saw room for improvements. He expanded Strong's curriculum, strengthened its faculty by hiring only teachers who held degrees in their speciality area, and persuaded the school board to add new classrooms to the facility and build a new cafeteria. On the nonacademic front, Johnson was able to motivate parents and school patrons to purchase new uniforms for the school's marching band, football and basketball teams, and majorettes. Johnson's tenure in Marianna, however, was during troubled times. The Lee County School District was going through a very controversial desegregation process, which began with "freedom of choice" as a first step toward desegregation. Since black and white students did not "choose" to change schools, the faculties of Strong and T. A. Futrell (the local white high school) were the first to experience "involuntary desegregation." This process cost Johnson some of his best teachers. Johnson was also the last principal of Strong High School because when the Lee County School District completed the desegregation process in 1970, Strong became a junior high school and all high school students were assigned to the new Lee High School, which had been specifically constructed to accommodate desegregation. As for Johnson, despite his proven administrative ability, he was not assigned a principalship in the newly desegregated school district; rather, he was "promoted" to the position of assistant superintendent of the Lee County School District where he served during the 1970–1971 school year. For a man who had become accustomed to using his own mind and operating his own school, the position of assistant superintendent offered few challenges to Johnson's intellect. He accepted a more challenging position as the assistant principal of the Dunbar Junior High International Studies/Gifted and Talented Magnet School in Little Rock where he worked until his retirement in 1991. While at Dunbar, Johnson served under seven different principals and was, on more than one occasion, offered the principalship of the school. He refused each offer. During his career in public education, Johnson served a two-year term as president of the all-black Arkansas School Administrators Association and received numerous plaques and awards for outstanding leadership and service. He currently lives in Little Rock, Arkansas, where he is active in community and civic affairs and in the Retired Teachers Association of the city.

B. T. Johnson. From 1957 to 1959, Johnson was the principal of the George Washington Carver High School in Marked Tree (Poinsett County), Arkansas. During his administration, Johnson strengthened the curriculum of George Washington High by making chemistry a graduation requirement. The Marked Tree School District, which had only a small black student population, was one of the earlier ones in Arkansas to desegregate, and when the process was completed the Carver High School became a junior high and its faculty, including the principal, was forced to seek employment elsewhere.

Emma S. Davis. Mrs. Davis was the principal of three elementary schools in the Lee County School District headquartered in Marianna, Arkansas: Strong Elementary, 1957–1970; Whitten-Nunnaly, 1970–1979; and a second tour of duty at Strong Elementary, 1979–1984. She retired at the end of the 1983–1984 school year. While Davis was at Strong Elementary, it was an all-black school, but when the Lee County School District completed the desegregation process in 1970, Davis was transferred from Strong to the principalship of the formerly all-white Whitten-Nunnaly Elementary School. She was the first black principal of Whitten-Nunnaly and was assigned to the school because of her proven administrative, communicative, and leadership skills and because of the respect she had built in the black and white communities over a number of years prior to desegregation. One of the highlights of her administration prior to desegregation was the presentation of the "Operetta," a play which featured the more disadvantaged pupils in the elementary school as well as those identified as at-risk students. The purpose was to improve self-esteem. Another highlight of Davis's administrative career in the Lee County School District was the establishment of the district's first kindergarten program. While serving as an administrator in a newly desegregated school system, Davis found the time to be quite active in her professional organizations. She was a member of the Arkansas Elementary School Council, the Arkansas Administrators Association, and the Arkansas Advisory Council for Title IV Programs, and was appointed by Governor Bill Clinton to a term on the board of the state's Children and Families at Risk Program.

Jesse W. Cooper. Cooper was a career educator in the West Memphis (Crittenden County) School District. He began his career in the district as a classroom teacher and was named principal of the Jackson Elementary School in 1965. He only spent one year at Jackson Elementary, but it was a productive one. Jackson received little support from the local planter-controlled school board and suffered from neglect. Cooper, however, was able to overcome the neglect through galvanizing community support for the school. He reorganized Jackson's Parent Teacher Association and with its support was able to purchase textbooks and other learning materials for his underfunded school and poverty-stricken students. He also implemented an individualized instruction program that resulted in an increase in the reading and comprehension level of Jackson's students. Following his successful year at Jackson Elementary, Cooper was named the successor of L. R. Jackson as principal of Wonder High School where he served from 1966 until 1973. In 1973 the West Memphis School District had completed the desegregation process, and Wonder High School became Wonder Junior High School and Cooper was "promoted" from his principalship to the position of assistant superintendent of schools. He served in this position until his retirement in 1993. Cooper, an ordained minister, still lives in West Memphis (2000) where he is active in local community affairs and pastors a church.

Roland A. Carpenter. The principal of the Mildred Jackson High School at Hughes (St. Francis County), Arkansas, 1961–1971, Carpenter was a dedicated educator who was determined to provide students in this rural agricultural community with a quality education. The odds appeared to be against him, however, because the white planters in St. Francis County were not known for their support of black schools. Carpenter was able to overcome the odds against him by organizing an effective Parent Teacher Association and with its support was able to secure "new" state-issued textbooks for his school, replacing the used, damaged, and outdated books that had been traditionally passed down from the white school. With the strong support of the Mildred Jackson PTA, Carpenter was also able to persuade the local school board to separate the elementary grades from the high school and construct a new elementary school which contained a library and a modern cafeteria. Carpenter's principalship was during the period of increased desegregation of public schools, and he realized that if his teachers were to keep their jobs in the newly desegregated schools, they would need to be well qualified. Consequently, he strongly encouraged those on his staff who had not completed their college degree programs to do so and refused to hire new teachers who did not hold degrees in their spe-

ciality areas. He even personally helped his nondegree faculty members obtain loans and scholarships to attend summer school in order
to complete their degree programs. Unfortunately, Carpenter's
accomplishments and emphasis on educational excellence did not
translate into a continued principalship when the Hughes School
District completed the desegregation process in 1971. Following the
desegregation of Hughes's public schools, Carpenter resigned to
accept a position with the Arkansas Department of Education. He
later was promoted to the position of associate director of federal
programs, from which he retired in 1987.

Louvenia Clark. Clark was a teacher in the Forrest City (St.
Francis County) School District before serving as the principal of
the district's Stewart Elementary School, 1960–1970. Stewart was
the typical black school in the Arkansas delta: underfunded, staffed
with an overworked faculty, and attended by poverty-stricken students who lived on area plantations and farms. Clark, however,
believed that poverty and culture were not obstacles to learning if
students were exposed to good teachers and were taught to feel good
about their heritage and themselves. Clark believed that it was
never too early to begin the learning process. She also believed that
students should learn not only about their own culture and history,
but also that of other cultures. This type of learning, she believed,
would broaden the students worldview and help them adjust to an
increasingly multicultural society. When the Forrest City School
District completed the desegregation process in 1970, Clark was
"promoted" and became a supervisor for elementary education and
a district grant writer. The change of position, however, did not
change her views of what students should learn in elementary school
in addition to basic educational skills. Subsequently, in 1971 she
wrote and received a federal grant for the implementation of an
individualized social studies program at the sixth-grade level, and
in 1973 she received another grant for the implementation of a for-
eign language program at the same level. Mrs. Clark retired in 1980.

Tempie W. Morehead. This graduate of AM&N College at Pine
Bluff (B.A.) and Georgia's Atlanta University (M.A.) did further
study at Arkansas State University (certification in elementary education administration), Indiana University, and the University of
Texas at Austin. She began her career in public education in

Arkansas as an elementary teacher in the Forrest City (St. Francis County) School District in the early 1950s. In 1967, Morehead was named principal of the Stewart Memorial Elementary School in the Forrest City School District. (Stewart Memorial and Stewart Elementary were two separate schools on the same campus, each with its own principal. One covered grades 1–3 and the other grades 4–6.) Morehead, who retired in 1990, stressed quality instructions and student achievement, which was reflected in improved standardized test scores of her students.

Albert Williams. Williams has spent his entire administrative career in the public schools of Osceola (Mississippi County), Arkansas. From 1981 to 1982, he was the principal of the Wilson Elementary School. After one year at Wilson, he was transferred to the Shawnee Elementary School where he worked from 1982 to 1993. The Osceola School District is located in an overwhelmingly rural portion of Mississippi County where farming, not education, is the top priority. Williams has, however, throughout his career stressed the importance of regular school attendance, academic excellence, and a college education.

Central Arkansas

When compared to other areas of Arkansas with a significant black population prior to the advent of public school desegregation, central Arkansas contained some of the better black public schools in the state, particularly those in Little Rock and North Little Rock. It also had some of the best-qualified faculties, but when compared to white schools in the area these schools and their administrators still suffered from discrimination in terms of facilities, teacher salaries, and general support from their local school boards. Because of their education, location, administrative skills, and commitment to quality education, many of the black administrators in central Arkansas schools emerged as leaders in the battle for educational equity and fairness, following the desegregation of the area's public schools.

Lloyd W. Black. A native of Eudora, Arkansas, Lloyd Black, the last of seventeen children, went on to become one of Arkansas's distinguished black educators. He was educated in Louisiana public schools, at AM&N College in Pine Bluff (B.A.), the University of Arkansas at Fayetteville (M.Ed.), and completed additional studies at Southern University (Baton Rouge, Louisiana), Arkansas

State University at Jonesboro, the University of Central Arkansas at Conway, and the University of Arkansas at Little Rock. He began his career in public education in the Brinkley (Arkansas) School District where he taught social studies, 1954–1960. His administrative career began in the heat of the desegregation era when he was named principal of the all-black George Washington Carver High School in Clarendon (Monroe County), Arkansas, where he served for eight years. During his tenure at Carver, Black persuaded the all-white school board to abolish the split school term which he believed restricted student learning. He also strengthened Carver's curriculum, which led the state to change its rating from "C" to "A," the highest state classification. The impact of Black's leadership was clearly reflected in the graduation and college attendance rate of Carver students. Carver's college attendance rate increased from 10 to 80 percent during Black's eight-year tenure. While at Carver, Black also served as president of the Monroe County Teachers Association, on the board of the Arkansas Teachers Association, and as president of District V of the ATA, which included Monroe, Lee, Phillips, and St. Francis Counties.

In 1968, Black took his educational skills and administrative experience to Helena, Arkansas (Phillips County), where he served as principal of the Westside Elementary School, 1968–1975, in the Helena-West Helena School District. The Helena-West Helena School District desegregated during Black's tenure in the district but he, unlike many black administrators during the era, was retained as principal of Westside. The school was reorganized; the teaching staff was desegregated; and the students served changed from grades 1–6 to grades 3–4. In this newly desegregated situation, Black, once again, proved to be an effective leader. He piloted a successful reading program for the school, employed the Westside's first black male special education teacher, and prepared the school for accreditation by the North Central Association of Colleges and Schools. In 1975, Black resigned from his principalship in the Helena-West Helena School District in order to accept a position in the Little Rock School District where he served as principal of the George Washington Carver Elementary School, 1975–1980. During his five years at Carver Elementary, Black again demonstrated his educational know-how and leadership skills. He spearheaded the establishment of a totally desegregated and effective

Parent Teacher Association and led the school to full accreditation by the North Central Association. In 1980, Black left Carver to accept an assistant principalship position at Sylvan Hills in the Pulaski County Special School District. The following year he was named principal of the district's Wakefield Elementary School. During his tenure at Wakefield, Black helped organize a strong desegregated PTA, which elected, for the first time in the school's history, a black president. He also led the school through its reevaluation by the North Central Association of Colleges and Schools. In 1987, due to a federal court order, the Pulaski County Special School District lost Wakefield and thirteen other schools to rapidly expanding Little Rock School District. Black, however, had a proven administrative record, and with the strong support of the Wakefield PTA and other school patrons, he was retained as the school's principal and served until his retirement in 1993. His second tour of duty in the Little Rock School District was characterized by several notable achievements. These included the recruitment and hiring of twenty-one new teachers in the summer of 1987 and the employment of a teaching staff at Wakefield that was 55 percent white and 45 percent black. Wakefield was the first school in the Little Rock School District to have this black/white teacher ratio, which was maintained throughout Black's tenure. Under Black's leadership, Wakefield was also one of the first schools in the Little Rock School District to be wired for cable television, which was used as a teaching aid, and was the first to develop an educational partnership with AT&T. During Black's tenure at Wakefield, the school developed a culture that revolved around the theme "The Best and Nothing Else." This school culture had a positive social, intellectual, and psychological impact, not only on the school, but also on the local community.

While Black was leading Wakefield to new educational heights, he was also very active in his professional associations and in civic affairs. He was a charter member of the Arkansas Association of Elementary School Principals and served on different occasions as the organization's secretary-treasurer, as its vice president, and as its first black president. Black also served as president of the Pulaski County Special School District Principals Association and the Little Rock Principals Association. Nationally he served on the board of directors of the National Association of Elementary School

Principals (NAESP), and was the NAESP's first black representative from Arkansas. He also received numerous honors and awards for his years of dedicated professional service. In 1975, Black was honored by being selected as Principal of the Year, as the recipient of NAESP's Laurel M. Pennock Goldbuster Membership Award (1983), the Phi Delta Kappa Frank Cannady Award, and upon his retirement the Arkansas Association of Elementary School Principals (AAESP) Service and Life Membership Award. According to Black, one of his greatest honors was the opportunity to introduce Governor Bill Clinton to a national audience in Washington, D.C. The Arkansas governor went on to become president of the United States in 1993. Black currently (2000) lives in Little Rock, where he continues to be involved in civic and educational affairs. He is an active member of the National Association for the Advancement of Colored People, the Pecan Lake Property Owners Association (past-president), the Greater Little Rock AM&N/UAPB Alumni Association, and the Retired Educators of Little Rock and Other Public Schools. He is also the director of Area VI of the Retired Teachers Association. Black's church, the Greater Archview Baptist Church in Little Rock, takes up much of his time. He serves as one of the church's deacons and chairs several committees. Black is truly an outstanding educator and public servant, one of Arkansas's "unsung heroes."

Curtis H. Sykes. A well-known and respected native of North Little Rock, Curtis Sykes is sometimes referred to as the state's black historian. He was educated in the public schools of North Little Rock and earned the B.A. degree at Arkansas Baptist College. He also studied in Texas (Bishop College at Marshall) before returning to Arkansas and earning the M.S. degree at Harding University in Searcy. He was the first black to earn an advanced degree from Harding. Sykes completed additional graduate studies at Texas State College (Tyler), State College of Arkansas at Conway (currently the University of Central Arkansas), Henderson State University (Arkadelphia), the University of Iowa (Iowa City), the University of Wisconsin at Madison, and the George Peabody College for Teachers in Nashville, Tennessee (currently Vanderbilt University).

Sykes began his long career in Arkansas's public schools as the principal of the Woodruff County Training School at Augusta,

1957–1965. From Augusta, he returned to the Little Rock School District where he taught and coached basketball at the Gibbs and Carver Elementary Schools before being named the principal of the Booker T. Washington Elementary School, 1969–1973. He was later transferred (1973) to the Woodruff Elementary School, where he became its first black principal in the era of desegregation. He served Woodruff until his retirement in 1985. Following his retirement, Sykes settled in North Little Rock and devotes much of his time to the upkeep of his neighborhood, to civic affairs, and to the collection and preservation of the history of notable black Arkansans. Currently (2001), he is the president of the Dark Hollow Neighborhood Association. The association works to keep the neighborhood physically attractive and drug free.[33]

Although Sykes is deeply involved in the activities of the Dark Hollow Neighborhood Association, he is also the driving force behind the collection and preservation of black Arkansas history. During several years of teaching the history of Arkansas and black American history at Arkansas Baptist College, he discovered that there was little information readily available about the history of influential black Arkansans. Subsequently he, almost singlehandedly, launched a campaign to collect and have deposited in the state's public schools the history of notable black Arkansans. He was aided in his quest by state senator Jean Edwards (D—Jefferson County), who was successful in getting Act 326 of 1997 through the state legislature. The statute required the teaching of black history in all of the state's public schools throughout each school year. Sykes believed that all public school students should be cognizant of the contributions of blacks to the state's development and history. Many public schoolteachers, however, argued that they could not meet the requirements of the law because needed materials were not available. To correct this problem, Sykes worked diligently with representatives from the state Department of Education in the development of teaching materials for units on black history. While working with the representatives of the Arkansas Department of Education, Sykes was also working with blacks in the state legislature who were pushing through that august body an act that established the Arkansas Black History Advisory Committee. The committee, which is currently (2001) chaired by Sykes, works with the Arkansas History Commission to collect, preserve, and make

available to historical researchers and the general public information relative to the history of black Arkansans.[34]

Sykes, who is a natural leader and a life member of the Alpha
Phi Alpha Fraternity, is also interested in the moral development
of young men. He played a major role in persuading the Little Rock
chapter of his fraternity to purchase a house for its meetings and
community activities. One of the programs operated through what
is known as the Alpha House is SANIC (which means "first roots").
The program, directed by Sykes, is a mentoring program for young
men ten to fourteen years of age that stresses the value of education
and good moral character. Sykes also organized a similar program
for seventh graders in North Little Rock's Eastgate Community.
The Eastgate program is funded by the Darkhollow Community
Development Corporation, which Sykes was instrumental in founding. He also organized the Midnight basketball program in North
Little Rock in an effort to keep young men off the streets and away
from criminal activity. Not only is Sykes concerned about the moral
development of today's youth, he is also concerned about the historical continuity of the black community. Consequently, in 1981,
he led a successful campaign to get the street on which Jones High
School once stood renamed Jones Street because the name of the
school had been changed and no longer served as a point of historical identity for the black community. In recognition of his dedicated service to his community, Sykes was the recipient of the
Salute to Greatness Community Service Award in 1998. In addition to his community service activities, Sykes is an active member
of the Prince Hall Masons and his church—King Solomon
Baptist—where he serves as a trustee, a Sunday School teacher, and
a church historian.

William H. Fowler. Fowler spent the majority of his career as a
public school principal in the schools of Pulaski County and the
city of Little Rock, Arkansas: Woodson Elementary, 1947–1948;
Cook Elementary and High School, 1948–1954; Capitol Hill,
1960–1961; and Rightsell Elementary, 1961–1967. While at
Rightsell, Fowler improved the school's curriculum and academic
standards, oversaw the construction of a new library, and sponsored
a successful campus beautification program. By 1967 public school
desegregation in Little Rock and throughout Pulaski County was
near completion and many black administrators were being

removed from administrative positions in individual schools and "promoted" into the administrative ranks of the Little Rock School District. Fowler was one of those and he served as the district's first black assistant superintendent, 1967–1980. In recognition of his service to the public schools and to his community the Board of Trustees of Philander Smith College (Little Rock, Arkansas) bestowed upon him an honorary doctorate of human letters in 1970. He also served as special assistant to the superintendent for administration, 1981–1982. In 1983, he left the Little Rock School District and accepted a position as vice president for administrative services with Philander Smith College, a local black Methodist-sponsored private school. Fowler left Philander Smith in 1985 and accepted a position with the University of Arkansas at Little Rock in its Career Planning and Placement Center where he worked as a job development specialist until retirement.

Edwin L. Hawkins. This outstanding educator began his long administrative career in Clow (Hempstead County), Arkansas, where he was the principal of the Clow Training School, 1945–1952. In 1952, Hawkins left Hempstead County for the Little Rock School District where he served as principal of four schools: Bush Elementary, 1952–1954; Dunbar Junior High School, 1954–1958; Horace Mann High School, 1958–1971; and Central High School, 1971–1974. As a principal, Hawkins is best known for his work at Horace Mann and Central High Schools. At Horace Mann, the largest black high school in Arkansas, Hawkins had a gifted faculty, and he led the school to state, regional, and national academic recognition. During his tenure at Central High, where he was the first black principal of the formerly all-white school, Hawkins used his administrative and communication skills to provide invaluable leadership in creating order out of chaos during the critical years following desegregation and the "Little Rock school crisis." One of the first steps he took toward settling a potentially explosive racial situation at Central was the establishment of a biracial committee that conducted symposiums on race relations. He also expanded Central's curriculum to include courses in black history and literature. His administration was well received by Central's black and white students, who mourned his loss after his untimely death in 1974. The students of Central honored Hawkins by dedicating one of its bicentennial projects to his legacy. The projects involved the creation of silver and bronze commemorative medallions featuring a portrait of Hawkins on the front with a ribbon underneath which read:"With Liberty and Justice for All." The back of the medallion featured, in high relief, a picture of Central and its mascot, the Tiger. Proceeds from the sale of the medallions were deposited in the Hawkins Memorial Scholarship Fund established by the students of Central High.

Hawkins was not only an effective public school administrator, he was also an outstanding president, 1964–1966, of the all-black Arkansas Teachers Association. During his ATA presidency, Hawkins lobbied the state legislature and the Arkansas Department of Education for more support for black schools and for equalization of teacher salaries. To position the ATA so that it could better serve its members, Hawkins called for the organization of a speakers bureau to assist its affiliates across the state in developing and implementing more diversified activities, and for the coordination of the association's three departments—classroom teachers, administrators, and higher education—in order to promote quality teaching, expand public school curricular, and improve teaching conditions. One of the many achievements of Hawkins's ATA presidency was the completion of the construction and furnishing of the new ATA headquarters building, which was officially dedicated on April 11, 1965.[35]

James L. Wise. Wise was a well-known educator and administrator who played a major role in the battle for equalization of black and white teacher salaries in Arkansas following the 1945 victory of Susie Morris in her salary equalization suit against the Little Rock School Board. Wise began his career as an educator in the early 1950s in the Gould (Lincoln County) Special School District where he worked as a social studies teacher, a coach, and a school bus driver for $175 per month. White teachers in the district performing the same job earned considerably more than Wise, and when the district refused to increase his salary he filed a salary equalization suit against the Gould School District in 1953 on behalf of himself and other underpaid black teachers. He was immediately fired, and the black teachers who added their names to the suit were fired at the end of the 1952–1953 school year.[36] Wise was well aware of the risk involved in filing his suit and was willing to face it in the interest of equity.

Wise had filed his salary equalization suit against the Gould School District with the support of the Arkansas Teachers Association, and after his dismissal by the district he worked for the association during the 1953–1954 school year and completed his master's degree program at the University of Arkansas at Fayetteville. In 1954, with the support of the ATA, Wise was hired as a teacher in the Pine Street High School in Conway (Faulkner County). In the fall of 1967, Wise began his long career as a public school administrator when he was named principal of the Granite Mountain Elementary School in the Little Rock School District, serving until 1970. He also served as principal of a number of other schools in the Little Rock School District: Carver Elementary School, 1970–1975; Dunbar Junior High, 1975–1981; Horace Mann Junior High, 1981–1986; and Forrest Heights Junior High, 1986–1990. During his tenure, Wise earned a reputation as a good administrator and became a role model for students, black and white.

Willie Thompson. Thompson was the principal of three schools in central Arkansas: Nelson Junior High in Scott (Pulaski County Special School District), 1959–1963; Henderson Junior High, 1971–1981; and Dunbar Junior High, 1981–1986, both in the Little Rock School District. At each stop Thompson challenged students with stay-in-school projects. He also introduced the use of educational films with follow-up evaluations to increase student learning. The stay-in-school projects and educational films resulted in an increase in attendance and student performance on standardized test. The highlight of Thompson's career came when Dunbar Junior High School was placed on the National Registry of Historic Places.

Rachel A. Myers. Myers was also one of the first black principals of a formerly all-white elementary school in the Little Rock School District following desegregation, Forrest Park Elementary, 1968–1973. Myers began her career in the Little Rock School District as an elementary teacher and served her first principalship at Ish Elementary School, 1965–1968. Her leadership of the Ish and Forrest Park Elementary Schools drew the attention of the central administration for the district, and she quickly moved up the administrative ladder. From 1985 to 1987, she was the administrative assistant of the superintendent of the district, and in the fall of 1987 she was promoted to the position of assistant superintendent, where she served until retirement. During her administrative career, Myers directed several district programs: the Program for Effective Teaching (PET); the Mastery Learning Program; the Classroom Management Program; the Teacher Expectation and Student Achievement Program (TESA); the Clinical Supervision and Turnkey Training Program; and the Early Prevention of School Failure Program.

Andrew Power. Power, who was an experienced teacher, began his administrative career as principal of Carter G. Woodson Elementary School (Pulaski County) in North Little Rock, where he served from 1968 to 1969. When the North Little Rock School District completed the desegregation of its public schools, Power, like many other competent and experienced black principals across the state, was "promoted" to the position of assistant superintendent for educational projects and student affairs, where he served from 1969 until 1989. During his tenure in the North Little Rock School District, Power was active in the civic affairs of the local community. He worked as a volunteer for the North Little Rock mayor's Office of Volunteer Service and as a commissioner of the North Little Housing Authority. The latter position was of special importance for the local black community because Power's sound, well-reasoned decisions helped to solve many of their public housing problems.

Dr. J. J. Lacey Jr. Dr. Lacey is a native of Mississippi who earned a B.A. at the University of Arkansas at Pine Bluff and his M.A. and Ed.D. at Indiana University (Bloomington). He began his career in public education as a teacher at the Eliza Miller Junior High School in Helena (Phillips County), where he worked until beginning his administrative career as the principal of Johns Elementary School in Eudora (Chicot County) in 1967. After two years in Eudora, Lacey accepted the principalship of the George Washington Carver High School in Clarendon (Monroe County), where he served one year, 1969–1970. In 1970, the Clarendon School District desegregated and George Washington Carver High School was reorganized into a middle school. The all-white Clarendon School Board did not retain Lacey as principal of either the new middle school or the newly desegregated Clarendon High School. He was "promoted" to the position of director of federal programs. After serving one depressing year in that position, Lacey decided to leave public education and return to graduate school to complete work on his doctorate in education. In 1973, after earning his degree in higher education, Lacey returned to Arkansas and accepted a position as an assistant professor of education at the University of Arkansas at Little Rock. In 1974, the Little Rock School District, seeking to add blacks with experience in public education, persuaded Lacey to join its ranks as director of federal programs. He served in that position five years, 1974–1979. He is still employed by the Little Rock School District and has held several administrative positions since 1979, including special assistant to the superintendent for desegregation, director of the Office for Special Programs, and evaluation specialist in the district's Office of Planning, Research, and Evaluation.

Verma Releford Isum. Mrs. Isum was an experienced elementary teacher in the Little Rock School District before being named principal of Pfeifer Elementary School in 1969. During her tenure at Pfeifer, 1969–1972, Isum wrote a manual for kindergarten instructional programs that was later adopted by the Little Rock School District. In 1973, Isum was assigned the principalship of Romine Elementary, where she served until her retirement in 1981. She counted among her major achievements the development of an instructional manual for kindergarten programs and the role she played in the establishment of the district's Head Start Program.

Otis Harris. Harris was the first principal, 1963–1970, of Booker Junior High in the Little Rock School District. The school, named after J. R. Booker, a prominent black civil rights lawyer, educator, and political activist, was located near Booker Homes, a public housing project for low-income families in the overwhelmingly black East End community of Little Rock which was underdeveloped and poverty stricken. When the Little Rock School District expanded its borders to include the area, it experienced a tremendous amount of difficulty in finding a principal and staff for the school. After several experienced administrators in the district refused to accept the principalship of Booker Junior High, Harris, a teacher at Dunbar Junior High, was persuaded to accept the position in August of 1963. His teaching staff, "drafted" primarily from the prestigious Dunbar Junior High, showed up for the first day of work with tears in their eyes, fearful of what they would encounter. Harris clearly recognized the challenge he faced and immediately attacked potential problems. He quickly established student discipline and a sound curriculum and won the respect and support of his staff, students, and the local community. During his administration, Booker Junior High became a school in which the local community took pride. One of Harris's teachers later commented: "He was truly an unsung hero, a portrait in courage."

Dr. Joseph Hale. Hale was an experienced administrator and educational consultant who had served in several positions before joining the Little Rock School District. He began his administrative career in Prescott, Arkansas, where he was the principal of the McRae High School, 1957–1969. When the Prescott School District desegregated in 1969, the district, following the familiar pattern established during the early years of desegregation, made Hale an assistant principal. After running his own school for twelve years, the assistant principal's position did not challenge Hale's intellect, and he left after one year and accepted a position with Ouachita Baptist University in Arkadelphia as a desegregation consultant, 1970–1973. His experience as a public school principal and knowledge of desegregation issues led to Hale being hired as principal of the newly (1970) desegregated Lee High School in Marianna (Lee County), where he served from 1973 to 1975. In 1970 the Lee County School District was going through turbulent times as a result of a local boycott of white-owned businesses, protest by black students against the administration and student privileges, and conflicts over staff appointments. After two years in this unsettled situation, 1973–1975, Hale moved on to the comparatively quieter Little Rock School District where he served as the assistant principal of the Metropolitan Vocational and Technical High School, 1975–1983, and Central High School, 1983–1988. At the end of the 1987–1988 academic year, Hale left the public schools for Arkansas Baptist College where he currently (2000) serves as an associate professor in the Department of Education. While teaching at Baptist, Hale earned an Ed.D. from Grambling State University in Louisiana.

Charlie Barkins. Barkins was a principal in the Pulaski County

Special School District, where he served the all-black Harris High School at McAlmont, Arkansas. McAlmont was a poor and overwhelmingly black rural community on the northern edge of the city of North Little Rock and the school drew little support from its school board or the impoverished black community. Barkins experienced one frustration after another while in McAlmont due to the refusal of the school board to provide his school with new books instead of outdated and damaged ones passed down from the local white school and his inability to protect competent teachers who openly disagreed with school board policies. "Not only were these people competent teachers," recalled Barkins, "they were also my friends and coworkers, but the board told me who to fire and this was a frustrating experience." Barkins, however, did not let the dictatorial tactics of his board, nor the lack of support from the local community, keep him from encouraging students to strive for academic excellence or from encouraging teachers to complete their college degree programs in order to increase their mobility. One of his students took his words quite literally and went on to become principal of McClellan High School in Little Rock.

Barkins left Harris High School in 1966 to become the first black principal of the formerly all-white Joe T. Robinson High School in Pulaski County, where he served from 1966 to 1977. This position also frustrated Barkins because the school board of the Pulaski County Special School District felt he needed to be "schooled" on how to operate the school. His schooling, recalled Barkins, "consisted of being told to not get upset if he was called names and to be calm and composed at all times." Barkins knew that he had accepted a controversial position and did not need the lectures, but he also realized that the board was trying to prepare him for a possible hostile reception from angry whites who might not accept him as the principal of "their school." Although the students at Joe T. Robinson accepted Barkins and applauded his first speech to an all-school assembly, the fears of the school board about how he would be received by the local white community were not unwarranted. According to Barkins, he received several threatening phone calls and seriously considered resigning and that only the counsel of Little Rock civil rights attorney John W. Walker kept him from doing so. Walker convinced Barkins that he was being closely observed by black and white educational leaders across the state and that his performance could possibly influence the fate of other blacks who aspired to become administrators in desegregated schools. Barkins persevered and served as principal of Joe T. Robinson for eleven years, he then accepted a position in the district personnel office where he worked until his retirement in 1985.[37] His career in the Pulaski County Special School District can easily be described as a "portrait in courage."

Maeleen Claye Arrant. "Mrs. A," as she was affectionately called by those with whom she worked, began her educational career as public school home economics teacher. During her early years in administration, she served as the principal of several rural elementary schools, including the Immanuel School in Almyra, Arkansas. In the late 1950s she became the first black supervisor of elementary education for the state Department of Education and subsequently played a significant role in the desegregation of the state's public schools. During her career, she served on the Governor's Committee for the Integration of Institutions of Higher Education and as the assistant director of the National Retired Teachers Association. Arrant was also the recipient of numerous certificates and citations for professional and humanitarian service. In recognition of her service and professionalism, the Arkansas Education Association established a scholarship in her name in 1980.

Dr. W. T. Keaton. A graduate of AM&N College at Pine Bluff (B.A.) and New York University (M.A.), Dr. Keaton also did further study at the University of Texas at Austin, Memphis State University (Tennessee), and the University of Arkansas at Fayetteville and was the superintendent of the Howard County School District in Tollette, Arkansas, in the early 1950s. He left Howard County in 1956 for Menifee (Conway County), where he served as superintendent of the Conway County Training School, 1956–1961. After leaving Conway, Keaton served as a public school principal in Bearden (Ouachita County) and Garland (Miller County) before accepting a position with the state Department of Education as a supervisor of vocational, technical, and adult education, where he worked until his retirement.

Bernice S. Moore. Mrs. Moore was the principal of Stephens Elementary School in the Little Rock School District from the 1950s to the 1970s. Moore, who was an avid reader, believed that reading was the key to the mastery of all subject areas. When she became principal of Stephens, the school, like the vast majority of black elementary schools during the period, did not have a library, a situation Moore found unacceptable. When she failed to persuade the school board to appropriate the funds for a library, she went directly to Governor Winthrop Rockefeller (Arkansas's Republican governor, 1967–1971) and appealed for library funds. Governor Rockefeller, who was also a wealthy philanthropist, was impressed by Moore's enthusiasm and gave her a substantial cash donation, which led to the establishment of a well-stocked library at Stephens Elementary School. As a result of Moore's persistence, Stephens Elementary became the first elementary school in the Little Rock School District to have both a library and a certified librarian. When the library was well established, Moore initiated an advanced reading program where students came to her office and selected classic literature to read and discuss with her.

David L. Lyons Sr. Lyons was the principal of three schools in Pulaski County: College Station Elementary, 1949–1962; J. C. Cook Elementary (Wrightsville, Arkansas), 1962–1976; and Fuller Elementary, 1977–1978. Although details of his accomplishments are unavailable, Lyons was an exceptional leader and during his tenure at J. C. Cook, he was recognized as one of the outstanding principals in Arkansas by the South Central District of the National Association of Elementary School Principals. His accomplishments continued at Fuller Elementary where he designed, secured the necessary funding, and oversaw the construction of a school library. The library was named, posthumously, in his honor.

Frank W. Smith. This native of Brookhaven, Mississippi, was the first executive secretary of the Arkansas Teachers Association, the official voice of black administrators and teachers in the state, and a renowned Arkansas educator. He graduated from Branch Normal High School on the campus of AM&N College. He went on to earn a B.A. from AM&N College and an M.A. from the University of Arkansas at Fayetteville. He spent over three decades mentoring black teachers and students in the state.

Smith began his career in public education in Arkansas as the principal and vocational agriculture teacher in the schools of Rison (Cleveland County), Clarendon (Monroe County), and Almyra

(Arkansas County). On two different occasions, 1946–1950 and 1961–1972, he served as the superintendent of the East Side School District in Menifee (Conway County). While serving the East Side School District, Smith was instrumental in getting a $250,000 physical plant constructed for the district and in securing federal funding for several district projects.

During Smith's tenure as executive secretary of the ATA, he tremendously improved communications between the organization and its statewide county affiliates through his skillful use of the *Bulletin*, the official journal of the organization. The Education Communication Service, an organization that judged and evaluated educational journals, said that the *Bulletin* "stood among the best educational journals." In 1955, with the advent of public school desegregation in Arkansas, Smith took a leave of absence from the ATA to serve as Arkansas's field representative of the National Association for the Advancement of Colored People. He was responsible for helping black public school administrators, teachers, and the general black public prepare for desegregation and associated problems. The position was a "natural" for him because his previous travels through the state and his communications with policymakers and state leaders. In 1961, Smith returned to the superintendency of the Conway County Training School where he served until 1972. He then left the public school to become mayor of Menifee, serving until his death in 1979.

Jethro A. Hill. Hill served as the principal of two rural Arkansas public schools, Lakeview High School at Lakeview (Phillips County), 1941–1942, and Landwood High School at Rison (Cleveland County), 1942–1948. Hill later moved to Little Rock, where he spent the remainder of his career as a mathematics teacher and a public school administrator in the Little Rock School District. In the district he was the principal of Metropolitan Vocational and Technical High School, 1967–1969, and Booker Junior High School, 1969–1971; and he was vice principal of Parkview High School, 1971–1981. During his years in the Little Rock School District, Hill served as president of the Principals Roundtable and was an active member of the Arkansas Education Association, the National Education Association, and the National Association of Secondary School Principals. He also served on the advisory board of the YWCA.

Nexton P. Marshall. Marshall, a native of the poverty-stricken Arkansas delta (Helena in Phillips County), became one of the more respected and innovative educational leaders in Arkansas. He was a graduate of Eliza Miller High School in Helena, Tennessee State University in Nashville (B.A.), and the University of Arkansas at Fayetteville (M.A.). Marshall also completed advanced study courses at the Universities of Iowa and Illinois and the George Peabody College for Teachers at Nashville, Tennessee. He began his career in public education as a teacher in the public schools in his hometown of Helena, Arkansas, and his administrative career in the North Little Rock Public School District, where he was the outstanding principal of Hillside Elementary School, 1954–1956, and Lincoln Elementary School, 1956–1978 (renamed the Seventh Street Elementary School after desegregation). During his tenure at Lincoln, Marshall was recognized as an exceptional administrator and was one of three hundred principals from across the nation selected to attend an educational workshop for administrators at George Peabody College for Teachers in Nashville. During the workshop he drew the blueprints for a state-of-the-art elementary school that featured collapsible walls for intermediate classroom instructions and a media center. Lincoln Elementary was later remodeled to fit Marshall's design and became the first elementary school in the North Little Rock School District with its features. Under Marshall's leadership, Lincoln Elementary also became the first elementary school in the district to receive full accreditation by the North Central Association of Colleges and Schools.

Marshall was not only an exceptional public school administrator, he was also an outstanding leader of the Arkansas Teachers Association, the statewide organization that represented black educators, during his presidency, 1962–1964. As president of the ATA, Marshall was one of the outspoken leaders in the fight for the equalization of black and white teacher salaries and for the improvement of black schools. Although Marshall pushed for the improvement of black public schools, his ATA presidency occurred during the push for the desegregation of public education in the aftermath of the *Brown* decision. Because Marshall realized that black public schoolteachers would have to be well qualified if they were to keep their positions in desegregated schools, he urged them to complete their undergraduate degree programs and to pursue graduate study.

Not only were public schools being desegregated during Marshall's ATA presidency, the organization was engaged in merger discussions with the all-white Arkansas Education Association, the statewide organization that represented white educators, and Marshall was one of the leaders in those discussions which culminated with the merger of the two organizations in 1969. In 1978, Marshall retired from public education after forty-one years of service. During his outstanding career, he accomplished a number of firsts: first black to serve a term on the Board of Directors of the National Education Association, 1970–1976; first black president of the North Little Rock Elementary Principals Association; and the first black to serve on the State Board of Collection Agencies. He was appointed to the latter position by Governor Bill Clinton. He was also a member of the National Council of State Association Presidents and an alternate member of the NEA's resolutions committee.[38] In 1981, as a tribute to Marshall's educational legacy, the ATA established a scholarship in his honor, and in an effort to increase the awareness of public school students and the general public of the contributions of blacks to Arkansas's history, sixteen posters of famous black Arkansans have been created and one of them features Marshall.[39]

Winston J. Muldrew. Muldrew, a long-term Arkansas educational administrator, left a legacy of achievements wherever he served before moving to the Little Rock School District in 1969 where he completed his career. He began his career as a teacher and first became a principal at the Dora E. Perkins Elementary School in Barton (Phillips County), where he served from 1951 until 1960. Barton was a rural agricultural community controlled by local white planters whose first priority was not the education of their cheap labor force, which meant that Perkins Elementary had little local financial support. Muldrew, however, was able to persuade the local school board to abolish the school's split-session school year so that students could realize the benefits of a continuous nine-month education. A dedicated educator who pushed high standards for his staff, Muldrew motivated his teachers to complete their undergraduate degree programs and pursue graduate study. He also expanded Perkins curriculum to include industrial arts and music appreciation. Many of Dora Perkins's students were from poverty-stricken farm families who could not afford to purchase school lunches for their children. Muldrew, who believed that hunger inhibited student learning, also established the school's first free lunch program for economically deprived students.

In 1960, Muldrew took his administrative skills to El Dorado (Union County), Arkansas, where he had accepted the principalship of the Carver/Morning Star Elementary School. During his tenure at Carver/Morning Star, 1960–1965, Muldrew developed and implemented a faculty evaluation plan and a school-wide reading and student-testing program. Due to his administrative success at the elementary level, Muldrew was promoted in 1965 to the vice principalship of Washington High School and to the full principalship the next year. He was Washington High School's last black principal, 1966–1968, because at the end of the 1967–1968 school year, the El Dorado School District desegregated, and Muldrew, despite his accomplishments as a public school principal, was demoted and assigned to the formerly all-white El Dorado High School as a vice principal, where he served from 1968 to 1969. Following the 1968–1969 school year, Muldrew left the El Dorado School District for the Little Rock School District, where he had accepted a position as assistant principal of the predominantly black Dunbar Junior High School. After one year at Dunbar, 1969–1970, Muldrew was promoted to the principalship of both the Granite Mountain and Gilliam Park Elementary Schools in the Little Rock School District, where he served from 1969 until 1979. Once again in charge of his own school and its educational programs, Muldrew established individualized instructional programs in the elementary schools and led them to full North Central Association accreditation. Muldrew spent the final years of his productive career as principal of Carver Elementary School, 1979–1985, and in the central office, 1985–1990, of the Little Rock School District.

Ulysses McIntosh. Unlike most public school administrators who had several years of teaching experience before they moved into the ranks of administration, McIntosh's venture into the administrative ranks was almost immediate. He was hired as a teacher in the Sweet Home Elementary and High School in the Pulaski County Special School District in 1954 and was named principal of the school after only a few months on the job. Apparently his performance was satisfactory because he spent the next two years, 1955–1957, as the principal of the J. C. Cook High

School at Wrightsville. McIntosh's first three years in administration was equivalent to on-the-job training because he was told by the superintendent of the district to "make use of whatever resources were available." Since few resources were available in terms of books and other teaching materials, McIntosh devoted the majority of his time emphasizing basic education skills and trying to motivate students to learn. In 1961 he was sent back to J. C. Cook where he worked until being transferred, in 1965, back to where he had begun his administrative career, Sweet Home Elementary and High School, where he worked until 1970. In that year he was again transferred, this time to the principalship of Fuller Junior High School where he served until his retirement in 1972. By the time McIntosh became principal of Fuller Junior High School, he was an experienced administrator and had developed an expertise in motivating students to learn and strive for academic excellence.

David Boswell. The son of a well-known and respected black doctor in Little Rock, Boswell earned a reputation of his own as an outstanding science and mathematics teacher. He began his career as a public school administrator in 1948 when he was hired as the principal/superintendent of the Conway County Training School. During his tenure at the training school, Boswell worked to strengthen the school by hiring only teachers who had completed their undergraduate degree programs. In 1954, Boswell carried his commitment to academic excellence to the Turrell (Crittenden County) High School. He left Turrell after two years, 1954–1956, because he found little support for public education and returned to Little Rock, where he served as the principal of the Panky High School, 1957–1966, which was in the Pulaski County Special School District. The superintendent of the school district was so impressed with Boswell's administrative ability that he was given the added responsibility of supervising the district's other black schools. Boswell's administrative abilities attracted the attention of the state Department of Education, which offered him a position as a supervisor of secondary education. He accepted the offer and worked for the department until his retirement in 1982.

Elbert E. Benton. This native of Louisiana was educated in Texas, B.A. and M.A. degrees, and moved to Arkansas in 1950 to chair the Department of Education at Shorter College in North

Little Rock. He held this position until being named academic dean of the college, serving from 1952 to 1956. At the end of the 1956 academic year, Benton resigned from his position at Shorter College and accepted the principalship of Carver Elementary School in the North Little Rock School District. He was the principal of Carver between 1956 and 1968. Under his leadership the faculty was encouraged to pursue graduate education, and Carver's students became known for their academic skills. Benton's success at Carver attracted the attention of the state Department of Education, which persuaded him to join its staff as a state supervisor of elementary education. In this position, 1968–1986, he was responsible for and successfully executed his duties of helping elementary schools throughout the state upgrade their academic programs so they could qualify for accreditation by the North Central Association of Colleges and Schools.

In addition to his professional responsibilities, Benton was actively involved in the civic affairs of the North Little Rock community. He was a member of the Urban League, worked with the Watershed Project and the NAACP, and served as chair of the building/fund committee at his church. Benton was also a lifetime member of the Phi Beta Sigma Fraternity and provided yeomen service for the organization. He served as the fraternity's southwest regional director and helped establish Sigma chapters on college and university campuses throughout his region, including chapters on the campuses of the University of Arkansas at Fayetteville, the University of Central Arkansas at Conway, and Arkansas Baptist College in Little Rock.

Dr. Samuel Branch. Dr. Branch is a native of Watson, Arkansas, where he received his elementary school education. He completed his high school education in Tillar, Arkansas, and went on to earn degrees in higher education at the AM&N College (B.S.), and Kansas State University, master's in 1979 and doctorate in 1998. Branch began his career in public school education in Tillar as a classroom teacher at the B. B. Pruitt Elementary School, 1970–1977. In 1977 he relocated to Pine Bluff (Jefferson County), where he taught at the Indiana Street Elementary School, 1977–1979. His administrative career began in the fall of 1979 when he assumed the principalship of the Altheimer-Sherrill School in Altheimer (Jefferson County), where he worked from

1979 to 1987. While leading the Altheimer-Sherrill School, Branch also taught courses in elementary education at the University of Arkansas at Pine Bluff, formerly AM&N College. Branch left the Altheimer-Sherrill School at the end of the 1987 academic year and briefly worked full-time at UAPB before moving to Little Rock, where he served as principal of the Mitchell Elementary School, 1993–1999, and of Forrest Park Elementary, 1999. While executing his principalship responsibilities in the Little Rock public schools, Branch also served as an evaluator of elementary education programs for the Arkansas Department of Education.

In addition to his professional responsibilities, Branch is an active participant in the civic affairs of his community. He is a member of the Royal Knights and Kiwanis Clubs, works as a volunteer 4-H Club leader, coaches pee-wee baseball, and mentors selected students enrolled in Little Rock's public schools.

Jodie T. Carter. Carter has spent the majority of his career in public education in the Little Rock area where he served as principal of Sylvan Hills Junior High in the Pulaski County School District, 1981–1983, and in the Little Rock School District at Hall High School, 1983–1988, and John L. McClellan High School, 1989–1999. At McClellan, Carter introduced the community school concept, developed the curriculum for the magnet school program, established computer laboratories on campus, and helped the school become the number-one business high school in Arkansas and one of the best in the nation.

Lucious Powell. Prior to becoming an assistant principal at Central High School, 1969–1971, in the Little Rock School District, Powell, who was trained in guidance and counseling, worked in the district as a teacher. In 1971, he left Central for a similar position at Hall High School, 1971–1974. Powell's years of service as an assistant principal helped to prepare him for a full principalship, and he was eventually named principal of Forest Heights Junior High School, where he served from 1974 to 1975. Following one year of service as a guidance counselor at Forest Heights, Powell returned to the teaching ranks and accepted a position at the Parkview Arts and Science Magnet School in the Little Rock School District. He served in this position until his retirement. In addition to being an educator and administrator, Powell is an accomplished vocalist who is known throughout the state for his melodious tenor voice.

Etta May Quick. Known as a dedicated teacher, organized administrator, and firm disciplinarian, Quick was the principal of two schools in the Pulaski County School District, Ish Elementary, 1971–1973, and Western Hills Elementary, 1973–1975.

Sadie M. Mitchell. This talented administrator is a native of Hope (Hempstead County), Arkansas, and a graduate of its public schools and Henderson State University at Arkadelphia. She began her career in Arkansas's public schools as a special education teacher in England, Arkansas, where she worked before accepting a similar position at Forest Park Elementary School in the Little Rock School District. After five years in the district, she began to move rapidly up its administrative ranks: assistant principal, Rockefeller Elementary School, 1989; principal, Cloverdale Elementary, 1990–1994; and in 1994 she was selected as the first principal of the newly constructed Dr. Martin Luther King Elementary, where she served from 1994 to 1995. Because of her administrative skills, Mitchell served as an assistant superintendent for elementary education in the Little Rock School District, 1995–1998, and as associate superintendent in 1998. While moving up the administrative ladder in the district, Mitchell was also expanding her educational credentials and is currently (2001) pursuing graduate studies at the University of Arkansas at Fayetteville. Her rapid ascent in the Little Rock School District is indicative of her commitment to public education and administrative skills.

Fred Oakley Jr. Oakley, like the majority of black public school administrators in Arkansas, began his career as classroom teacher. From 1955 to 1962, he taught high school agriculture at Carthage (Dallas County). His administrative career began at the J. E. Wallace High School, also in Dallas County, where he was principal from 1962 until 1970. As a former agricultural education teacher, Oakley stressed science education during his tenure at J. E. Wallace, the school's students won several first- and second-place awards at regional science fair competitions. Although he was a successful public school administrator, Oakley was lured away from the public schools by the University of Arkansas at Little Rock, where he served as director of institutional research, 1972–1976, and director of Trio Programs, 1976–1986. Although Oakley's move into higher education was a rewarding professional move, it also represented a loss for public education.

Frankie Rutherford. A dedicated, energetic, and entertaining educator, Rutherford was the principal of the Booker T. Washington Elementary School in the Little Rock School District, 1976–1985. Using the slogan "The Wonderful World of Washington," Rutherford improved the skills of her teachers, student learning, and community support for Washington Elementary.

Vernon Smith Sr. Smith began his administrative career in public education in the Helena-West Helena (Phillips County) School District where he held the dual positions of principal of Central High School (1980–1985) and coordinator of federal programs (1982–1985). Where Smith worked between 1985 and 1996 is unclear, but he served as named principal of Forest Heights Junior High School in the Little Rock School District, 1996–1999, and Hall High School, 1999. Students in the schools where Smith was the principal improved their daily attendance and academic performance, especially on standardized tests, because he was able to persuade teachers to adopt his educational philosophy: "Every child can learn if you work hard enough with him (her)."

Rowan J. Altheimer Jr. This innovative educator began his career at Horace Mann High School in Little Rock (Pulaski County), where he taught business education and consumer mathematics, 1962–1963. In the fall of 1963, Altheimer began teaching a new course at Mann—distributive education and diversified occupations. This was the first course of its kind to be taught in the Little Rock School District and proved to be immensely popular and successful. The course placed students in trainee positions at Little Rock's Union Bank and First Commercial Banks, Montgomery Ward, Sears, J. C. Penney, and a number of other private businesses in the Little Rock community. Many of these positions had been previously unavailable to blacks. Because of the success of this course, the Little Rock School District named Altheimer chair of the Mann High School Vocational Education Department, which he headed for two years, 1966–1968.

As chair of Mann's vocational education department, Altheimer's administrative and communication skills attracted the attention of the central office of the Little Rock School District, and he was promoted to the vice principalship of the Metropolitan Senior High School in 1968. In 1972, Metropolitan was renamed and became the Metropolitan Vocational Technical Center and Altheimer continued as vice principal until being named principal of Horace Mann Junior High School, 1975–1980. In 1980, he was transferred to the principalship of Forest Heights Junior High, 1980–1982, and finally to the principalship of Parkview High School, 1982–1985, where he worked until retirement. As an administrator, Altheimer's philosophy was "fairness to all students." One area of unfairness that concerned him was the Little Rock School District's zero-hour class period. This period began at 7 A.M., when no classes were scheduled, and allowed teachers to leave school an hour early in the afternoon. Arguing that this period placed students who depended upon public transportation (city busses) to get to school at an educational disadvantage, he successfully petitioned the Little Rock School District to eliminate the zero hour. Altheimer believed that no classes should began before all students could get to school and take advantage of the skills taught.

Dr. Mary Guinn. Dr. Guinn was principal of the Carver Magnet Elementary School in the Little Rock School District from 1985 to 1994. During the 1988–1989 academic year, Guinn served not only as principal of Carver, but also as a special assistant to the superintendent of the school district. She quickly developed a reputation as an excellent administrator, and during her Carver principalship the school became a model magnet school for the district. Unfortunately, the Little Rock School District and Arkansas lost the administrative skills of Dr. Guinn when she accepted a position in the Monroe (Louisiana) city schools as assistant superintendent for educational quality. She worked in this position for four years, 1994–1998, before leaving to become superintendent of the Gary (Indiana) Community School Corporation, which she currently (2001) directs.

Herbert H. Denton. Well known and respected, Denton served as the principal of the Bush Elementary Schools in Little Rock, Arkansas, in the late 1950s.[40] From 1966 to 1967, he was the principal of the Carver-Pfeifer Elementary School in the Little Rock School District. In 1967, Carver-Pfeifer was separated, and Denton continued as principal of Carver. His tenure at Carver was amazing because of its impact on the school and the local community. Carver Elementary was located in Little Rock's poor and predominantly black east end community, an area which had shown little interest in the school. Denton, however, believed that if the students in the area attended a school in which they could take pride, it would increase attendance and academic performance. Subsequently, he was able to get Carver's students and parents involved in a school beautification program that drew citywide recognition. With the help of students and parents the school was cleaned inside and out, and the lawn looked as if it had been manicured by a professional. As a result of Denton's leadership, Carver won the "City Beautiful Award," a plaque given by the Little Rock School District to the school showing the greatest improvements of buildings and grounds. Because of the school pride Denton was able to instill in Carver's students and parents, the school won the award each year during his tenure and for several consecutive years after his departure.

Denton spent nineteen years as a principal before being named director of the district's Career Opportunity Program (COP) in 1970. COP was a new program in the district that worked with college and university students enrolled in teacher education programs and provided them with the opportunity to work with experienced public schoolteachers in order to develop the skills they would need as public schoolteachers. It was hoped that these students would seek employment in the Little Rock School District upon their graduation from college.

Roosevelt Early. Following the desegregation of the Crossett (Ashley County) public schools, Early became the first black principal in the district. He served as principal of three different schools: Norman Junior High School, 1975–1980; Daniel Middle School, 1980–1985; and Crossett High School, 1985–2001. During his career, Early has stressed individualized teaching techniques and motivational learning programs as ways of enhancing student achievement. He has developed an effective dialogue with parents and community leaders who often refer to him as their local "father of education."

Portia L. Power. Power is a well-known and highly regarded educator who spent most of her thirty years in public education in the North Little Rock (Pulaski County) School District. She began her administrative career as principal of the Rose City Elementary School. During her tenure at Rose City, 1978–1981, Power established a "mathematics center." Students rotated through the "center" by grade level and worked on general math skills and individualized learning projects. Subsequently, the performance of Rose City students on standardized mathematics tests showed significant improvements. Power's success at Rose City led to her being named principal of Lakewood Elementary School in 1981. She served in this position until her retirement in 1993. At Lakewood, Power established an after-school tutoring program for underachievers in language arts, social studies, and math. Amazingly, she was able to persuade her staff to remain after regular school hours to work in the program without extra compensation.

In 1992, in recognition of Power's student learning programs and her dedication to education in general, she was invited by the Department of Defense, in conjunction with the North Central Association of Colleges and Schools, to travel to Germany (Frankfurt, Boeblingen, Crailsheim, Goeppinghen, Nuremberg, and Stuttgart) and help evaluate military schools for membership in the accreditation association. The next year Powers dedication to the students of Arkansas's public schools was recognized when she was named "Administrator of the Year" by the Arkansas Parents and Teachers Association (APTA) during its annual convention. The APTA recognition award was presented by James Smith, the superintendent of the North Little Rock School District, who pointed out that among other positive things, Power knew all of the parents and students at Lakewood Elementary by name. Her comments, in response to receiving the award, clearly revealed why she was the recipient. "I feel very humble at Lakewood," she said, "because we live and work as a family. I have to forget about the title principal and remember that every person is a person of worth, and make decisions based upon what is best for them."

During her long and distinguished career in public education, Power was active in her professional organizations and in civic affairs. Professionally, she served as president of the North Little Rock Elementary Principals Association, 1975; as board member of the Fulbright School, 1980; and as an elementary education program evaluator for the North Central Association. In addition to her professional activities, Power was also active in the religious education programs of her church—Eighth Street Baptist Church, North Little Rock—where she served as a member of the missionary society and as a teacher in the Baptist Training Program.

Northwest Arkansas

John L Colbert. This groundbreaking educator began his career in public education in 1976 as the first black special education teacher at the predominantly white Bates Elementary School in the Fayetteville (Washington County) School District. Fayetteville is one of the largest cities in northwest Arkansas with a population of approximately fifty thousand, but its black population is less than 10 percent of that total. Colbert's appointment to the Bates school was, therefore, noteworthy. By 1980, he had become a sixth-grade teacher at Bates and the lead teacher in the building. In 1984, Colbert was lured away from Fayetteville and Bates Elementary by the Fort Smith (Sebastian County) School District, which named him principal of its Howard Elementary School. During his years at Howard, Colbert expanded the school curriculum through the addition of units in black history. He also helped organize a Parent Teacher Association that became active in its support of the school.

In 1987, Colbert was persuaded to return to Fayetteville as principal of the Jefferson Elementary School, thus becoming the first black principal in the desegregated Fayetteville public school system. As Jefferson's principal Colbert, working with the local University of Arkansas, established a Partner-in-Education Program, which exposed Jefferson's students to the latest developments in educational programming and provided teacher education majors at the university with the opportunity to work with students before they entered the teaching profession on a full-time basis. In 1995, Colbert recorded another first when he was named principal of the newly constructed Holcomb Elementary School in Fayetteville where he currently (2001) serves. In recognition of Colbert's administrative skills the Arkansas Parent Teacher Association named him "Administrator of the Year" in 1997.

CHAPTER 7

Continuing the Legacy

Challenges since *Brown*, 1970–1990

The unanimous decision of the United States Supreme Court in the case of *Brown vs. Board of Education*, which said "that in the field of public education, the doctrine of 'separate but equal' has no place," received a mixed acceptance in Arkansas. Blacks, who had been fighting for educational equality for decades prior to the decision, accepted it as the inevitable solution to the problem of educational discrimination. Though they were not integrationist, many preferred to have their own quality schools within the segregated system, but they saw a desegregated public school system as the only way to end inequality in public school funding by the state and local school boards. Many whites, however, reacted in horror to the Court's decision because they saw it not as an educational issue, but a social one that threatened white supremacy and racial purity. The journalist Curt Copeland, from Hot Springs, Arkansas, said that the decision was a scheme by a liberal court to "put the nigger in your bedroom." And James D. Johnson, the state's most devout and articulate segregationist, commonly referred to as "Justice Jim" in Arkansas, also believed that the decision would lead the nation down the road of racial amalgamation. "If I send my child to an integrated school, I might see the day when I'll be bouncing a half-nigger on my knee and have him call me grandpa."[1]

The Supreme Court, realizing that its *Brown* decision presented complex social problems for the states with segregated public school systems, gave the states the opportunity to offer suggestions for relief within the boundaries of its decision. The majority of the southern states, however, sought ways to evade rather than comply with the Court's decision. This noncompliance led the Court in May of 1955 to issue its "all deliberate speed" decision, sometimes referred to as *Brown II*. The ruling let the states know that the constitutional principles outlined in its original decision could not be compromised and ordered the states to make a "prompt and reasonable start toward compliance."

Initially it appeared that Arkansas would be one of the few southern states to comply with the Court's decrees without serious resistance. Commenting on the Court's ruling in *Brown*, Governor Orval E. Faubus said that public school integration was a local matter "with state authorities standing ready to assist in every way possible."[2] Subsequently in 1955, there was no opposition from the state when the Fayetteville School District decided to desegregate and began sending its small number of students to Fort Smith, approximately one hundred and twenty-six miles away, round trip. However, when the small rural Hoxie (Lawrence County) School District decided to follow Fayetteville's lead and incorporate its twenty-five black students into the local school system instead of sending them to Jonesboro (Craighead County), approximately eighty miles away, round trip, defiance developed when die-hard segregationists, organized as the White Citizen Council and led by "Justice Jim," descended upon the city to protest. With the support of the federal court, Hoxie was able to complete its voluntary desegregation process, but the actions of Johnson and the White Citizen Council were a prelude of what was to come as school districts across the state marshaled their forces to fight desegregation. Many blacks in the state turned to the federal courts in order to force their local school districts to comply with the *Brown* decision. While the White Citizen Council was fighting desegregation in Hoxie, black parents in Van Buren were suing their local school board to force compliance with *Brown*. And in 1956, Daisy Bates, president of the Little Rock chapter of the National Association for the Advancement of Colored People, filed a desegregation suit against the Little Rock School District.[3]

The desegregation process in Arkansas was a slow and troublesome one. In 1963, the Arkansas Advisory Committee of the United States Commission on Civil Rights reported that "Arkansas's public schools remain basically segregated."[4] In a similar vein Charles Wesley, in the 1969 edition of the *International Library of Negro Life and History*, reported that in 1966, twelve years after the *Brown* decision had outlawed public school segregation, "the facts of racial isolation in the public schools left the Negro as short-changed as before."[5] Wesley's report reflected the conclusion of a 1966 report by the United States Department of Education, which said that "American public education remains largely unequal in most regions of the country, including those where Negroes form any significant part of the population." Since the desegregation process in Arkansas was so slow, the vast majority of the administrators in black public schools continued to improve their professional credentials, implement the latest educational programs in their schools, and seek the equalization of teacher salaries and physical plants. In the mid-1960s, the federal courts increased the pace of desegregation through their interpretations of the 1964 and 1965 Civil Rights Acts and the 1965 Elementary and Secondary Education Act. Those statutes, among other things, prohibited racial discrimination by any school or agency receiving federal funds. Threatened with the loss of desperately needed federal aid, Arkansas's public schools quickened the desegregation process. The increased pace of desegregation, however, presented new challenges and concerns to black public school administrators. Black principals, even the most qualified ones, were now forced to fight to keep their jobs, and those of their teachers, and to protect the rights of black students in newly desegregated and often hostile environments. They also faced the challenge of competency testing. They met the challenges head on, with a significant degree of success, and continued the legacy of competence which they had demonstrated prior to desegregation.

Southwest Arkansas

Mildred L. Johnson Smith. An experienced public schoolteacher who had spent several years in the public schools of Little Rock and North Little Rock, Arkansas, 1960–1973, Smith's career as a principal began in Hope, Arkansas, where she was a teacher and an assistant principal from 1973 to 1987. In 1988 she was simultaneously named principal of the Lincoln High School in Washington (Hempstead County) and school district superintendent. She was the first female superintendent of the district, a position she held until her retirement in 1991.

James Williams. Unlike the vast majority of black principals following the *Brown* decision and the turbulent early years of desegregation, Williams's career was not directly impacted because he was the superintendent of the all-black Oak Grove School District in Nevada County, 1976–1977. He was not, however, immune to what was taking place in the state's public schools and realized that Oak Grove graduates would have to be able to compete in an increasingly competitive society. Williams believed that the best way to prepare students for future success was through early academic preparation. He, therefore, opened the first kindergarten center at Oak Grove during his tenure.

Robert McGhee. McGhee was the principal of several rural schools in Arkansas before accepting the superintendency of the Oak Grove School District (Nevada County), 1984–1986. During his tenure with the south Nevada County public school, he worked with parents and local public school officials to unify the county's five separate school districts.

Otis L. Brown. From 1974 to 1998, Brown served as the principal of four different schools in the Pine Bluff (Jefferson County) school system: Patterson High School, 1974–1976; Belair Junior High School, 1977–1985; Jack Robey Junior High, 1986–1992; and Dollarway Junior High, 1992–1998.

Caleb Bronson. Bronson was the progressive superintendent of the predominantly black Oak Grove School District in Rosston (Nevada County), Arkansas, 1977–1983. Bronson implemented the district's first elementary counseling program and was instrumental in getting a kindergarten center and a home economics building constructed in the district. He also played a major role in securing funds for the remodeling of the Oak Grove Cafeteria.

Northeast Arkansas

Milton L. Washington. Washington spent his entire administrative career in the predominantly black Osceola (Mississippi County) School District. From 1985 to 1986, he was the assistant principal of the Osceola High School, and from 1986 to 1989 he served as principal of the Osceola Middle School. By 1989, Washington had become a proven administrator and was rewarded by being promoted to the principalship of the Osceola High School where he had formerly served as the assistant principal. He was principal of the high school from 1989 until 1997. Because of his success as principal of Osceola High School, Washington was named assistant superintendent of the Osceola School District and currently serves in that position. During his tenure, Washington helped establish the Tech Program in the district and on the campus of the nearby Mississippi County College.

Vhaness W. Chambers. From 1973 to 1978, Mrs. Chambers was the principal of the DeRossit Elementary School in the Madison (St. Francis County) community near Forrest City, Arkansas. In 1978, Chambers took on her greatest challenge when she was offered and accepted the principalship of the rural and predominantly black Madison/Butler Montessori School where she labored from 1978 until her retirement in 1998. When she accepted the principalship of the school, the institution was comprised of only two crumbling buildings with a poor underachieving student body. Chambers, however, was able to raise enough funds to repair and modernize buildings, expand the curriculum, and lead the school to full North Central Association accreditation. The school eventually became one of the Forrest City School District's prized magnet schools under Chambers's leadership.

James E. McCoy. Talent, energy, commitment to high academic standards, educational vision, and effective leadership characterized the principalship of this Marianna (Lee County) educator. McCoy was first employed as a mathematics and science teacher in the Anna Strong High School in the Lee County School District in the mid-1960s. The Lee County School District completed, amidst some turmoil, its desegregation process in the early 1970s. During the desegregation process, the talent, energy, communication skills, and ability to solve problems were noticed by McCoy's superiors in the district's central office, and he was persuaded to accept the principalship of the Anna Strong Middle School, the all-black high school prior to desegregation, in 1975. He was the middle-school principal from 1975 until 1993. During his principalship, McCoy quickly developed a reputation as a strict but fair disciplinarian and expanded the school's curriculum and library. The improved library included the Compton Computer Encyclopedia Network, which tremendously expanded the educational horizons of students and enabled them to meet, and often exceed, state minimum requirements on standardized exams. To motivate effective teaching and student learning, McCoy played a major role in persuading the school district to adopt for use in the middle school the Teacher Expectation of Student Achievement

(TESA) and the Gender Expectation of Student Learning teaching models. Under his leadership, a beginners and intermediate band program was organized at the Strong Middle School, and parental involvement in student learning was increased through the implementation of the James P. Comer School Development Model for site-based management. Seeking to better utilize McCoy's skills, the central office of the Lee County School District drafted him into its ranks in 1993 where he served as an assistant superintendent until his resignation in 1999.

Howard McNeal. McNeal, a native of Osceola, Arkansas, and a graduate of the local Rosenwald public school, AM&N College at Pine Bluff (B.A.) and Arkansas State University at Jonesboro (M.A.), began his career in public education as a science teacher at his alma mater. From 1968 to 1970, he taught science and served as assistant principal and dean of men at Rosenwald. In 1970 he was named principal of the Osceola Junior High School. Following the desegregation of the Osceola public schools, McNeal was named principal of the desegregated Osceola (Mississippi County) High School. He served in this position, 1985–1998, until retirement. In the spring of 1990 he was honored by the mayor of Osceola and area state legislators as a public school administrator. In recognition of McNeal's leadership, the Osceola School Board declared March 8 of each year as the annual Howard McNeal Day in the Osceola School District.

Rogers Hurston Ford. A native of Turrell (Mississippi County), Arkansas, a rural farming community, Rogers Ford has a special affinity for public education. He grew up in the days of strict Jim Crowism in Arkansas and learned the value of education quite early. Ford graduated from the public schools in Turrell, Tuskegee Institute in Alabama (B.A.), and Arkansas State University in Jonesboro (M.A.), and did further study at the University of Memphis (Tennessee). Ford, who believed that education was the escape route from poverty and ignorance, decided early in life that he wanted to be a teacher and began his career in public education as a social studies teacher and guidance counselor at Wilson High School in Wilson (Mississippi County), Arkansas. There were five small independent public school districts in Mississippi County that competed for students. In 1971 the five districts (Wilson, Dyess,

Joiner, Kaiser, and Frenchman's Bayou), in order to save money and offer better student programs, consolidated and created Rivercrest High School. Ford was named principal of Rivercrest in 1985. The vast majority of Rivercrest students came from poor and uneducated farm families, and their standardized test scores were far below the state's average. Ford challenged these students to learn, and under his leadership, the standardized test scores of Rivercrest students improved dramatically and the college attendance rate more than doubled. As of 1999, Ford continues as principal of Rivercrest. He is also a successful local businessman and has served one seven-year term on the Board of Trustees of Arkansas State University.

Central Arkansas

Lonnie Sue Dean. Dean spent most of her professional administrative career, 1983–1995, in the Little Rock School District in Pulaski County. During her tenure in the Little Rock School District, Dean was the principal of Romine Elementary School, 1983–1985; Booker T. Washington Elementary, 1985–1988; Ish Elementary School, 1988–1991; Stephens Elementary, 1991–1994; and Baseline Elementary School, 1994–1995. In addition to her principalships, Dean helped write the district's revised desegregation plans and to implement its Major Enhancement Plan, the Racial Identification Plan, and the School Incentive Plan.

James A. Ziegler. Ziegler was a talented and innovative administrator who was able to maintain his position as a black public school principal during the controversial desegregation of the North Little Rock School District. He was employed as a teacher in the district before being named principal of the Redwood Elementary School in 1970. Ziegler served Redwood until being named principal of the Meadow Park Elementary School in 1986, where he served until his retirement in 1994. During his tenure in the North Little Rock School District, Ziegler led the Redwood Elementary School to full accreditation by the North Central Association of Colleges and Schools. He also played a major role in the smooth transition of the Redwood school from segregation to desegregation. One of the major programs he developed to aid in that process was a weekly communication system designed to keep parents informed about the academic and social progress of their children. Ziegler was also an influential member of the North Little Rock Principals

Association and the district's Staff Development Steering
Committee.

Cherrie R. Johnson. This native Arkansan was educated in the
public schools of Desha County, Arkansas, the University of
Arkansas at Pine Bluff (B.S., elementary education), and the
University of Central Arkansas at Conway where she earned a master's degree in elementary education and administrative supervision. She began her career in public education in South Bend,
Indiana, in 1965 as an elementary classroom teacher, but yearned
to return home to Arkansas and the Little Rock area. Following a
few years of teaching in Indiana, Johnson returned to Arkansas
where she had accepted a teaching position in the J. C. Cook
Elementary School in Wrightsville, an institution in the Pulaski
County School District. She has worked in the district since that
time. Cherrie proved to be an excellent teacher and motivator at
J. C. Cook and served as principal of Mabelvale Elementary School
for five years, 1982–1987.

Following her successful tenure at Mabelvale, Johnson was
moved to the principalship of the newly constructed Bates
Elementary School where she served from 1987 to 1992. Bates
Elementary was named in honor of Daisy Bates, the leader of the
successful movement to desegregate Little Rock Central High
School in 1957, and Johnson played an instrumental role in the
naming of the school. After five years at Bates, Johnson moved on
to become principal of Scott Elementary, 1992–1994, and Harris
Elementary, 1994–2001, where she currently serves the Pulaski
County School District. During her tenure at Bates, Johnson implemented an elementary mathematics and science education program
and LEAP, a Language Enrichment Activities Program for at-risk
students. As an administrator, Johnson's philosophy centers around
the belief that a high-quality instructional program must strive to
meet the needs of all students and must be preceded by the establishment of a vision for the school, a mission statement, general and
specific goals and objectives. She also believes that all staff members should develop their potential to the fullest. To this end she
strongly encourages her teachers to participate in staff development
in-service programs, to attend professional meetings, to develop
meaningful grade-level meetings, and to participate in peer obser-
vations to further enhance their instructional skills. Johnson also

meets regularly with her staff to listen to their concerns and share ideas.

To support classroom learning life experiences, Johnson has successfully recruited eleven business partners for the school (Harris Elementary) and organized a Dads on Campus Club, and she uses volunteer professional parents to strengthen weak areas of the curriculum such as physical education and music. She has also infused economic education throughout the Harris curriculum and even into behavior management. These programs/activities offer students the opportunity to experience real-life situations early and helps students to make sound decisions. Johnson is recognized as one of the Pulaski County School District's outstanding administrators, and in 1996 she was nominated for the prestigious Arkansas Principal of the Year award and the National Distinguished Principal Award in 1997. She continues in her present position to strive to reach her fullest potential as an administrator.

Lionel Ward. Ward is one of those black educators who has used his administrative skills to eliminate the suspicion held by many white superintendents, especially during the early years of desegregation, that black principals lacked competency. He demonstrated his excellent administrative skills while serving as the principal in several schools in the Little Rock School District: Rightsell Elementary, 1980–1987; Romine Elementary, 1987–1994; Mabelvale Elementary, 1994–1995; and Garland Academy, 1995–1999. While at Rightsell, Ward introduced the Program for Effective Teaching, the Teacher Expectation of Student Achievement teaching model, and computer usage as teaching models/strategies. During his tenure at Mablevale, Ward developed a parent/teacher handbook and at Garland Elementary he has introduced the Effective Learning in Technical Environments (ELTE) teaching program which enhances learning through the utilization of a four-day academic core curriculum combined with project-based instructions, staff development opportunities, and a student academic activities day.

Eleanor Cox. Mrs. Cox was one of several talented black principals in the Little Rock School District whose leadership skills could not be ignored. Consequently, she was named principal of the district's Bale Elementary School. Her appointment to Bale was significant because it represented a decision by the Little Rock School District to assign black principals to schools outside of the city's historical black population centers. Following three years of service at Bale, Cox held other positions in the district, including principalships at Gibbs Elementary School and Geyer Springs Elementary. In 1995, Cox was transferred to the principalship of the Baseline Elementary School where she currently (1999) serves. In addition to being one of the first principals from a segregated school to lead a formerly all-white elementary school in the Little Rock School District, Cox counts among her many achievements the successful implementation of the Success-for-All Reading Program in schools where she served.

Shirley Jones. In 1984, Jones became the principal of Fuller Junior High School in the Pulaski County Special School District where she currently serves (1999). During her tenure in the district, she has focused her energies upon staff development opportunities that will help her better serve students, teachers, and parents.

Dr. Marian G. Lacey. The Little Rock School District, because of its location in the state's largest metropolitan area and its reputation for educational excellence and above-average salaries, attracted some of the state's best black teachers and administrators; one of those was Dr. Lacey. Lacey began her administrative career in the Little Rock School District as the principal of Dunbar Junior High School, 1986–1988. From Dunbar, she was transferred to the principalship of the Mann Arts and Sciences Magnet School where she served from 1988 until 1998. Following her tour of duty at the magnet school, Lacey became an assistant superintendent in the district. She is a very talented and productive administrator who, in 1997, received the $25,000 Miliken Family Foundation National Education Award for excellence in education. In 1998, Lacey was the recipient of the impressive AM&N College/UAPB (class of 1970) Profile Salute to Excellence Award and was recognized by the *Arkansas Democrat Gazette* (one of Arkansas's two statewide newspapers at the time) as its ideal principal and role model for the year. Among the many awards and citations she received was one of special significance to this outstanding educator—a plaque from the Parent Teacher Association of Dunbar Junior High School which saluted her for ten years of dedicated service.

Catherine Jewell Gill. This native of West Memphis, Arkansas, was recognized as an outstanding elementary teacher in several schools in the Little Rock School District—Gibbs, Rightsell, and Brady—before serving as the principal of Fair Park Elementary, 1978–1991. During her tenure at Fair Park, Gill established the first banking project for elementary students, which taught them how the nation's economic system worked and the value of saving. This unique project became a nationally recognized Economic Education Program. In 1991, Gill became the supervisor of the Little Rock School District's Incentive Program and an influential member of the district's Parent Involvement Council. During her career, Gill has received educational awards and is listed in the current (1999) edition of *Personalities of the South in Education*.

Rudolph Howard. Known for fostering sound academic programs and student discipline, Howard served as principal of the Cotton Plant High School in Cotton Plant (Woodruff County), Arkansas, 1974–1978; Southwest Junior High School (Pulaski County) in the Little Rock School District, 1985–1987; and McClellan High School, 1987–1990. Because of his ability as an educational problem solver, especially in the areas of race relations and desegregation, the Little Rock School District, assigned Howard to serve as the district's student hearing officer, 1990–1993. Because of his administrative skills and reputation for fairness, Howard was named principal of the historic Central High School in 1993. Although he was a strict disciplinarian and stressed academic excellence, Howard was well received by Central's students, who appreciated his fairness, academic emphasis, and problem-solving skills. They showed their appreciation through a passage included in the 1999 Central yearbook, the *Tiger*, which read:

> Central is very privileged to have an outstanding leader such as Mr. Howard. He is extremely dedicated to his work and takes great pride in it. He constantly tells us to be mindful and to remember this (school day) is not the weekend and to focus on our studies. He encourages students to stay on track and to stay out of trouble. Mr. Howard doesn't take any "mess" when it comes to disruptive behavior and disorderly conduct. To sum him up, Mr. Howard is a great guy and a joy to have at our school.

Bobbie Hawkins Goodwin. Goodwin was the principal of five elementary schools in the Little Rock School District: Garland Elementary, 1977–1981; Oakhurst/King Elementary, 1981–1988; Carver Magnet Elementary, 1988–1989; Washington Elementary, 1989–1990; and Rightsell Elementary, from which she retired. The Little Rock School District was still in the desegregation process when Goodwin first became a principal, and she played an influential role in the smooth transition to desegregation at the elementary level. In 1988 she received special recognition from the school district for her outstanding educational service, and in 1991 the National Committee for School Desegregation presented her with a Certificate of Merit for her outstanding contributions to the desegregation of public education.

Dr. Morris L. Holmes Jr. This very capable administrator was the principal of three schools in the Little Rock School District: Opportunity High School, 1970–1971; Forrest Heights Junior High School, 1973–1974; and the historic Central High School, 1974–1979. While at Opportunity High, a school for students who experienced disciplinary problems in the regular school setting, Holmes established a learning program that served as a model for similar schools. During his tenure at Forrest Heights, he was particularly disturbed by the lack of student academic achievement and worked hard to secure and use Title I federal funds for the implementation of mathematics and reading programs, which significantly enhanced student learning and improved standardized test scores.

Holmes faced his greatest challenge as an administrator when he accepted the principalship of Central High School in 1974. He was only thirty-four years old, one of the youngest principals of a major high school in Arkansas, and one of a very small cadre of blacks to head a predominantly white high school. Upon his arrival at Central, Holmes announced that his first priority was to create an atmosphere conducive to student learning. During his tenure at the school, students regularly encountered him in the hallways, in the cafeteria, and at sporting events. No matter where he came into contact with students, he always reminded them to stay in school and study because "now is the time to prepare for the future." He also worked closely with Central's teachers, and they became accustomed to his regular visits to their classrooms. According to ABC Television personality Geraldo Rivera, who interviewed Holmes

and featured Central during one of his Good Morning America tele-
casts, Central, under Holmes's leadership, was a model school.

Dr. Holmes's administrative success at Central High brought
him to national attention, which he used to become associate director of the Arkansas Department of Education, associate superintendent of the Fort Worth (Texas) Public School System, and
superintendent of public schools in New Orleans, Louisiana.

Gail Anderson (McLaughlin). Anderson began her career in
public education in the North Little Rock School District in Pulaski
County as a junior high school teacher. Her first administrative
position in the district was an assistant principalship at Sylvan Hills
Junior High School, 1979–1980. After only one year in the North
Little Rock School District, Anderson left to accept a similar position at the North Junior High School in Jacksonville (Pulaski
County Special School District), Arkansas, where she worked,
1980–1981. While at North Junior High, Anderson strengthened
the school's curriculum through the addition of the performing arts.
In 1982, Anderson was employed in the Little Rock School District
as the assistant principal of Cloverdale Junior High School,
1982–1987, and as principal of Southwest Junior High School,
1987–1989. During her tenure at Southwest, Anderson developed
the New Futures Program and an after school tutorial program for
students experiencing academic problems. She also developed a program to assist student teachers from the University of Arkansas at
Little Rock to adjust to the public school teaching environment.
Anderson left Arkansas's public schools in 1990 in order to pursue
a doctorate in educational administration.

Troy Lowe. Mr. Lowe has served as a public school principal for
nine years. His administrative career began in 1982 when he was
named an assistant principal at Robinson Junior High School in the
Pulaski County School District. He was later (1990) promoted to
the principalship of the Jacksonville Junior High School. In 1997
the district adopted the middle-school concept, and the Jacksonville
Junior High became a middle school, grades 6–7. Lowe chose to
remain in Jacksonville as the principal of the middle school. Under
his leadership, the middle school has exceeded all expectations.
Lowe's strong leadership was recognized in 2000 when the Arkansas
Association of Secondary School Principals selected him as the

Principal of the Year. The award, given each year, honors a middle-school principal who demonstrated a willingness to take risk in order to improve student learning, anticipate problems, apply appropriate solutions, and create a school climate conducive for learning.

Eddie Davis Brown. Brown (1910–1977) was a graduate of Haygood High School in Pine Bluff (Jefferson County), Arkansas, Dunbar Junior College in Little Rock, AM&N College at Pine Bluff, and Columbia University in New York. During his teaching career he taught at the Lincoln Junior High School in Fayetteville (Washington County) and at the Carver High School in Augusta, Arkansas. He began his administrative career as principal of the Nelson High School in Scott, Arkansas, and concluded it as the principal of the White County Training School in Searcy. Prior to desegregation, Brown was the only black principal in White County. During Brown's administrative career there were few black teachers in White County, but he was able to keep up with what was taking place in public education through maintaining an active membership in the Arkansas Education Association and the National Teachers Association. After his retirement, Brown became an active member of the Retired Teachers Association.

Larry S. Robertson. This native of Louisiana was educated in the public schools of that state, at Philander Smith College in Little Rock (B.S., elementary education), at the State Teachers College in Conway, where he earned the M.S.E. degree in early childhood education, and at Atlanta (Georgia) University where he has completed all requirements for the doctorate in education except the dissertation. In 1968, Robertson began his career in public education as a teacher in a Pulaski County Headstart Program operated by the federal Office of Economic Opportunity. In 1970, as a Educational Professional Development Act Fellow, Robertson taught kindergarten in the Little Rock School District. In 1972, because of his outstanding performance in the kindergarten program, he was offered and accepted a position with the Arkansas Department of Education as a kindergarten specialist. He moved rapidly up the administrative ranks of the Arkansas Department of Education, becoming an educational administrative supervisor, a coordinator of elementary education programs, and a coordinator of K-12 supervision. In 1990, the Little Rock School District persuaded Robertson to rejoin its ranks as an assistant superintendent for educational programs and staff development. In 1993 the district named him the assistant superintendent for student discipline. He served in this position until his retirement in 1996. The Department of Education continues to consult Robertson on procedures for implementing new educational programs.

During his professional career, Robertson was active in numerous professional organizations. He was an associate director for elementary education for the North Central Association of Colleges and Schools; a consultant for the Arkansas Council on Elementary Education; a member of the Arkansas Accreditation Committee for public and private schools; a member of the Arkansas Child Facility Review Board; and a member of the Arkansas Department of Education Equity Team, which was responsible for developing the agency's position on equity issues in education. Although retired, Robertson is still an active member of his church (Mount Pleasant Baptist, Little Rock), the NAACP, and his fraternity, Kappa Alpha Psi.

Coy W. Franklin. In the early 1940s, Franklin became the first black principal of the George Washington Carver High School in Marked Tree (Poinsett County), Arkansas. Located in an area dominated by large white-owned plantations, Carver received little support from the local school board nor the impoverished black farm community. Franklin, however, was able to improve and expand the school's curriculum and lead it to full state accreditation. He also worked closely with the parents of Carver's students in an effort to get them to send their children to school and to college. Franklin left Marked Tree to become principal of Lee High School in Marianna (Lee County), Arkansas. Lee County, which had a countywide school system, desegregated in 1970, and Franklin was the first black principal of the newly desegregated Lee High School. He served there until poor health forced his retirement in 1973.

Othella Faison. This talented native Arkansan was educated in the public elementary school in Holly Grove (Monroe County), Arkansas, and her high school education at the privately operated Fargo Training School of Floyd Brown near Brinkley (Monroe County), Arkansas. She went on to earn a B.A. in English and music at Philander Smith College in Little Rock, and an M.A. in English at the University of Arkansas at Fayetteville. Additional studies were completed at Texas Southern University (Houston) and the University of Central Arkansas (UCA) at Conway.

During the Little Rock School District's early years of desegregation, Mrs. Faison was one of the first black teachers to be assigned to a predominantly white school as a teacher of English. Because of her superb communication skills and teaching ability, she was selected to serve as the principal of four consecutive sessions of summer school, 1981–1985, at Central, Hall, and Parkview High Schools. Although Faison was not trained as an administrator, the summer-school sessions proved to be valuable training for her future in the Little Rock School District, because in 1990 she was named principal of the district's alternative school for junior high school students where she proved to be an excellent administrator. Within her first two weeks on the job, Faison compiled a student handbook and met with the parents of students. She encouraged and motivated her staff to work with students on an individual basis to improve their skills and to identify special needs. Once the individual needs of students had been identified, Faison secured a grant from the state Department of Education, which afforded students the opportunity to participate in hands-on learning activities, including the building of transistor radios and computers. These items became the property of the participating students upon completion of the program.

In addition to being an innovative educator, Faison is also a talented musician (piano and organ) and a celebrated soloist and the first black soloist to perform with the predominantly white Arkansas Choral Society. She is also a singer/soloist with the well-known Art Porter Singers. In addition to her professional education career and musical involvements, Faison finds time to be active in her church (Bullock Temple C.M.E.), where she serves as the minister of music, and in volunteer service work in her community. She is a member of the Arkansas Health Board for Pregnant Girls and spends countless hours tutoring community youths in mathematics, music, and public-speaking skills, and helping them with routine school assignments. When asked what was the cost of all her time, she replied: "Just be somebody and whatever people do for you don't forget to say thank you."

Raymond Chambers. Chambers was the principal of the predominantly black East School in Menifee (Conway County), Arkansas, 1976–1980. Under his leadership the school improved from a state Department of Education rating of "C" to "A." His success at East led to his appointment as assistant superintendent of the 75 percent white·South Conway School District at Morrilton. He was the district's first black administrator. In 1998, Chambers became the district's full-time superintendent, another first. Because of the experience he gained working in a desegregated public school system, he served as a consultant on race relations for Ouachita Baptist University in Arkadelphia, Arkansas.

CHAPTER 8

Other Blacks Who Influenced Black Education in Arkansas

The influential role played by black administrators in the education and shaping of the future of Arkansas's black youths from the Reconstruction Era to the early 1970s goes unquestioned. They were the ones who struggled with white school boards, often dominated by white planters in rural areas and unresponsive to the educational needs of blacks, for funding for buildings, educational programs, equipment, transportation, adequate salaries for their teachers, and a host of other educational needs. They, however, were not alone in the battle. Arkansas has been a rural agricultural state throughout most of its history, and many black farmers and sharecroppers, especially for the 1870–1950 period, could not afford to send their children into the major cities (Little Rock, Pine Bluff, Hot Springs, Fort Smith, for example), to complete their high school education. The needs of these rural people and their children were often met by teachers paid with funds from northern philanthropic foundations (such as the Jeanes Fund, the Slater Fund, and the Rosenwald Fund) and from black assistant agents from the Arkansas Agricultural Cooperative Extension Service. Following the desegregation of Arkansas's public schools, many blacks continued to try to mentor and improve the education of black students through their administrative positions and through contacts in the business community.

Harvey C. Ray. From 1918 until 1952, Ray was an employee of the Arkansas Agricultural Extension Service and served the rural black population in Pulaski and adjoining counties. During the depression of the 1930s, he taught his clients how to preserve food, vaccinate livestock, grow more productive crops, conduct product demonstrations, hold public meetings, and develop other skills they needed to become successful farm families. And successful farm families often sent their children to public schools and on to college.

Ella P. Neely. Mrs. Neely was the home demonstration agent for the Arkansas Agricultural Extension Service in Pulaski County,

1920–1935. Working primarily with women in rural areas, Neely taught these farm women how to better preserve food, sewing and mattress-making skills, home-furnishing techniques, and other skills needed for self-sufficiency. She ended her career as a district home demonstration agent in southwest Arkansas.

Clifford Epps. From 1927 to 1934, Epps was an Arkansas Agricultural Extension Service agent in Pulaski County. Working primarily with independent black farmers, Epps taught his clients how to make yearly budgets, repair farm buildings and equipment, conduct public meetings, improve livestock production and health, and how to rotate crops. In 1934, Epps left the Extension Service to become an independent farmer and use his agricultural know-how to improve the quality of life for himself and his family. His desire to help others, however, did not end when he departed the Extension Service. He took on a new role as a teacher of adult education classes in Pulaski County. He also taught wayward black youth at the Boys Training School in Wrightsville (Pulaski County), Arkansas.

Leonard Lawrence Phillips. Phillips was another agent of the Arkansas Agricultural Extension Service who served the state's rural black population. To Phillips, the skills he taught his clients were essential to their self-sufficiency and survival. He taught black farmers, like most extension agents, how to improve food crop production, when to plant and rotate crops, how to repair buildings and equipment, and how to improve poultry and pork production. From October of 1937 through July of 1946, he was the extension agent for Lee and Monroe Counties in eastern Arkansas. In February of 1938, he was assigned exclusively to Lee County where he worked until 1946. Because of his success in Lee County, Phillips was transferred to Phillips County and given the responsibility of directing thirty-two thousand young black men and women who were enrolled in the Extension Service's 4-H Club programs supervised by black county extension agents. He successfully supervised these agents and their programs until public school desegregation led to the merger of black and white 4-H Club programs in 1965. Following the merger, Phillips accepted a position on the Extension Service's statewide 4-H Club programs staff where he worked until being named director of the 4-H Club Rural Civil Defense Program.

This program, designed to prepare junior and senior high school students for emergency civil defense activities, was implemented in fifty-two rural school districts in Arkansas and drew national attention under Phillips's leadership.

Marguerite Pearson Williams. This native of Pine Bluff (Jefferson County), Arkansas, was honored in 1998 as the first home economics teacher to graduate from AM&N College at Pine Bluff. She went on to become a noted public school teacher and agricultural home economist for the Arkansas Agricultural Extension Service. After graduating from college, Williams taught home economics in the black public schools at Dermott and Wabbaseka, Arkansas. In 1935, she began a twenty-two-year career with the Arkansas Agricultural Extension Service as an assistant home demonstration agent for blacks in Union County. In 1958, Williams was promoted to the position of district supervisor for the Extension Service's black home economists. In 1967, this talented and energetic woman was named an extension specialist at the University of Arkansas's (Fayetteville) Cooperative Extension Service. She remained in this position until her retirement in 1975. During her career, Williams traveled throughout Arkansas training people who served as judges of competitive home economics exhibits at county fairs how to recognize and rank quality exhibits.

Williams held membership in several state and national professional associations and in numerous community clubs. She was a Baptist in her religious work and a member of the executive board of the National Baptist Convention. She authored two books for the convention. In her local church, Mount Zion Baptist Church in Little Rock, she was the director of the Board of Christian Education, and she organized the Widows' Club. She was the widow of C. P. Williams, who for many years served as the principal of Washington High School in El Dorado, Arkansas.

Eula Peeble. Described as "a charming and dignified lady who cared for people," Mrs. Peeble performed a valuable service to the rural black community as an area supervisor for the home vocational education program of the Arkansas Agricultural Extension Service from 1942 into the early 1960s. Trained as a home economist, Peeble not only directed vocational education projects for rural women and girls, she also spent a great deal of her time working with senior home economics majors at AM&N College. She was invaluable in helping these students make lesson plans for their initial ventures into public school teaching and in helping them adjust to the public school teaching environment.

LaVerne Williams Feaster. This native of Cotton Plant, Arkansas, was educated in the public schools of that city; Swift Junior College in Rogersville, Tennessee; Tennessee (Nashville) State University, B.S., vocational home economics, 1949; and the University of Arkansas at Fayetteville, M.A., 1966. She earned additional graduate credits at Fayetteville and at the University of Arizona. She began her career in public education in 1949 as a home economics teacher at Swift Junior College. She returned to Arkansas in 1950 where she taught home economics in the black high schools in Augusta, 1950–1953, and Dermott, 1953–1960.

In August of 1960, Mrs. Feaster left Arkansas's public schools and accepted a position with the Arkansas Cooperative Extension Service as an assistant home demonstration agent in Clark County. In 1966, she was promoted to the position of associate home demonstration agent and given the responsibility for human relations and child-development programs. Four years later she was again promoted to the position of home economist for nutrition for Clark and Garland Counties. Her new position required her to develop home nutrition programs for low-income families. In 1971, Feaster was again promoted and assigned to the Extension Service's offices in Little Rock as the state agent for 4-H Club programs. She was the first black woman to hold this position, and she held the post until 1977. From 1977 to 1981, she served as the district home economist for the Northeast District. She was also the first black to hold this position. During her career, Feaster received several awards for outstanding service at both the county and state level.

Dr. Tandy Washington Coggs. Dr. Coggs (1887–1992), whose parents were former slaves, was born in Crawford County near Van Buren, Arkansas. He received his high school education in the high school branch of Arkansas Baptist College in Little Rock and remained at the institution to earn a B.A. degree. He later attended Hampton Institute in Virginia and Tuskegee Institute in Alabama. While at Tuskegee, he studied under Booker T. Washington, the celebrated black educator and leader of his people.

Coggs began his career in the education of Arkansas's black youths when he accepted a position with Arkansas Baptist College as an instructor in carpentry in 1912. He left Baptist in 1915 to accept a position with Branch Normal College (AM&N) in Pine Bluff—the newly established position of director of trades and industry. In 1928, Coggs left Branch Normal to become the first black superintendent of the Negro Boys Industrial School at Pine Bluff. When he accepted the position the Boys Industrial School existed only on paper. Coggs was hired to build this school for black boys who were incarcerated in the state prison with hardened adult criminals. He was responsible not only for building the institution, but also for the development of its educational programs. His outstanding performance as superintendent of the Boys Industrial School led the Board of Trustees of Arkansas Baptist College to offer him its presidency. Coggs accepted Baptist's offer and served as president of the institution for eighteen consecutive years. During his tenure, Arkansas Baptist College experienced unprecedented growth: four brick buildings were renovated, enrollment increased four-fold, and the school was officially accredited as a Junior College by the state's Department of Education. Upon his retirement as president of Arkansas Baptist, Coggs accepted the principalship of the Sweet Home Elementary School (Pulaski County), where he continued to mold and shape young black minds for future progress.

During his long and productive career, Dr. Coggs was active in professional educational associations, especially the all-black Arkansas Teachers Association. He served two terms, 1938–1940, as president of the ATA, and he served as its treasurer for sixteen years, 1940–1956. In 1956, he became the organization's executive secretary and served in that position until his retirement in 1961. Upon his retirement, the ATA honored him with an award for more than fifty years of service to education in Arkansas and named him executive secretary emeritus. Shortly after the merger of the ATA and the all-white Arkansas Education Association, the teacher in-service grants of the old ATA were permanently named in his honor. He also received numerous other awards and citations including an honorary doctorate from AM&N College and being named vice president emeritus of Wings Over Jordan after having served on its board of directors for seventeen years.

Ila D. Upchurch. Stationed in Prescott, Arkansas, Ms.

Upchurch was a Jeanes supervisor for black schools in Nevada County, 1924–1943, where she worked with rural families on projects involving cooking, canning, cleaning, and health care. She did not, however, confine her activities to those job requirements. Upchurch also worked closely with parents and school officials in the successful effort to consolidate the various black schools in Nevada County into the Oak Grove Consolidated School District. The consolidated schools, she believed, reduced costs and afforded students better educational opportunities. In 1929, she also helped the consolidated district secure its first buses for student transportation.

Fannie M. Boone. Mrs. Boone began her career in education in Arkansas as a teacher and summer school principal in Mississippi County. She left the public schools to accept a position with the Arkansas Agriculture Cooperative Extension Service as a home demonstration agent for "Negro Work" in Lee County, 1942–1951. Boone took a leave of absence for the 1951–1952 year. She returned to the Extension Service in late 1952 as a district agent and worked in that position until her retirement in 1958. During her career, Boone taught her clients food preservation methods, how to make household furnishings, how to make family clothing, and how to make other products out of common, but overlooked, materials. Her clients competed in ham and egg shows, bread and dress shows, county fairs, and numerous other programs designed to improve the quality of rural life.

Tee Roy Betton. Educated at AM&N College (B.S., agriculture) and the Michigan State University (M.S.), Betton made a significant contribution to improving the quality of life for blacks throughout Arkansas. He began his career as an agriculture teacher in Warren (Bradley County), Arkansas, in 1933. Because of his performance and interpersonal skills the National Youth Administration (NYA), a major depression-era program designed to keep young people in school and off welfare lines, selected Betton as one of its regional directors. He worked with the agency two years, 1937–1939, before resigning to accept a position as a teacher of agriculture in the school for blacks in Fayetteville (Washington County), where he worked two years. Betton's abilities and reputation for hard work attracted the attention of the Arkansas

Agriculture Extension Service, who hired him as the assistant county agent for "Negro Work" in Howard and Nevada Counties. His performance in this position led to his promotion to district agent for "Negro Work," which he held from 1943 to 1967. Betton was a resident of Pulaski County and returned to his home county in 1967 as the Extension Service's farm specialist for farm safety programs. His service in this position, as in previous ones, was above standard, and he was promoted in 1969 to the position of assistant director of special programs for the state. This position required Betton to work with a wide variety of people in developing pro-grams for the state Cooperative Extension Service. Sensing that better use could be made of Betton's talents and communication skills, he was promoted to the position of coordinator of extension economic development where he served until retirement.

During his career with the Agriculture Extension Service, Betton earned the respect and support of people throughout Arkansas, black and white. He received numerous citations and awards for his professional work. He also served as the president of the National Alumni Chapter of AM&N College (UAPB) and as a deacon in his local church, Mount Zion Baptist Church in Little Rock.

William M. Pierce. Bill, as he was affectionately called, was a native of Hampton, Virginia, and the son of a pace setter in the Agricultural Extension Service. His father, John B. Pierce, was the first black agricultural extension agent in America. He was appointed by James Wilson, secretary of agriculture, in 1906. His son, Bill, following the lead of his father, went on to make a name for himself on his own merits. Bill was educated in the public schools of Hampton and earned a B.S. degree at South Carolina (Orangeburg) State College in 1939. Following his graduation from college, he began his career with the Agricultural Extension Service by accepting a position as assistant county agent in South Boston, Virginia. The position required him to collect, interpret, and dis-tribute information relative to county-level Extension programs. In 1948, Pierce accepted a similar position with the Extension Service at El Dorado (Union County), Arkansas, where he worked until 1955. While working in Union County, Pierce helped establish the Rural Life Conference, which meets annually at the University of Arkansas at Pine Bluff, and worked closely with the United States

Department of Agriculture. He was also instrumental in establishing agriculture education programs and college scholarships for both rural and urban young people. As of this writing (2000) forty scholarships have been granted. From 1955 to 1972, he worked with the Extension Service's statewide office and the Farmers Home Administration to help develop and build five Vegetable Marketing Co-Op Sheds in Phillips, Lee, Cross, St. Francis, and Crittenden Counties. These sheds afforded farmers the opportunity to supplement their farm income through growing in the summer months while waiting on their major crops (cotton, soy beans, rice, etc.) to mature for harvest in the fall.

Between 1972 and 1975, Pierce received grants from the Department of Commerce for the establishment of the first Office of Minority Business (OMB) in the nation. This office aided minority business development throughout Arkansas. Pierce served as the OMB's first president, executive director, and later as chairman of the board. From 1975 to 1983, Pierce served as a senior vice president for business development at Union National Bank in Little Rock. In this position he was responsible for the development of new businesses, expanding existing ones, community relations, major depositor solicitation, minority employment and development, and the overall decision-making process at the bank. During this period he also became the first black to serve as a director, and later chairman, of the Little Rock branch of the Federal Reserve Bank at St. Louis, Missouri, Eighth District. Bill's impact on the economic development of Arkansas, especially its black community, is immeasurable.

Arthur Cartledge. Following the desegregation of the Helena-West Helena public schools, Cartledge, a specialist in curriculum design and grant writing, served as the school district's deputy superintendent, 1988–1994. The district, located in the Arkansas delta (Phillips County), was one of the poorer in Arkansas, and Cartledge used his grant-writing skills to secure several state and federal grants for curriculum and physical plant improvements. These curriculum grants were critical because they helped to improve the learning of black students who, before desegregation, had attended schools that were poorly funded and could not afford the latest in educational learning materials.

Sterling Ingram. This native of Little Rock, Arkansas, was educated in the city's public schools, at Tennessee (Nashville) State University (B.S., music education), and at the University of Arkansas at Fayetteville (M.S., music education). He also completed additional graduate work at Memphis (Tennessee) State University, the University of Oklahoma, and the University of Arkansas at Little Rock. He was an instrumental music teacher in the Little Rock School District for fifteen years with teaching assignments at Horace Mann High School, Mann Junior High School (after desegregation), and Parkview High School. Because of his intricate knowledge of music, Ingram became a noted musical adjudicator throughout Arkansas, Louisiana, and Texas.

Ingram, who currently (2000) serves as director of staff development for the Little Rock School District, held a number of administrative positions in the district and at the state level before this latest appointment, including associate to the deputy superintendent; director of planning, research, and evaluation; associate director of planning and development with the Arkansas Department of Education; supervisor of music for the Little Rock School District; and as president of the board for the Arkansas Federal Teachers Credit Union. While serving in these various professional positions, Ingram did not neglect community and religious service. He served as a member and director of the Art Porter Singers and as president of Art Porter Sr. Music Education. In his church, St. Peters Rock Baptist (Little Rock), he serves as the choir director.

Cora Duffy McHenry. McHenry began her career in public education as a teacher of English and French in the black high school in Camden, Arkansas. She was a talented and popular teacher who was very active in the affairs of the Arkansas Teachers Association, the voice of black teachers in Arkansas before desegregation. McHenry's involvement with the ATA led to her election to the organization's board of trustees in the early 1960s. In 1969 the ATA merged with the all-white Arkansas Education Association, the AEA kept its original name, and McHenry served on the board of directors of the new organization and later as its assistant director for instruction and human relations. She served in a number of AEA staff positions before serving as the executive secretary of the organization, 1985–1999, the first black to hold this position. McHenry was also the first woman to serve on the Board of Trustees of Arkansas Tech University at Russellville. Throughout her career the education of youths, especially black youths, was one of her first priorities.

Lucille McCall. During a thirty-seven-year career in public education in Arkansas, she left a profound impact on the education of black youths and education in general. She joined the Arkansas Department of Vocational Education (ADVE) in 1966 as its first black supervisor of home economics education, and she served in this position longer than any other black in the history of the department. She was also a member of the State Advisory Board, 1965–1966, when the New Homemakers of America, the organization for black students in the public schools, and the Future Homemakers of America, its white counterpart, were merged. During her career, she served as a consultant/writer for departmental publications, including curriculum guides for home economics courses and manuals for preparing students and others for the "World of Work."

Lendora Early. In 1959, Early was the supervisor for educational programs in the all-black schools of Crossett (Ashley County), Arkansas, and established the first Cooperative Special Education Supervision Program in the county. Under her leadership, the program has grown from one special education teacher to fourteen and three speech pathologists. Early has also been successful in securing federal grants for programs in psychological testing, physical therapy, and occupational therapy. She also serves on the Board of Trustees of the University of Arkansas at Monticello.

Joyce Littleton. Following the desegregation of the public schools in Hot Springs (Garland County), Arkansas, Littleton served as an assistant principal of the desegregated high school, 1987–1993. Her administrative abilities were noticed almost immediately by the Hot Springs School Board, and in 1993 she was promoted to the position of assistant superintendent. She was the first black to be appointed to this position in which she currently (1999) serves.

Ora Barnes Stevens. This native of Marianna (Lee County), Arkansas, is a graduate of the all-black Robert R. Moton High

School, AM&N College (B.S., with honors in home economics education), and Arkansas State University at Jonesboro where she earned an M.S. in secondary administration and special education, and a specialist degree in curriculum design and assessment. She has also studied at the University of New York in Albany, and is currently pursuing an educational doctorate at the University of Mississippi, Oxford. Stevens worked as a teacher and administrator in a number of school districts in New York, Illinois, and Arkansas before accepting a position in the Lee County Public School District in her hometown of Marianna.

Stevens joined the Lee County Public School District in 1978 as the director of curriculum and instruction. She served in that position until being promoted to the principalship of Whitten Elementary School where she served from 1987 until 1990. During her tenure at Whitten, Stevens helped establish an effective Parent Teacher Association and implement a program for gifted and talented students. In 1990, she left the public schools for the Arkansas Department of Education where she had accepted a position in the department of curriculum and instruction for middle-level education. which she held from 1990 until 1996. She was later promoted to the position of director of curriculum and assessment for workforce education, where she currently (2000) serves. In addition to her professional responsibilities, Stevens remains active in community affairs. She currently serves as president of the Robert R. Moton High School Alumni Association, which she was instrumental in getting organized. The association, in addition to organizing school reunions every two years, annually grants a scholarship to a graduate of Lee High School, the only high school in Marianna following the desegregation of the Lee County School District. She is active in her church, Mount Pleasant Missionary Baptist, and in her beloved Delta Sigma Theta Sorority.

Elizabeth Jackson. Jackson began her career as a classroom teacher in the black schools of Hot Springs (Garland County), Arkansas. She was one of the survivors of the controversial early desegregation years in the Hot Springs School District. After twenty-nine years as a classroom teacher, Jackson was promoted to the position of coordinator of federal programs where she served from 1973 to 1988. In this position she worked to secure federal funds for reading laboratories throughout the district. These laboratories tremendously enhanced student performance, especially minority students, on standardized tests.

James E. Wilson. Wilson began his career in public education as a science teacher at Immanuel Elementary and High School in Almyra (Arkansas County) in 1957. The school was closed during the early years of desegregation, and Wilson, who was not retained as a principal in the school district, moved on to work in other Arkansas school districts. In 1970, Wilson was employed by the Arkansas Department of Education as an educational service manager. He worked in this position for twenty-five years. During his career with the Department of Education, Wilson coordinated a nationwide computer program for collecting, storing, and distributing educational and health-care data relative to migrant children.

Dr. Jesse Rancifer. Rancifer, a native Arkansan, was born in McGhee (Desha County), where he received his public school education. He received his college education at AM&N College (B.S., mathematics education), Tuskegee (Alabama) Institute (M.S., mathematics and science education), and at Kansas State (Manhattan) University (Ph.D., mathematics). Postgraduate studies were also completed at the University of Arkansas at Fayetteville. Rancifer began his Arkansas career in public education as a mathematics teacher in the Pine Bluff (Jefferson County) public school system. He left the public schools, however, to accept a position in higher education at the University of Arkansas at Pine Bluff where he was an associate professor of mathematics, 1978–1980. From 1980 to 1984, he served as the assistant dean of the School of Education at UAPB and as its certification officer for teacher education programs. Rancifier returned to public education in 1984 when he accepted a position as an associate superintendent in the Little Rock School District, where he worked until 1988. Rancifer enjoyed his years in public education, but higher education had become his first love and he left the Little Rock School District to accept a position as an associate professor of educational administration in the College of Education at the University of Central Arkansas at Conway. He held this post from 1988 until his retirement in 1999.

During his varied career in public and professional education,

Rancifer was, and continues to be, active in civic affairs. He is a member of Little Rock's Twentieth Century Club, and chairman of the board of COPE (Community Organizations for Poverty Elimination). As chairman of COPE, Rancifier was instrumental in getting this organization to restore its many social services to the Little Rock community. His other civic activities include working as a volunteer with Vision Little Rock and serving on the board of Little Rock's Museum of Discovery. Rancifer and his family are members of the Allison Presbyterian Church in Little Rock, where he spearheaded the construction of a new sanctuary for the church.

Dr. T. Josiha Haig. Dr. Haig hold degrees in education from Providence College (B.A.), Providence, Rhode Island; Rhode Island College (M.Ed., educational administration); and Boston University (Ed.D.), Chestnut Hill, Massachusetts. He also earned the Ph.D. in literature at Upsala College (East Orange, New Jersey), and a law degree at the University of Florida at Gainesville. In 1979, this well-qualified educator was brought to the Little Rock School District as director of human resources. In this position he was responsible for recruiting, interviewing, and hiring all staff (teachers and mid-level managers) in the district. He was also responsible for the development and implementation of an employee benefit program. Haig's tenure in the Little Rock School District was brief, but he served with distinction. Since leaving the district, he has worked throughout the nation as a deputy superintendent of schools, a director of secondary school operations, a superintendent/chief school executive, an adjunct professor, and an educational consultant.

Estelle Mathis. Mathis began her career in Arkansas in 1957 in the Augusta (Woodruff County) School District as a special education teacher. In 1975, she was awarded two state grants for her innovative special education projects. Because of her expertise in working with handicapped children, Mathis served from 1978 until 1989 as the district's first director of special education. This position afforded Mathis the opportunity to demonstrate her administrative skills, and in 1989 she was appointed the district's associate superintendent for curriculum. She served in this position until being named the district's interim superintendent in 1993. Mathis was the first black, and the only woman, to hold this position in the state's largest school district. Her leadership skills were recognized in a special tribute paid to her by Bill Clinton, president of the United States. After one year as the interim superintendent of the Little Rock School District, Mathis became the district's deputy superintendent and served in that capacity until her retirement in 1996. During her administrative career, Mathis served as the Little Rock School District's representative to the Pulaski County Magnet Schools Review Committee, Special Education Advisory Board (1980), and as a board member of the Arkansas Autism Society (1986).

CHAPTER 9

Conclusion

Challenges of the 1990s and the New Millennium

As public education in Arkansas completed the 1990s and entered the new millennium, the number of black administrators in the state's public schools, especially principals, had declined dramatically since the onset of desegregation in the late 1950s. This is due, in part, to the fact that since the 1970s other avenues of employment have been opened to talented blacks (offering higher salaries than public education) and to a changing public school system in which administrators have less and less authority to direct their schools in the way that they believe best benefits students. Black administrators prior to desegregation were in almost complete control of their schools, curricula, and extracurricula programs. They dedicated much of their time and energies to molding and shaping young black minds so they would be able to take advantage of the limited opportunities available to them in a segregated society. As Arkansas moves into the new millennium, the days of segregated public schools and all their inequities continue to exist only in the memories of senior black educators and have become historical abnormalities for many black students. Black students are no longer forced to attend school in substandard buildings, attend school during the hot summer months of split sessions without the benefit of modern air conditioning, use worn-out handed-down textbooks, or try to prepare for participation in modern society with underfunded and outdated educational programs. Black administrators and teachers, particularly those in predominantly white school districts, are no longer forced to plead with insensitive school boards for adequate facilities, funding for updated educational programs and equipment, and equal salaries. For those, however, who still labor in small predominantly black school districts, and there are several in Arkansas as the state enters the new millennium, little has changed.

In the 1990s and into the 2000s, the struggle of black administrators to mold and shape the minds of young blacks continues, and educators face challenges that once were considered to be minor or that did not exist during the era of segregation. They face the challenge of racial discrimination within desegregated school systems, which impacts not only their own self-esteem, but also that of black students. Many senior black administrators in the 1990s who had been successful high school principals and role models for black students during the era of segregated schools were demoted to assistant principalships or, more often, "promoted" to positions as supervisors of special programs and hidden away in central offices where they had little or no contact with black students. Consequently, the students often found themselves isolated in their respective classes. They suffered from the loss of role models with whom they could identify and the loss of self-esteem, as they were denied roles in school plays, on the debate team, in student government, and in other student activities in which they were formerly active. To confront these challenges, black administrators sought position in desegregated schools that were both educationally and professionally rewarding for themselves and beneficial for black students. These administrators, often allied with black teachers, devoted much of their time toward helping black students adjust to desegregation, to retaining their self-esteem and self-worth, and to discovering their own individual identities. To this end they also pushed for the establishment of courses in black history, literature, art, music, and various programs in ethnic sensitivity training.

In helping to structure curricula for their schools, black administrators of the late 1990s not only pushed for curricula that had some relevancy for black students, they also faced the challenges of curriculum revision, state-mandated competency testing, bussing for racial balance, school disparities in student performance and graduation rates, black/white teacher ratios, and the very noticeable absence of young black men in the classroom as teachers. They sought to overcome these challenges through calling for alternative education programs, counseling and tutoring programs for those experiencing academic difficulties, the establishment of college programs designed to encourage black males to enter the teaching profession, and more input into the decision-making process at the highest levels of administration. In addition, they pushed for the monitoring of disciplinary policies and school activities such as student government elections, the selection of cheerleaders, and other student body representatives in an effort to make sure that black students were included and could feel as if they were part of the overall school program.

Political changes also influenced public education and the opportunities afforded students. School districts often follow the lead of their state government or the federal government, and in Arkansas, the political climate was not conducive for progress in public education during the late 1950s and early 1960s under the administration of the state's segregationist governor, Orval E. Faubus. In the late 1960s, the educational atmosphere slightly improved when Winthrop Rockefeller, a liberal Republican, defeated Faubus for the governorship in 1966. Rockefeller, who served two terms as governor, 1967–1971, supported public education but was unable to significantly improve the hostile racial climate in the state's public schools due to the Faubus legacy, statewide public unrest caused by the civil rights movement of the 1960s, and a conservative Democratic legislature that refused to enact programs designed to support public education. In 1970, Rockefeller was defeated in his bid for a third term as governor by Dale Bumpers, a Democratic moderate. Bumpers, who served two terms as governor, 1971–1975, before moving on to represent Arkansas in the United States Senate, supported public education and was able to get the legislature to enact many of the educational programs proposed by his predecessor, including increased taxes to support public schools, and the establishment of kindergartens and community colleges.[1]

In 1974, David Pryor was elected governor of Arkansas. He publicly voiced support for public education and the expansion of opportunities for minorities, but under a strict economic retrenchment program, he did little before moving on to the United States Senate in 1979. He did, however, publicly recognize Mattye Woodridge, an innovative black public schoolteacher from Helena (Phillips County), as the founder of National Teachers Day. Pryor was succeeded as governor in 1979 by Bill Clinton, a man who had a special interest in improving public education. Clinton believed that improved and expanded educational opportunities for *all* Arkansans would in turn improve the state's agriculture based economy by making the state more attractive to industry.[2] During his administration, he pushed through the legislature statutes designed to improve teacher salaries, student performance, course offerings, and teacher training. But these measures, although they did improve public education in the state, did not solve black educational problems created by hundreds of years of slavery which were followed by decades of rigid Jim Crowism. The desegregation of public schools and the Clinton initiatives only dented some of the problems and created monumental new ones for black administrators at the close of the 1990s decade. As Charles Wesley succinctly pointed out in his article, "The Quest for Equality: From Civil War to Civil Rights,"

> For those who had pinned their hopes on racial integration occurring promptly and smoothly after the Supreme Court rulings of the 1950s, the next decade was to prove a trying time period . . . [Blacks] would not reach equal status in clerical jobs until 1972, among skilled workers until 2005, among professionals until 2017, among sale workers until 2114, and among business managers until 2130.[3]

Wesley's article was published in 1969 and, as Arkansas and the nation heads into the new millennium, none of his projections have materialized. The challenge ahead for black administrators, and educators in general, is as it always has been: To mold, shape, and nurture young black minds so they will be able to define for themselves who they are and develop a sense of self-worth and self-esteem that will enable them to take advantage of the opportunities available in an increasingly competitive and technological world society.

In the early years of public school education for blacks, black administrators often took little—pitiful funding, used and outdated textbooks, inadequate facilities, split school sessions, limited educational materials and equipment—and produced high school graduates who went on to proudly represent their people in all facets of American society throughout the nation. The great majority of black leaders in the 1990s who are over fifty years of age are graduates of all-black high schools and colleges and were nurtured by black administrators. The challenge for young black administrators in the new millennium will be the same that it was for their predecessors: to continue the productive legacy of black administrators while fighting more subtle, but just as damaging, forms of racism in both the educational academies and the private sectors of American society. They must accept, as did their forefathers, the challenge to keep the rich legacy of black educational achievements alive, not only for themselves, but for future generations.

Appendix

As stated in the preface to this volume, this is not a definitive or all-inclusive work. Many of the principals/educators who labored to brighten the future for Arkansas youths have been identified, but they left no written records, nor have the editors and researchers been able to gather an adequate oral history. Their names and periods of service are listed below along with those whose stories are discussed in the preceding pages. All collected materials not used in this book will be placed on file at the Arkansas History Commission.

1899–1929
Allen, Charles
Barr, Zelmon Emerson
Barron, R. C.
Black, Nellie
Blakely, K. J. I.
Boone, Fannie Mae (supervisor)
Braggs, W. F.
Branch, W. F.
Brantley, M. L.
Brown, G. P. A.
Buchanan, W. C.
Carr, Coy
Chanay, Reuben Napoleon
Childress, Rufus Charles
Clark, Sarah Elizabeth Perry
Coggs, Tandy W.(Arkansas
        Teachers Association)
Coleman, C. P.
Corbin, Joseph C.
Davis, Leslie V.
Dean, W. P.
Dykes, J. R.
Epps, Clifford (supervisor)

Eskridge, Alma
Gillam, Issac T.
Goldstein, Percy
Green, C. E.
Green, Charles C.
Greene, C. M.
Hamilton, H.
Hammonds, O. S.
Harris, James
Harrison, James
Holmon, L. D.
Hunter, W. J. C.
Ish, George W.
Jackson, Beecher H.
Jackson, N. F.
Jamerson, D. W.
Johnson, F. D.
Jones, Theron
Lewis, John Henry
Long, Frank
Madison, Eddie
Massie, Samuel P.
McAllister, J. H.
McCoy, L. M.

McCraw, L. M.
Nelson, Cynthia
Nelson, Samuel Paul
Patterson, James
Pettis, Pearl Franklin
Ray, Harvey C. (supervisor)
Russell, M. L.
Ryan, S. E.
Shepperson, Archie
Smith, C. S.
Strong, Anna M. P.
Townsend, William
Trent, Edward Ozro

Trust, C. B.
Turner, Fred C.
Upchurch, Ila D. (supervisor)
Van Pelt, P. J.
Wallace, James Edward
Watkins, Charles
Watkins, P. W.
Wilborn, M. M.
Williams, Charles L.
Williamson, Llewellyn Wilburn
Willis, Mary E.
Yeager, Henry Clay

1929–1941

Albritton, D. J.
Allen, Steve W.
Anderson, C. W.
Anderson, Granville
Bayless, Edwin
Bazzelle, Mattie
Bonds, A. A.
Boone, A. C.
Caesar, R. C.
Claye, Clifton Maurice
Clowers, C. C.
Conley, W. O.
Daley, J. B.
Daniels, T. W.
Douglas, Julius
Draper, Coy E.
Hanson, W. D.
Haraway, Calvin Coolidge
Harris, Hattie
Hicks, Charles A.
Hicks, French J.
Hill, J. H.

Hill, Jonah
Ivory, George S.
Jeffers, Leo D.
Johnson, David
Johnson, L. W.
Johnson, P. J.
Johnson, R. W.
Jones, W. R.
Kennerson, E. E.
King, Hyman
King, J.
Lewis, John Henry
Lindsey, Lillie B. Jones
Mason, Jessie W., Sr.
Maxwell, Gertrude Preston
Mazique, L. A.
McBeth, James Roy
McIntosh, Stanley
McNeil, Le Roy
Milan, Walter N.
Minor, Samuel L.
Neely, Ella P. (supervisor)
North, Cross E.

Palmer, A. L.
Parr, U. S.
Peyton, Emma (supervisor)
Phillips, Lawrence Leonard
    (supervisor)
Porter, J. R.
Ridley, Elmo
Ridley, Hazel
Roland, E. P.
Shumpert, Paul
Sims, Julia
Smith, C. E.
Smith, James Madison, Sr.
Stewart, Edith
Stidham, Sarah
Stilson, Myrtle B.
Story, Alma
Talley, Edith

Tanner, Hiram
Taylor, Edward Everett
Terry, C. M.
Vines, J. W.
Watson, John Brown
Weddle, George W.
White, John Henry
Wilborn, E. C.
Williams, Albert M.
Williams, Benjamin George
Williams, Chester P.
Williams, Marguerite P.
    (supervisor)
Willis, E. E.
Wilson, Mamie Boyd
Winters, Beatrice
Wright, H. M.

1941–1954
Arrant, Maeleen
Bailey, Edward E.
Baxter, Albert
Benton, Elbert E.
Betton, TeRoy
Black, Luther H.
Booker, Lillian Cannon
Branch, Corneilus
Brown, Eddie David
Brown, Elmyra
Buchanan, Roland Leon, Sr.
Buffington, F. B.
Bullock, S. E.
Champion, Eugene
Chanay, Reuben N.
Cheney, Wayman T.
Christophe, LeRoy Matthew

Clayton, Rucker E.
Cobbs, Codie T.
Collier, Mattie L.
Cook, J. C.
Cooper, Jobe Vaughn
Coppage, S.
Craft, Curtis
Currie, W. L.
Curry, F. L.
Davis, Marie
Davis, Richmond
Davis, T. D.
Denton, Herbert H.
English, J. W.
Floyd, Gwendolyn M.
Fowler, William Harry
Franklin, Coy W.
Franklin, Lonnie

Golden, Iredell
Golden, W. M.
Green, C. M.
Griffin, Annie
Hamilton, Carmen D.
Hawkins, D. D.
Hawkins, Edwin L.
Henderson, Hovey A.
Hill, Jethro A.
Hunter, Elza H.
Isum, Verna R.
Jackson, Leroy
Johns, G. C.
Johnson, D. J.
Johnson, Sadie
Jones, Carl
Jones, Emanuel N.
Jones, Horace
Jordan, M. D.
Kimbell, George
Landers, E. G.
Lowe, Thomas J.
Lyons, David L., Sr.
Mabins, J. N.
Martin, Margaret
Martin, William Harris
Meekins, George Alvin
Mercer, C. C.
Miller, Hazel K.
Mitchell, Fred
Moore, Bernice
Moseley, Mott
Muldrew, Winston J.
Nelson, Leon
Newton, McKinley
Owens, Joyce

Patterson, Thomas E.
Peebles, Eula
Phillips, Irwin P.
Porchia, Seth
Potts, Walter C.
Richardson, W. L.
Robinson, Edward Daniels
Robinson, Sandy
Roland, S. B.
Rutherford, Will V.
Shaw, Eddie
Smith, Alfonzo C.
Smith, Frank W.
Smith, William M.
Tate, A.
Terry, C. M.
Tollette, Sandford Bernard
Toney, Clyde N.
Toney, Elton
Tuggle, Sopronia
Wallace, Eula B.
Walter, Otis
Watkins, P. W.
White, C. V.
White, Chester A.
White, Robert L.
Wiley, Robert
Williams, H. O.
Williams, Sadie
Williams, Willis "Big Bill"
Williamson, E. M.
Williamson, R. B.
Williamson, Saner W.
Williamson, W. S.
Wilson, Maggie
Woodridge, Mattye Mae

After 1954
Adkins, Henry
Altheimer, Rowan
Anderson, Gail
Babbs, J. C., Sr.
Baker, Sherman
Baltimore, Argeri
Banks, Alice B.
Barkins, Charlie
Barnes, William
Barry, James
Bell, Johnnie
Bingham, W. E.
Black, Lloyd W.
Black, Louis Thomas, Dr.
Blathers, L. O.
Bomar, Faustenia
Boswell, David S.
Boy, Henry
Bradford, Clifford L.
Branch, Samuel
Briggs, Edward
Bronson, Caleb
Brown, Coley
Brown, Otis L.
Brown, Pamela
Brown, Robert
Brunson, Thomas C.
Buckner, Jeanette S.
Bunton, Frank
Burl, Tom
Burns, Sidney
Butler, Charles
Calhoun, Norman
Carpenter, Roland A.
Carr, Jeff J.
Carruth, Sylvia
Carson, Leon

Carter, Jodie T.
Carter, Lillie B.
Chambers, Clarence, Jr.
Chambers, Raymond
Chambers, Vhanesa
Chanay, Earl Nelson
Chapman, Robert
Chatmon, Ozy
Clark, Louvenia J.
Colbert, John L
Cooper, Jesse W.
Courtney, T. R.
Cox, Eleanor
Cox, Robert
Cunningham, Calvin
Currie, W. L.
Dalton, H. I.
Daniels, Roy
Davis, Emma S.
Davis, Levi
Davis, Oscar
Dean, Hyacinth
Dean, Lonnie Sue
Dean, Patricia B.
Doug, J. L.
Early, Lendora (supervisor)
Early, Roosevelt
Easter, Caldwell
Easter, Marvin T.
Edwards, Jean
Evans, Paul L., Sr.
Evans, Robert A.
Faison, Othella
Faison, Peter G.
Feaster, Laverne (supervisor)
Finn, William
Ford, Oscar J.
Ford, Roger Houston

Garmon, Bertran
Gill, Catherine Jewell
Golston, Mary Ruth
Goodwin, Bobbie Hawkins
Green, Charles A.
Green, Charles E.
Green, Ruel
Grisby, Louis
Grundy, Louis D.
Guinn, Mary
Haig, Josiaha
Hale, Joseph A.
Hall, Donna
Hamilton, Elizabeth
Hamilton, Oscar
Harper, Willie D.
Harris, Otis
Harris, Tyrone
Hawkins, Russell
Henderson, Jonnie Belle
Henderson, L. F.
Henton, Gene E.
Hertz, George E.
Hickman, John
Hobbs, Felicia
Holmes, Morris L., Jr.
Horn, Clarence
Howard, Rudolph
Ingram, Sterlin (supervisor)
Isum, Verma Releford
Jackson, Elizabeth (supervisor)
Jackson, L. R.
Johnson, Acie L.
Johnson, B. T.
Johnson, Cherrie
Johnson, James W.
Johnson, Jean
Johnson, Sadie B.

Jones, Beverly
Jones, Curtis
Jones, Lamar
Jones, Thelma
Jones, William
Jones, X. L.
Jordan, Cartheu
Keaton, William T.
Kendall, John E.
Kennedy, Dessie P.
Lacey, Jesse L.
Lacey, Marion G.
Latimer, Charles J.
Lever, Ben F.
Leverette, Juanita
Lewellen, John
Littlejohn, Walter
Littleton, Joyce (supervisor)
Lowe, Troy
Marshall, Nexton P.
Martin, Fred, Jr.
Mathis, Estelle (supervisor)
McCall, Lucille (supervisor)
McCoy, James
McGhee, Robert
McGraw, Linel
McHenry, Cora (supervisor)
McIntosh, Ulysses G.
McKinda, Q. R.
McNeal, Howard
Metcalf, Vernard
Miller, A. M.
Mitchell, Deborah
Mitchell, Marylene
Mitchell, Sadie
Mixon, Archie
Moorehead, Tempie W.
Morris, Parker Edison

Mosby, Jimmy J.
Moss, Wilmar B., Jr.
Myers, Rachel
Neel, Karen Buchanan
Nelson, Leon
Nelson, Robert
Nichols, George C.
Nichols, Lloyd G.
Norman, Cassandra
Oakley, Fred
Owens, Joyce L. Cowan
Pain, J. D.
Pearson, Jewell
Penix, Levenis
Pettis, Eula Mable
Phillips, John L., Jr.
Phillips, Leon A., Jr.
Pierce, William (supervisor)
Piggee, Roland H.
Porchia, Raymond
Power, Andrew
Power, Portia
Powell, Lucious
Ouick, Etta Mae
Rancifer, Jesse (supervisor)
Reynold, William
Roland, Mitchell
Rosborough, Mozella
Ross, Lester
Rush, William
Rutherford, Frankie
Sain, Lloyd
Scott, Mary (supervisor)
Scott, Robert L.
Shaw, Eddie David
Shepherd, C. Darline
Simpson, Earnest
Sims, Earnest

Smith, Lettie Ann
Smith, Mary S.
Smith, Mildred L.
Smith, O. Z.
Smith, Richard
Smith, Sheryl
Smith, Vernon, Jr.
Staples, Raymond
Stevens, Ora B. (supervisor)
Sykes, Curtis H.
Terry, Denita
Thompson, Charles A.
Thompson, Clyde
Thompson, Nelson
Thompson, Willie
Tim, W. C.
Townsend, William
Twillie, Manuel A.
Waddington, W.
Walker, Fulton W.
Walton, Tommy
Ward, Lionel
Washington, Milton
Watkins, Homer Lee
Watson, Hugh Perry, Jr.
White, Abel
Wilburn, Issac G.
Whiting, Samuel
Wiley, Robert
Williams, Albert
Williams, Ava Vann
Williams, Charles A.
Williams, Earnest
Williams, Garfield
Williams, James
Williams, Joyce
Willis, Harry D.
Wilson, George

Wilson, Henry Franklin
Wilson, James (supervisor)
Wilson, Levanna N.
Wilson, L. W.
Wise, James LeRoy

Woodard, Abraham
Woods, Dorthuelia
Ziegler, Gwendolyn S.
Ziegler, James A.

Periods of Service Unavailable
Adams, Mary L.
Anderson, Elo
Anderson, Linda
Anthony, Frank
Beckley, Ethel
Berry, James
Bizzell, Ethel
Brown, E. "Bear"
Bruce, Linda
Bryant, Melvia
Burton, Evelyn
Carey, Dena
Carter, Bishop
Carter, Willis
Cheatham, C. L.
Christopher, F. D.
Coleman, Rosie
Cooper, Emma
Cooper, Nolan
Coppage, F. L.
Crombly, Jack
Daniels, J. C.
Daniels, Leroy
Daniels, Theodore
Davis, Albert
Davis, Robert
Delaney, Wilma Pitts
Dickens, Inez
Dodson, Arthur
Douglas, J. L.
Dukes, J. R.

Edwards, Plymouth
Ford, Glenn
Foster, H. C.
Gathen, Thomas
Gray, Annie Rycraw
Green, Charlese
Hannon, Olive B.
Haraway, J. W.
Harris, E. M.
Hodges, Jewell
Holmes, L. D.
Jackson, L. H.
James, Annie
Johnson, Aretha
Johnson, Florence
Johnson, H. D.
Johnson, S. C.
Johnson, S. E.
Jones, C. E.
Jordan, Youstin C.
Kimbell, Docie
King, Alfred J.
Lawson, Samuel
Liggins, Edwards
Madison, Eddie, Sr.
Maiden, James
McDavid, J. C.
McKinney, Alberta
McQueary, Arthur
Mills, Wilbur
Moore, Charlie
Morris, Parker Edison

Muldrew, Kenneth
Neal, Pearlie
Nelson, Electra
Patterson, Azell
Patterson, Mattie
Perkins, Dora
Reed, Alfonzo L.
Roberts, Lunnetta
Robinson, Charles
Russell, M. L.
Smith, William L.
Stamps, Z. T.
Stroughter, Emma
Suggs, Arizona
Sullivan, L. W.
Tate, A.
Taylor, John A.
Thomas, Marshall
Trotter, Nicie
Tucker, Arthur
Turner, Alfonzo

Turner, Leon Franklin, Jr.
Tyus, G. L.
Vaster, Sam
Wade, Geraldine
Walker, Johnetta
Walker, L. W.
Walton, Lois H.
White, J. E.
White, M. R.
White, Major
Williams, A. W.
Williams, E. G.
Williams, Lorene
Williams, Willis C.
Williamson, Andrew W.
Williamson, E. M.
Williamson, R. B.
Williamson, Saner W.
Wilson, Harold L.
Yerger, Georgia

Notes

Chapter 1. The Unfolding History of Black Educational Administrators in Arkansas: Reconstruction to Progressivism, 1865–1895

1. Bobby L. Lovett, "African Americans, Civil War, and Aftermath in Arkansas," *Arkansas Historical Quarterly* 42 (Autumn 1963): 349.

2. Ibid.

3. Quoted in Thomas C. Kennedy, "Southland College: The Society of Friends and Black Education in Arkansas," *Arkansas Historical Quarterly* 42 (Autumn 1963): 208. Kennedy provided a detailed discussion of the Friends educational activities in Arkansas, especially in Phillips County. For a discussion of the activities of the AMA in Arkansas, see Larry Wesley Pearce, "Enoch K. Miller and the Freedmen's Schools," *Arkansas Historical Quarterly* 31, 4 (Winter 1972): 305–27.

4. Lovett, "African Americans, Civil War, and Aftermath in Arkansas," 349 and 353.

5. Sondra Gordy, "Charlotte Andrews Stephens," in Nancy A. Williams, ed., *Arkansas Biography: A Collection of Notable Lives* (Fayetteville: University of Arkansas Press, 2000), 271–72.

6. Thomas C. Kennedy, "The Rise and Decline of a Black Monthly Meeting," *Arkansas Historical Quarterly* 50, 2 (Summer 1991): 116.

7. Quoted in Lovett, "African Americans, Civil War, and Aftermath in Arkansas," 351.

8. Michael B. Dougan, *Arkansas Odyssey: The Saga of Arkansas from Prehistoric Times to Present* (Little Rock, Ark.: Rose Publishing Co., 1994), 252.

9. Allen is quoted in Lovett, "African Americans, Civil War, and Aftermath in Arkansas," 351.

10. William P. Vaughan, *Schools for All: The Blacks and Public Education in the South, 1865–1877* (Lexington: University of Kentucky Press, 1974), 3.

11. Clark is quoted in Kennedy, "Southland College: The Society of Friends and Black Education in Arkansas," 211.

12. Washington County Retired Teachers Association, *School Days, School Days: The History of Education in Washington County, 1830–1950* (Fayetteville, Ark.: Fayetteville High School, 1986), 52.

13. Lovett, "African Americans, Civil War, and Aftermath in Arkansas," 353.

14.   Fon Louise Gordon, *Caste and Class: The Black Experience in Arkansas, 1880–1920* (Athens: University of Georgia Press, 1995), 95.

15.   John W. Graves, *Town and Country: Race Relations in an Urban Rural Context, Arkansas, 1895–1905* (Fayetteville: University of Arkansas Press, 1990), 58.

16.   Ibid., 252.

17.   Ibid.; Dougan, *Arkansas Odyssey*, 253.

18.   Lucius J. Barker and Mark H. Jones, *African Americans and the American Political System* (Englewood Cliffs, N.J.: Prentice Hall, 1994), 105.

19.   Gordon, *Caste and Class*, 96.

20.   Lovett, "African Americans, Civil War, and Aftermath in Arkansas," 352–53.

21.   Gordon, *Caste and Class*, 98–100.

22.   Records of the General Education Board: Early Southern Programs, Series 1: Appropriations; Subseries 1: States; Arkansas. Microfilm Roll 17, File 214. Microfilm copies of these records can be found in the Arkansas History Commission, One Capitol Mall, Little Rock, Arkansas.

Chapter 2. Black Educators in the Progressive Era: Progress in the Midst of Prejudice, 1895–1920

1.   C. Vann Woodward, *Origins of the New South, 1877–1913* (Baton Rouge: Louisiana State University Press, 1951), 373, and *The Strange Career of Jim Crow* (New York: Oxford University Press, 1966), 91. See also, David A. Shannon, *Twentieth-Century America: The Progressive Era*, vol. 1 (New York: Rand McNally, 1974), 98–99; and August Meier, *Negro Thought in America, 1880–1915* (Ann Arbor: University of Michigan Press, 1966), 164–65.

2.   T. Basket, ed., *Persistence of the Spirit: The Black Experience in Arkansas* (Little Rock: Arkansas Endowment for the Humanities, 1986), 21.

3.   C. Fred Williams et al., *A Documentary History of Arkansas* (Fayetteville: University of Arkansas Press, 1984), 124.

4.   Basket, *Persistence of the Spirit*, 22.

5.   John W. Graves, *Town and Country: Race Relations in an Urban Rural Context, Arkansas, 1895–1905* (Fayetteville: University of Arkansas Press, 1990), 216–17.

6.   Ibid.

7.   C. Fred Williams et al., *A Documentary History of Arkansas*, 163.

8.   C. Calvin Smith, "Black Organization and White Suppression: The Elaine Race Riot, 1919," *Craighead County Historical Quarterly* 12, 3 (Summer 1974): 2–3; Arthur I. Waskow, *From Race Riot to Sit-in, 1919 and the 1960s* (New York: Doubleday, 1967), 122–23; Jeannie M. Whayne, "Low

Villians and Wickedness in High Places: Race and Class in the Elaine Race Riots," *Arkansas Historical Quarterly* 58, 3 (Autumn 1999): 309–10.

9.   *Arkansas Gazette*, January 30, 1891; C. Fred Williams et al., *A Documentary History of Arkansas*, 156.

10.   See notes 3 and 6; W. D. Baker, *Minority Settlement in the Missouri River Counties of the Arkansas Delta, 1870–1930* (Little Rock: Arkansas Historic Preservation Program, 1991).

11.   T. E. Patterson, *History of the Arkansas Teachers Association* (Washington, D.C.: National Education Association, 1981).

12.   S. B. Weeks, *History of Public Education in Arkansas* (Washington, D.C.: Government Printing Office, 1912), 81.

13.   Department of the Interior/Bureau of Education, *Negro Education: A Study of the Private and Higher Schools for Colored People in the United States*, Bulletin No. 39, vol. 2 (Washington, D.C.: Government Printing Office, 1917).

14.   Anderson, *The Education of Blacks in the South, 1850–1935*, 170.

15.   Department of the Interior, *Negro Education*, 12.

16.   Records of the General Education Board, Early Southern Programs, Series 1: Appropriations; Subseries 1: State, Arkansas, Microfilm Roll 17, File 214.

17.   Gladys D. Mays, "Black Business Community Prosper with City," *Newport Daily Independent*, August 11, 1975.

18.   The Jackson County Medical Registry of Physicians record that Dr. Craigen was licensed to practice medicine in the county on April 12, 1905; G. P. Hamilton, *The Bright Side of Memphis* (Memphis, Tenn., 1908), 32.

19.   T. M. Stinnett and C. B. Kennan, *All This and Tomorrow Too: The Evolving and Continuing History of the Arkansas Education Association* (Little Rock, Ark.: Pioneer Press, 1969).

20.   Patterson, *History of the Arkansas Teachers Association*, 12.

21.   Ibid., 30.

22.   Ibid., 33.

23.   Ibid., 34.

24.   Ibid.

25.   Baker, *Minority Settlement in the Missouri River Counties of the Arkansas Delta, 1870–1930*, 9.

26.   Catalog, University of Arkansas at Pine Bluff, 1999–2001, 7.

27.   Patterson, *History of the Arkansas Teachers Association*, 46.

28.   Ibid., 22.

29.   Ibid., 27.

30.   Patterson, *History of the Arkansas Teachers Association*, 46.

31.   Ibid., 27.

Chapter 3. Educating the Mind and the Spirit: The 1920s

1.   Bishop Conner and E. C. Morris are quoted in Fon Louise Gordon, *Caste & Class: The Black Experience in Arkansas, 1880–1920* (Athens: University of Georgia Press, 1995), 127.

2.   William Curtis Mears, "L. S. (Sharpe) Dunaway," *Arkansas Historical Quarterly* 13 (Spring 1954): 77.

3.   Scott is quoted in David M. Kennedy, *Over There: The First World War and American Society* (New York: Oxford University Press, 1980), 284.

4.   C. Fred Williams et al., *A Documentary History of Arkansas* (Fayetteville: University of Arkansas Press, 1984), 28.

5.   Bishop Conner is quoted in Gordon, *Caste and Class*, 124.

6.   Thomas E. Patterson, *History of the Arkansas Teachers Association* (Washington, D.C.: National Education Association, 1981), 40.

7.   Xavier Z. Wynn, "The Development of African-American Schools in Arkansas, 1863–1963: A Historical Comparison of Black and White School with Regards to Funding and the Quality of Education" (University of Mississippi, doctoral dissertation, 1995), 129.

8.   *The Bulletin of the State Department of Education*, June 30, 1919, 7–8. See also Gordon, *Caste and Class*, 98.

9.   Patterson, *History of the Arkansas Teachers Association*, 44–45.

10.   *The Bulletin of the State Department of Education*, 1919, 4–5.

11.   *The Merrillean*, 1945–46 Yearbook, Merrill High School.

Chapter 4. The Depression Era: Black Administrators in Arkansas, 1929–1941

1.   Xavier Z. Wynn, "The Development of African-American Schools in Arkansas, 1863–1963: A Historical Comparison of Black and White Schools with Regards to Funding and the Quality of Education" (University of Mississippi, unpublished doctoral dissertation, 1995), 121 and 140.

2.   Tom Basket Jr., ed., *The Persistence of the Spirit: The Black Experience in Arkansas* (Little Rock: Arkansas Endowment for the Humanities, 1986), 32.

3.   Thomas E. Patterson, *History of the Arkansas Teachers Association* (Washington, D.C.: National Education Association, 1981), 57.

4.   Quoted in Michael B. Dougan, *Arkansas Odyssey: The Saga of Arkansas from Prehistoric Times to Present* (Little Rock, Ark.: Rose Publishing Co., 1994), 439.

5.   Patterson, *History of the Arkansas Teachers Association*, 57.

6.   T. H. Alford, *Biennial Report of the State Commissioner of Education, State of Arkansas, 1936–1938* (Little Rock, Ark.: State Department of Education, 1938), 46. Hereafter cited as Reports of the State Department of Education.

7.   Ibid., 1932, 63.

8.   Wynn, *The Development of African-American Schools in Arkansas*, 171.

9.   Unsigned letter to the editor, *Arkansas Gazette*, December 31, 1934.

10.   *Arkansas Gazette*, January 15 and 16, 1935.

11.   David E. Rison, "Arkansas during the Great Depression" (Los Angeles: University of California, unpublished Ph.D. dissertation, 1974), 78.

12.   *Arkansas Gazette*, March 5, 1935.

13.   Ibid.

14.   Wynn, *The Development of African-American Schools in Arkansas*, 173.

15.   Ibid., 181; Report of the State Department of Education, 1938–1940, 39.

16.   Ibid., 40.

17.   Two accounts discuss the establishment of the Oak Grove School District: W. L. Bazzelle, *A Developmental History of Oak Grove School District #4, Nevada County, Rosston, Arkansas* (Magnolia: Southern Arkansas University, 1984) and Willard B. Gatewood, "Wortham Gymnasium," in Mark K. Christ and Cathryn H. Slater (eds.), *Sentinels of History: Reflections of Arkansas Properties on the National Register of Historic Places* (Fayetteville: University of Arkansas Press, 2000), 125–29.

18.   Interview with Miss Ila Upchurch, a ninety-year-old (1981) former teacher and resident of Prescott, Arkansas. During her teaching career she was Jeanes supervisor for black schools in Nevada County and played a major role in the formation of the Oak Grove Consolidated School District which led to the establishment of the Nevada County Training School for blacks.

19.   Ibid.

20.   Ibid.

21.   Gatewood, "Wortham Gymnasium," 126.

22.   Ibid.

23.   Bazzelle, *A Developmental History of Oak Grove School District #4*, 27.

24.   Harry L. Tanner, "Malvern Negro Public School Prior to WWII," *Heritage* 10 (1983): 127–34.

25.   Report of the State Department of Education, 1938–1940.

26.   Samuel Minor had a long career in education in Arkansas, spanning the period 1930–1964. After serving nineteen years as principal of Mount Holly, he moved on to Sanders, Arkansas, 1949–1954, and from there to Sweet Home, Arkansas, 1954–1964.

27.   Patterson, *History of the Arkansas Teachers Association*, 57.

28.   The black school in McCrory was not named after anyone in particular and was simply called the McCrory Colored School.

29.   Interview with Mrs. Thelma Parks, one of Turner's students at Booker T. Washington, May 10, 2001. Mrs. Parks lives in Jonesboro, a few blocks from the old B. T. Washington High School, which is currently the E. Boone Watson Community Center.

30.   Leo M. Favrot to Director, Jeanes Fund, January 31, 1914, Records of the General Education Board.

31.   Patterson, *History of the Arkansas Teachers Association*, 49.

32.   For details of the Key Schools Program, see Reports of the State Department of Education, 1934–1940.

33.   This organization was founded in 1904 as the National Association of Teachers in Colored Schools and became the American Teachers Association in 1939.

34.   Patterson, *History of the Arkansas Teachers Association*, 49–50.

35.   For a brief history of black public schools in Washington County, see *Washington County Retired Teachers Association, School Days, School Days: The History of Education in Washington County, 1830–1950* (Fayetteville, Ark.: Fayetteville High School, 1986).

36.   Julianne L. Adams and Thomas A. DeBlack, *Civil Obedience: An Oral History of School Desegregation in Fayetteville, Arkansas, 1954–1965* (Fayetteville: University of Arkansas Press, 1994), 4.

37.   Hazel D. Peagues, "Negro High Schools in Fort Smith," *Fort Smith Historical Society Journal* 9 (April 1985): 13–17.

38.   Ibid.

39.   Wynn, "The Development of African-American High Schools in Arkansas," 118.

40.   J. H. Lewis, "News from the Schools," *Bulletin of the Association of Teachers of Negro Youth of Arkansas* 4 (July 1931): 8.

Chapter 5. Winds of Change and Educational Progress, 1941–1954

1.   T. M. Stinett and Clara B. Kennon, *All This and Tomorrow Too: The Evolution and Continuing History of the Arkansas Education Association* (Little Rock: Arkansas Education Association, 1969), 181.

2.   *Arkansas Gazette*, December 15, 1940.

3.   Ibid., February 6, 1940.

4.   Geoffrey Perrett, *Days of Sadness, Years of Triumph: The American People, 1939–1945* (Baltimore, Md.: Penguin Books, 1973), 338; *Arkansas Gazette*, May 12, 1943.

5.   *Arkansas Gazette*, April 17 and October 15, 1943.

6.   *Arkansas Democrat*, October 21, 1943; *Arkansas Gazette*, October 21, 1943.

7.   Ibid., January 5, 1944.

8.   Ibid., October 24, 1943.

9.   Thomas E. Patterson, *History of the Arkansas Teachers Association* (Washington, D.C.: National Educational Association, 1981), 85; Xavier Z. Wynn, "The Development of African-American Schools in Arkansas: A Historical Comparison of Black and White Schools with Regards to Funding and the Quality of Education" (University of Mississippi: Unpublished doctoral dissertation, 1995), 209.

10.   *Arkansas Gazette*, March 24, 1940.

11.   Report of the State Department of Education, 1938–1940, 39–40.

12.   *Arkansas Gazette*, March 24, 1940.

13.   Patterson, *History of the Arkansas Teachers Association*, 85–86; *Arkansas Gazette*, March 1, 1942; Wynn, "The Development of African American Schools in Arkansas,"213.

14.   Lois B. Moreland, *White Racism and the Law* (Columbus: C. E. Merrill Company, 1970), 10.

15.   *Arkansas Gazette*, March 1, 1942; *Arkansas Democrat*, March 1, 1942.

16.   *Arkansas Gazette*, March 3, 1942.

17.   Ibid., May 21, 1942; *Arkansas Democrat*, March 9, 1942.

18.   *Arkansas Gazette*, September 29, 1942.

19.   Ibid.

20.   Ibid., October 3, 1943.

21.   Ibid., March 9 and October 3, 1942.

22.   *Arkansas Democrat*, October 3, 1942; *Arkansas Gazette*, October 3, 1942.

23.   Ibid.

24.   Ibid., January 6, 1944; *Arkansas Democrat*, January 6, 1944.

25.   *Arkansas Gazette*, January 9, 1943.

26.   Patterson, *History of the Arkansas Teachers Association*, 90; *Arkansas Gazette*, June 10, 1945.

27.   Ibid., 90.

28.   *Arkansas Gazette*, May 27, 1942.

29.   Ibid., March 27, 1949.

30.   *Time Magazine*, March 21, 1949.

31.   *Arkansas Gazette*, March 27, 1949.

32.   For a brief history of black education in northwest Arkansas, see Washington County Retired Teachers Association, *School Days, School Days: The History of Education in Washington County, 1830–1950* (Fayetteville, Ark.: Fayetteville High School, 1986).

33.   *Bulletin of the Arkansas Teachers Association* 20 (April–June 1948): 2.

34.   Patterson, *History of the Arkansas Teachers Association*, 92.

35.   Albert S. Baxter, "Status and Characteristics of Displaced Negro Teachers in Arkansas, 1954–1968" (University of Arkansas at Fayetteville: Unpublished Ed.D. Dissertation, 1970).

36.   Patterson, *History of the Arkansas Teachers Association*, 88–93.

37.   Ibid., quoted in, 94.

38.   The Eliza Miller Award was named in honor of Mrs. Eliza Miller, who was a member of one of the oldest black families in Phillips County. She was a successful and well-respected local business woman (real estate, movie houses, etc.) who donated to the city of Helena the land upon which the Eliza Miller High School was constructed.

39.   Telephone interview with Dr. Charles A. Hicks (currently ninety-two years of age), August 26, 2000. Mr. Hicks is a resident of Atlanta, Georgia.

40.   *Phillips County Progress*, November 20–21, 1992, No. 49.

41.   Ibid.

42.   Patterson, *History of the Arkansas Teachers Association*, 131.

43.   *Bulletin of the Arkansas Teachers Association* 16, 2 (April–June 1944): 5.

44.   *Arkansas Gazette*, August 28, 1964.

45.   Obituary of Sylvia Victoria Tallier Caruth, Mount Zion Baptist Church, Little Rock, Arkansas, April 23, 1994.

46.   Ibid., 101–3.

Chapter 6. From "Separate but Equal" to "All Deliberate Speed"

1.   *Public Education in Arkansas, 1963: Still Separate and Still Unequal* (Washington, D.C.: United States Commission on Civil Rights: A Report by the Arkansas Advisory Committee on Civil Rights, September 1963), 1.

2.   Michael B. Dougan, *Arkansas Odyssey: The Saga of Arkansas from Prehistoric Times to Present* (Little Rock, Ark.: Rose Publishing, 1994), 465; Thomas E. Patterson, *History of the Arkansas Teachers Association* (Washington, D.C.: National Education Association, 1981), 92.

3.   *Arkansas Gazette*, March 21 and April 16, 1941; *Arkansas Democrat*, March 1, 1942.

4.   *Arkansas Gazette*, March 27, 1949.

5.   Ibid.; Dougan, *Arkansas Odyssey*, 484.

6.   *Arkansas Gazette*, March 27, 1949.

7.   *Public Education in Arkansas*, 2.

8.   Patterson, *History of the Arkansas Teachers Association*, 101–2.

9.   Ibid., 101.

10.   Julianne L. Adams and Thomas A. DeBlack, *Civil Obedience: An Oral History of School Desegregation in Fayetteville, Arkansas, 1954–1965* (Fayetteville: University of Arkansas Press, 1994), 4.

11.   Ibid., Bates quoted in, p. 2.

12.   There is no need here for a detailed discussion of the Little Rock desegregation crisis since a number of books have been written on the issue,

some of the more interesting ones are Daisy Bates, *The Long Shadow of Little Rock* (New York: David McKay Co., 1962); Robert R. Brown, *Bigger Than Little Rock* (Greenwich, Conn., 1959); Elizabeth Huckaby, *Crisis at Central High, Little Rock, 1957–1958* (Baton Rouge: Louisiana State University Press, 1980); Tony Freyer, *The Little Rock Crisis: A Constitutional Interpretation* (Westport, Conn., 1984). The crisis is also well covered in articles published in numerous professional journals; some of the better ones are Neil R. McMillen, "White Citizens Council and Resistance to School Desegregation in Arkansas," *Arkansas Historical Quarterly* 30 (Summer 1971): 95–122; and David Wallace, "Orval Faubus: The Central Figure at Little Rock Central High School," *Arkansas Historical Quarterly* 39 (Winter 1980): 314–29.

13.   *Public Education in Arkansas*, 4 and 8.

14.   Albert Sidney Baxter, "Status and Characteristics of Displaced Negro Teachers in Arkansas, 1954–1968" (University of Arkansas, Fayetteville, unpublished doctoral dissertation, 1970), 12.

15.   Robert W. Hooker, *Displacement of Black Teachers in the Eleven Southern States* (Nashville, Tenn.: Race Relations Information Center, 1970), 14.

16.   Baxter, "Status and Characteristics of Displaced Negro Teachers in Arkansas," 1.

17.   Xavier Z. Wynn, "The Development of African-American Schools in Arkansas, 1863–1963: A. Historical Comparison of Black and White Schools with Regards to Funding and the Quality of Education" (University of Mississippi, unpublished doctoral dissertation, 1995), 267.

18.   Professor Baxter is quoted in Hooker, *Displacement of Black Teachers in the Eleven Southern States*, 14.

19.   Ibid., 34; Patterson, *History of the Arkansas Teachers Association*, 156.

20.   For a detailed discussion of these cases, see Baxter, "Status and Characteristics of Displaced Negro Teachers," 33–40; Patterson, *History of the Arkansas Teachers Association*, ch. 9.

21.   Baxter, "Status and Characteristics of Displaced Negro Teachers," 33–40; Patterson, *History of the Arkansas Teachers Association*, ch. 9.

22.   Ibid., 154 and 156.

23.   The majority of the following information was derived from inter-views with the person being discussed or was contributed by family and friends. Where independent documentation could be found to collaborate their stories, it has been cited.

24.   Patterson, *History of the Arkansas Teachers Association*, 166–67.

25.   Ibid., 168–69.

26.   Ben J. Altheimer was the son of Joseph Altheimer, for whom the town of Altheimer is named, and a prominent Pine Bluff attorney,

landowner (ten thousand acres), and philanthropist. In 1940 he established the Ben J. Altheimer Foundation for the benefit of Arkansas schools, churches, and civic organizations. For more information on Altheimer, see Nancy A. Williams, ed., *Arkansas Biography: A Collection of Notable Lives* (Fayetteville: University of Arkansas Press, 2000), 9–10.

27.   *The Emissary*, Forrest City High School newspaper, May 1971; Obituary of C. T. Cobb, October 15, 1988.

28.   Interview (telephone) with Edward William, a former Lincoln High School basketball player who graduated in 1955, April 18, 2001. William currently lives in St. Louis, Missouri. Eighth Street Baptist Church, North Little Rock—where she served as a member of the missionary society and as a teacher in the Baptist Training Program.

29.   Homecoming and Dedication of Cobb Field Program, October 16, 1965.

30.   Cobb is quoted in the *Tiger*, Lincoln High School Yearbook, 1965, 3.

31.   Patterson, *History of the Arkansas Teachers Association*, 151–52.

32.   *Time Magazine* reprinted the editorial from the *West Memphis News* and sent a team of its own reporters to the city to investigate the situation. The results of their investigation was published in *Time*, March 21, 1949.

33.   *Arkansas Democrat Gazette*, December 11, 2000.

34.   The Arkansas Black History Advisory Committee is not under the auspices of the Arkansas History Commission. The committee is independently funded by the legislature and its members are nominated by the governor and confirmed by the Arkansas Senate.

35.   Patterson, *History of the Arkansas Teachers Association*, 119–20.

36.   Ibid., 101–2.

37.   The information on Barkins's career came from a personal interview with him by two members of the Retired Teachers Association of Little Rock and Other Public Schools.

38.   Ibid., 118–19.

39.   In addition to Patterson's *History of the Arkansas Teachers Association*, information about Marshall's long career was obtained through a personal interview with four members of the Retired Educators Association of Little Rock and Other Public Schools.

40.   Several senior citizens in Little Rock remember Denton's principalship at Bush Elementary, but the specific dates of his tenure have not been located.

Chapter 7. Continuing the Legacy: Challenges since *Brown*, 1970–1990

1.   Copeland and Johnson are quoted in Michael B. Dougan,

Arkansas Odyssey: The Saga of Arkansas from Prehistoric Times to Present (Little Rock, Ark.: Rose Publishing, 1994), 496–97.

2.   Ibid., quoted in, 497.

3.   Numerous books and articles have been written on the Little Rock desegregation crisis, some of the more interesting ones include the following: Daisy Bates, *The Long Shadow of Little Rock: A Memoir* (New York: David McKay Co., 1962); Elizabeth Huckaby, *Crisis at Central High, Little Rock, 1957–1958* (Baton Rouge: Louisiana State University Press, 1980); Sara Alderman Murphy, *Breaking the Silence: Little Rock's Women's Emergency Committee to Open Our Schools, 1958–1963* (Fayetteville: University of Arkansas Press, 1997); and Neil R. McMillen, "White Citizen Council and Resistance to School Desegregation in Arkansas," *Arkansas Historical Quarterly* (Summer 1971): 95–122.

4.   *Public Education in Arkansas, 1963: Still Separate and Unequal* (Washington, D.C.: United States Commission on Civil Rights: A Report by the Arkansas Advisory Committee on Civil Rights, September 1963), 1; Albert S. Baxter, "Status and Characteristics of Displaced Negro Teachers in Arkansas, 1954–1968" (University of Arkansas, Fayetteville, unpublished doctoral dissertation), 12. Also see the introduction to chapter 6 of this document.

5.   Charles H. Wesley, "The Quest for Equality: From Civil War to Civil Rights," *International Library of Negro Life and History* (New York: Doubleday, 1969), 109.

Chapter 9. Conclusion: Challenges of the 1990s and the New Millennium

1.   T. Harri Baker and Jane Browing, *An Arkansas History for Young People* (Fayetteville: University of Arkansas Press, 1991), 388.

2.   Ibid.

3.   Charles H. Wesley, "The Quest for Equality: From Civil War to Civil Rights," *International Library of Negro Life and History* (New York: Doubleday, 1969), 109.

Bibliography

Primary Sources

Bazzelle, W. L. *A Developmental History of Oak Grove School District, #4, Nevada County*. Hope, Arkansas, 1984.

Biennial Report(s) of the Arkansas State Commissioner of Education. Little Rock: Arkansas State Department of Education, 1920–1950.

Department of the Interior, Bureau of Education. *Negro Education: A Study of the Private and Higher Education Schools for Colored People in the United States*. Bulletin No. 39, Vol. 2. Washington, D.C.: Government Printing Office, 1917.

Records of the General Education Board: Early Southern Programs. Series I: Appropriations; Subseries I: States; Arkansas (Microfilm copies, Dean B. Ellis Library, Arkansas State University, Jonesboro).

United States Civil Rights Commission. *Public Education in Arkansas, 1963: Still Separate and Still Unequal. A Report by the Arkansas Advisory Committee on Civil Rights, September 1963*. Washington, D.C.: Government Printing Office, 1963.

Weeks, S. B. *History of Public Education in Arkansas*. Washington, D.C.: Government Printing Office, 1912.

Newspapers and Magazines

Arkansas Gazette

Arkansas Democrat

Arkansas Historical Quarterly

Bulletin of the Association of Teachers of Negro Education (1931). Little Rock: Arkansas History Commission

Eliza Miller High School (Helena, Arkansas), Yearbook, 1945 and 1946

Fort Smith (Arkansas) Historical Quarterly

Heritage Magazine (Malvern, Arkansas), 1983

The Motonite (Robert R. Moton High School Yearbook, Marianna, Arkansas), 1965

The Tiger (Central High School Yearbook, Little Rock, Arkansas), 1990

The Tiger (Lincoln High School Yearbook, Forrest City, Arkansas), 1965

The Tiger Tracks (Morrilton High School Yearbook, Morrilton, Arkansas), 1965

Time Magazine (1949)

Secondary Sources

Adams, Julianne, and Thomas A. DeBlack (eds.). *Civil Obedience: An Oral History of School Desegregation in Fayetteville, Arkansas, 1954–1965*. Fayetteville: University of Arkansas Press, 1994.

Baker, W. D. *Minority Settlement in the Mississippi River Counties of the Arkansas Delta, 1870–1930*. Little Rock: Arkansas Historic Preservation Program, 1991.

Baker, T. Harri, and Jane Browning. *An Arkansas History for Young People*. Fayetteville: University of Arkansas Press, 1991.

Barker, Lucius J., and Mark H. Jones. *African Americans and the American Political System*. Englewood Cliffs, N.J.: Prentice Hall, 1994.

Basket, Tom, Jr., et al. *The Persistence of the Spirit: The Black Experience in Arkansas*. Little Rock: Arkansas Endowment for the Humanities, 1986.

Bates, Daisy. *The Long Shadow of Little Rock: A Memoir*. New York: David McKay Co., 1962.

Billingsley, A. *Black Families in White America*. New Jersey: Prentice Hall, 1968.

Brisbane, R. H. *The Black Vanguard: Origins of the Negro Social Revolution, 1900–1960*. Philadelphia, Pa.: Judson, 1970.

Christ, Mark E., and Cathryn H. Slater (eds.). *Sentinels of History: Reflections of Arkansas Properties on the National Register of Historic Places*. Fayetteville: University of Arkansas Press, 2000.

Dougan, Michael B. *Arkansas Odyssey: The Saga of Arkansas from Prehistoric Times to Present*. Little Rock, Ark.: Rose Publishing, 1994.

Ferguson, J. L., and J. H. Atkinson. *Historic Arkansas*. Little Rock: Arkansas History Commission, 1966.

Gaines, D. B. *Racial Possibilities as Indicated by Negroes in Little Rock*. Little Rock, Ark.: Philander Smith College, 1898.

Gordon, Fon Louise. *Caste and Class: The Black Experience in Arkansas, 1880–1920*. Athens: University of Georgia Press, 1995.

Graves, John W. *Town and Country: Race Relations in an Urban Rural Context, Arkansas, 1895–1905*. Fayetteville: University of Arkansas Press, 1990.

Hooker, Robert W. *Displacement of Black Teachers in the Eleven Southern States*. Nashville, Tenn.: Race Relations Information Center, 1970.

Huckaby, Elizabeth. *Crisis at Central High, Little Rock, 1957–1958*. Baton Rouge: Louisiana State University Press, 1980.

Jones, Howard, et al. *African Americans: Their History*. New York: American Heritage Publishing, 1997.

McMillen, Neil R. "White Citizen Council and Resistance to School Desegregation in Arkansas." *Arkansas Historical Quarterly* (Summer 1971): 95–122.

Meier, August. *Negro Thought in America, 1880–1915*. Ann Arbor: University of Michigan Press, 1966.

Moreland, Lois B. *White Racism and the Law*. Columbus, Ohio: C. E. Merrill, 1970.

Murphy, Sara Alderman. *Breaking the Silence: Little Rock's Women's Emergency Committee to Open Our Schools, 1958–1963*. Fayetteville: University of Arkansas Press, 1997.

Patterson, Thomas E. *History of the Arkansas Teachers Association*. Washington, D.C.: National Education Association, 1981.

Shannon, David A. *Twentieth-Century America: The Progressive Era*. Vol. 1. New York: Rand McNally, 1974.

Stinett, T. M., and Clara B. Kennon. *All This and Tomorrow Too: The Evolution and Continuing History of the Arkansas Education Association*. Little Rock: Arkansas Education Association, 1969.

Thomas, C. E. *Jelly Roll: A Black Neighborhood in a Southern Mill Town*. Little Rock, Ark.: Rose Publishing, 1986.

Vaughan, William P. *Schools for All: The Blacks and Public Education in the South, 1865–1877*. Lexington: University of Kentucky Press, 1974.

Washington County Retired Teachers Association. *School Days, School Days: The History of Education in Washington County, 1830–1950*. Fayetteville, Ark.: Fayetteville High School, 1986.

Williams, C. Fred, S. Charles Bolton, Carl H. Moneyhon, and Leroy T. Williams. *A Documentary History of Arkansas*. Fayetteville: University of Arkansas Press, 1984.

Williams, Nancy A., ed. *Arkansas Biography: A Collection of Notable Lives*. Fayetteville: University of Arkansas Press, 2000.

Woodward, C. Vann. *Origins of the New South, 1877–1913*. Baton Rouge: Louisiana State University Press, 1951.

——. *The Strange Career of Jim Crow*. New York: Oxford University Press, 1966.

Unpublished Studies

Baxter, Albert S. "Status and Characteristics of Displaced Negro Teachers in Arkansas, 1954–1968." Doctoral dissertation, University of Arkansas at Fayetteville, 1970.

Rison, David E. "Arkansas during the Great Depression." Doctoral dissertation, University of California at Los Angeles, 1974.

Wynn, Xavier Z. "The Development of African American Schools in Arkansas: A Historical Comparison of Black and White Schools with Regards to Funding and the Quality of Education." Doctoral dissertation, University of Mississippi, 1995.

A Note on Contributors

This book was made possible as a result of the desire of the Retired Educators of Little Rock and Other Public Schools (RELROPS) to collect and distribute information relative to the historical struggles and achievements of black public school administrators from the Reconstruction Era through the 1990s. Representing RELROPS, Mrs. Frances Johnson and Lloyd W. Black discussed their ideas with Robert E. Bailey and Robin Giles, the director and associate director of the Arkansas Humanities Council (AHC), respectively. Those discussions led to a planning grant from the AHC and the Arkansas Black History Advisory Committee. Following the approval of the planning grant, a select committee of volunteers from RELROPS was organized and began the process of collecting information. Survey questionnaires were sent to educators and their families throughout Arkansas and other states, seeking information about past Arkansas educators. The committee analyzed and organized the returned questionnaires and asked Drs. C. Calvin Smith and Linda Joshua to put the information into proper historical context.

About the editors

Dr. Linda Walls Joshua, assistant editor. Dr. Joshua is a native of Little Rock, Arkansas, where she received her public school education. She earned two degrees at the University of Arkansas at Little Rock (B.A., history and English, and an M.A. in technical and expository writing) and a Ph.D. in statistics and secondary education from the University of Arkansas at Fayetteville. The first seventeen years of Joshua's professional career were spent in the public schools of Little Rock as a teacher of English. Since 1995, she has been on the faculty of the University of Arkansas at Pine Bluff where she is an assistant professor of education. Joshua has published several articles in her fields of study, including "DEMOS: Dialoguing, Experiencing, Modeling, Overlapping and Showing," in D. Fleniken and K. Atkins, eds., *Excellence in Education: An Arkansas Perspective* (Conway, Ark., 1997); "Welcoming Technology: The Arkansas Story," *SEDL Quarterly* 6 (1994); and "University Colleges of

Education and Public Schools: Vital Partners in Education Renewal,"
SRATE Journal 3 (Winter 1993). She has also conducted writing and
curriculum workshops throughout the state and presented a number
of papers at professional forums in her field.

Dr. C. Calvin Smith, primary editor, researcher, and coauthor.
Dr. Smith is a native of Marianna (Lee County), Arkansas, and was
educated in black public schools of that city. He received the first two
years (1961–1963) of his undergraduate college education at Arkansas
Baptist College in Little Rock and completed his undergraduate studies at AM&N College in Pine Bluff, Arkansas, where he earned a
B.A. degree in history and government. He went on to earn a master's degree in social science at Arkansas State University in Jonesboro
and a Ph.D. in recent American history at the University of Arkansas
at Fayetteville. He taught social sciences and coached football at
Strong High School in Marianna, his hometown, before joining the
faculty of Arkansas State University in 1970 as an instructor in history. He is currently (2001) a professor of history at ASU where he
has published widely in his field and received several honors. Included
in his many publications are *War and Wartime Changes: The
Transformation of Arkansas, 1940–1945* (Fayetteville: University of
Arkansas Press, 1986); coauthor, *African Americans: Their History*
(New York: American Heritage Publishing, 1997); "The Black Press
in Arkansas," in Henry L. Suggs, ed., *The Black Press in the South*
(Greenwood Press, 1983); and "Homer Martin Adkins, Governor of
Arkansas, 1941–1945" and "Junius Marion Futrell, Governor of
Arkansas, 1933–1937," in Nancy A. Williams, ed., *Arkansas
Biography: A Collection of Notable Lives* (Fayetteville: University of
Arkansas Press, 2000). Smith has also published more than twenty
articles in professional journals and presented numerous papers at professional meetings. One of his articles, "On the Edge: The Houston
Riot of 1917" (*The Griot* 10, 1 [Spring 1991]), was selected as the best
article published in the journal for the year by the Southern
Conference of Afro-American Studies. In 1994, he was honored by
the ASU Faculty Commencement Committee when he was selected
to deliver the fall commencement address. His address, "Arkansas
State University and the Challenge of the Arkansas Delta," was later
published in *Voices of State*, the university newsletter.

Research Committee of the Retired Educators of Little Rock and Other Public Schools

Frances Cole Johnson. Mrs. Johnson, project director for REL-ROPS, is one of five children born on a plantation near Birdeye (Cross County), Arkansas, to the late Mr. and Mrs. Jonnie Cole. She received her public education in the eighth-grade school at Birdeye and the Cross County Training School at Wynne, Arkansas (two years), and she graduated from Booker T. Washington High School in Jonesboro (Craighead County). Johnson began her undergraduate college education at Prairie View (Texas) A&M and completed the process at AM&N College in Pine Bluff (University of Arkansas at Pine Bluff) where she earned a B.S. degree in Home Economics. She later earned a master's degree at Tuskegee Institute in Alabama and completed additional graduate work at Michigan State University in East Lansing, Henderson State University in Arkadelphia, and the University of Arkansas in Fayetteville. While pursuing her undergraduate education, she met and married Acie L. Johnson, and to this union was born one daughter, Sharon D. Johnson Crowder.

Johnson began her career in public education as a home economics teacher at Eliza Miller High School in Helena (Phillips County), Arkansas. She has also taught at Field High School in Gould, Arkansas, Chicot County Training School in Dermott, and Strong Elementary in Marianna (Lee County), Arkansas. In 1971, she moved to Little Rock, Arkansas, where she became the first black home economics teacher at Central High School. She taught at Central for eighteen years, retiring in 1989. During her career in public education, Johnson was active in her professional organizations. She is a lifetime member of the National Education Association, and while teaching in Marianna, she played a major role in the organization of the Lee County Classroom Teachers Association. In recognition of her extensive contributions to public education, Johnson has received awards from Arkansas governors William "Bill" Clinton and Mike Huckabee and Central High School principals Morris Holmes and Richard Maples. Johnson is also a lifetime and active member of the AM&N College Alumni Association and has chaired the association's Green House Project. She is also an active member of Alpha Kappa Alpha Sorority.

Mary Scott Smith. Mrs. Smith, project chair, is one of seven children born to Arthur and Anna Harris Scott on a family-owned farm in Fordyce, Arkansas. Mary received her public school education, through the tenth grade, at the Calhoun County Training School and the Dallas County Training School (grades 11–12) at Fordyce, Arkansas. She received her college education at Arkansas Baptist College in Little Rock (B.A.) and the University of Wisconsin at Madison (M.A.). Additional graduate work was completed in Arkansas at Henderson State University in Arkadelphia and the University of Arkansas, Fayetteville. During her undergraduate years, Mary met and married Joe C. Smith. Two children were born to this union.

Mrs. Smith began her career in public education in Arkansas as an elementary teacher in the Banks Public School in Bradley County. After four years of service at Banks and twelve years in Dallas County, Smith moved to Little Rock, Arkansas, where she spent the next twenty-eight years as a first-grade teacher in the Little Rock School District. During her tenure in the Little Rock School District, she served on the textbook adoption committee, as the building representative of the Classroom Teachers Association, and helped establish the district's first Gifted and Talented Students Program. After thirty-six years in public education, Smith joined the faculty of Arkansas Baptist College where she served as an administrative assistant and as assistant professor of education.

Mrs. Smith has been recognized as a Distinguished Alumnae of Historically Black Colleges and Universities and is the recipient of numerous awards and honors for her contributions to education in Arkansas. Among these are the Pi Lamdba Theta National Honor Society Award for Women in Education, the Zeta Phi Beta Torchbearer of Academic Excellence Award, and the Lena Lockhart Award for Outstanding Community Service. In her community, Mary has participated in the Vision Little Rock Transportation Workshop and is an active member of the American Association of University Women, the Federated Women's Club, the Silhouettes of Kappa Alpha Psi, the Arkansas Baptist Alumni Association, and the Retired Educators of Little Rock and Other Public Schools.

Shirley Flenory Buckner. Mrs. Buckner is the second of three daughters born to Charles L. and Helen L. Flenory of Hope, Arkansas. She received her public school education in Hope, elementary through tenth grade, and at Langston High School in Hot Springs,

Arkansas, where her family had relocated. She earned her college degrees at Philander Smith College in Little Rock (B.A., elementary education) and the University of Central Arkansas at Conway (M.S., elementary education).

Mrs. Buckner began her career as a public schoolteacher at the Booker T. Washington Elementary School in Jonesboro (Craighead County), Arkansas, where she taught from 1963 through 1965. From 1965 until her retirement in 1986, she taught elementary education in the Little Rock School District. While pursuing her undergraduate education, Buckner met and married Randel Buckner and to this union was born one son, Dr. Edmond R. Buckner, who is an associate professor of education at the University of Arkansas at Pine Bluff. Since her retirement, Mrs. Buckner has worked extensively with the American Red Cross and its Camp Aldersgate Branch, serving two terms on the Board of Directors of the Little Rock Chapter and an additional two years as secretary for the board of the Camp Aldersgate Branch. She is an active member of the Retired Educators of Little Rock and Other Public Schools.

Juanita D. Edwards. Mrs. Edwards is the oldest of three children born to Ebenezer and Alberta Davis of Pine Bluff, Arkansas. She was educated in the black public schools in Pine Bluff, graduating from the city's Merrill High School. Her undergraduate college education began at Hampton Institute in Virginia and was completed at AM&N College in Pine Bluff. She later earned a master's degree at Ouachita Baptist College in Arkadelphia and completed additional graduate studies at the University of Arkansas at Fayetteville and the University of Central Arkansas at Conway. Prior to initiating her career in public education in the Little Rock School District, Edwards worked in private industry and in the business office of University of Arkansas, Pine Bluff, 1955–1968. She taught in the Little Rock School District until her retirement in 1989. In retirement, Edwards continues to serve on the supervisory committee of the Arkansas Teachers Federal Credit Union and is an active member of the Retired Educators of Little Rock and Other Public Schools. She takes pride in the fact that she persuaded two of her four children to become public school educators.

Acie Leon Johnson. Johnson, coordinator of facilities (for this project) and records for the Retired Educators of Little Rock and Other Public Schools, is the ninth of ten children born to a sharecropping family, James and Ora Lee Johnson, on a plantation near Helena (Phillips County), Arkansas. He began his public school education, grades 1–4, at St. Mary's Elementary in Helena. The family moved often before settling in Marvelle (Phillips County), Arkansas, where Acie completed the tenth grade in the Marvelle Colored School (1944). The agricultural teacher in Marvel, William Smith, recognized Acie's academic potential and, with the permission of his parents, took him to Pine Bluff, Arkansas, where he was enrolled in the J. C. Corbin High School on the campus of AM&N College. At Corbin, Acie excelled as a student and an athlete (all-state fullback).

In the fall of 1946, Johnson enrolled in AM&N College on an athletic scholarship and became a triple sport threat, but he excelled in football, earning Honorable Mention as an all-Southwest-Conference tackle. As a star athlete, Johnson did not neglect his academic requirements and completed his undergraduate education in four years. Following his graduation from AM&N, Johnson was employed by the institution as an instructor for black veterans of World War II. He held this position until being drafted into the army in 1951, where he served two years before being honorably discharged in 1953. Taking advantage of his GI benefits, Johnson returned to the academic world and earned a master's degree in educational administration at Michigan State University. While pursuing his undergraduate education and before his military experience, Johnson met and married Frances Cole. To this union one daughter, Sharon Denice Johnson, was born.

Johnson's administrative career in Arkansas public schools include principalships at the W. O. Field High School in Gould, Chicot County Training School in Dermott, and Robert R. Moton High School in Marianna, and he served as an assistant principal at the Dunbar Junior High International Studies/Gifted and Talented Magnet School in Little Rock. His accomplishments as a public school administrator are discussed elsewhere in this volume.

Wilhelmina Epps Lewellen. On December 8, 1937, Mrs. Lewellen was born to Clifford and Odelle Epps in Woodson, Arkansas. She was one of seven children born to the Epps, a family of black educators. All of the siblings went on to become college graduates. Lewellen received her public school education in the black schools of Pulaski County, grades 1–10, and at Dunbar High School in Little Rock, Arkansas (grades 11–12). Her graduating class at Dunbar (1955) was the last senior class to graduate from the historic institution. She went on to earn college degrees at AM&N College in Pine Bluff (B.A., sociology) and at Ouachita Baptist University in Arkadelphia (M.S., elementary education). While pursuing her undergraduate education, Epps met and married John M. Lewellen, a Democratic member of the Arkansas House of Representatives. Two daughters were born to this union.

Mrs. Lewellen began her career in public education as a social studies teacher in Hermitage (Arkansas) High School where she taught from 1959 to 1962. She left Hermitage for Altheimer, Arkansas, where she taught elementary education, 1962–1964. At the end of the 1964 academic year, Lewellen left the public schools to become a field training specialist for the Girls Scouts of America. She worked with the Girl Scouts until 1967 and then returned to her first love—public schoolteaching. She was employed by the Little Rock School District from 1967 until 1995. During her tenure in the public schools, Mrs. Lewellen was an active member of her professional educational organizations and the recipient of numerous awards and honors. Among these was the Arkansas Certificate of Merit, 1994; Certificate of Appreciation from the city of Little Rock, 1994; Certificate of Appreciation from RSVP, 2000; Capitol Citation from the secretary of state, 1994; and the Professional Achievement Award from her sorority, Alpha Kappa Alpha. She is also listed in *Who's Who in American Education* (1989–1990) and in *Who's Who Among American Teachers* (1994). After twenty-eight years in public education, Lewellen retired and accepted a position with the Arkansas General Assembly as a legislative clerk and currently (2001) serves in that position. She continues, however, to be an active member of the Retired Educators of Little Rock and Other Public Schools.

As the wife of a state legislator from Little Rock, Lewellen is quite active in local politics. She is a member of the local Democratic Caucus, the Pulaski County Democratic Women's Organization, and the Pulaski County Democratic Committee representing Justice of the Peace, District 6. She is also active in local community affairs: board member, Retired Senior Volunteers of Little Rock and the Vision Little Rock Committee; Arkansas Arts Center; Community Arts Committee; Wildwood State Arts Committee; and the National Association for the Advancement of Colored People.

Levada Levon Parker Mason. Mrs. Mason is the third of four children born to Mr. and Mrs. Arthur Parker Sr. of Washington (Hempstead County), Arkansas. Her parents were sharecroppers, but they recognized the value of education and encouraged their children to take advantage of every educational opportunity. As a child, Levada worked in the cotton fields and that experience motivated her to heed her parents encouragement to get a good education. She began her public school education in the one-room, one-teacher Sweet Home Elementary School in Nevada County. From Sweet Home she moved on to Childress Junior High School (Wynne, Arkansas), where she studied for two years, and she completed her public school education at the Nevada County Training School in Rosston, Arkansas. After graduating from high school, Mason enrolled at Philander Smith College in Little Rock, Arkansas, where she earned a B.A. degree. She later attended AM&N College in Pine Bluff, where she converted her B.A. degree into a B.S. degree in home economics. A graduate degree was earned at the University of Central Arkansas at Conway (M.S., home economics), and additional gradu-ate studies were completed at Prairie View (Texas) A.M. College, Tuskegee Institute (Alabama), and the University of Arkansas at Fayetteville. During her undergraduate studies, she met and married the late Jesse W. Mason Sr. Five children, all college graduates, were born to the Masons.

Mrs. Mason began her career in public education as a teacher in the Gurnsey Elementary School in Hempstead County. She taught vocational home economics and coached girls' basketball at Central High School in Parkin (Cross County), Arkansas, before leaving pub-lic education for the Arkansas Agricultural Extension Service where she worked as a demonstration agent for Negro work in Crittenden County. Teaching, however, was Mason's calling and she left the Extension Service and accepted a teaching position in West Memphis, Arkansas, at Wonder Elementary School. Mason also taught home economics at Eliza Miller Junior High School in Helena (Phillips County), Arkansas, and in the Little Rock School District at Booker Junior High, Southwest Junior High, and Hall High School. During her forty-two years of public service, Mason was active in her professional organizations and was the recipient of numerous awards. Professionally, she is a member of the National Education Association and the Arkansas Education Association, and she has supervised NHA and FHA organizations. Her many honors and awards include the Home Demonstration Agent of the Year Award, the highly prized State 4-H Club Loving Cup, Future Homemakers of America Award (Hall High School), and the Home Economics Award. Mason is also an active member of the NAACP, the Philander Smith College Alumni Association, and the Retired Educators of Little Rock and Other Public Schools.

Lloyd W. Black. This veteran of the Korean War and the past-president of the Retired Educators of Little Rock and Other Public Schools is the last of seventeen children born to Adolph and Rosa Moore Black. He holds degrees from AM&N College and the University of Arkansas at Fayetteville. He was the only male from his community in his age bracket to graduate from college, and he credits his parents with his success because "they taught me the value of goal setting and hard work." Black began his career in public education in Arkansas as a teacher in Brinkley and moved on to serve as principal of public schools at Clarendon, Helena-West Helena, the Pulaski County School District, and the Little Rock School District. Although retired, Black is an active member of the Retired Educators of Little Rock and Other Public Schools.

Elsie Beard Black. This native of Camden, Arkansas, is the fourth of nine children born to Mr. and Mrs. Elijah Beard. Elsie was educated in the black public schools of Camden and earned college degrees at Philander Smith College (B.A.) in Little Rock and at Southern University (M.A.) in Baton Rouge, Louisiana. She also earned additional graduate credits at the University of Central Arkansas at Conway and Ouachita Baptist University at Arkadelphia, Arkansas. Black began her career in public education in Arkansas as an elementary schoolteacher at Emerson. During her thirty-five-year career, Black also taught in Clarendon, Helena-West Helena, and the Little Rock School District. Exceptional teachers are sometimes recognized for their skills, and Black was one of those who received recognition. She was the recipient of an award for Instructional Leadership and was granted lifetime membership in the Parent Teachers Association. During her career, she was active in her professional organizations (the National Education Association and the Arkansas Education Association) and continues to serve as a board member of the Arkansas Teachers Credit Union. She is also active in the Retired Educators of Little Rock and Other Public Schools and was the recent recipient of the Special Retired Educators Award.

Marion "Ginger" Johnson Fowler-Armstrong. Born on October 7, 1922, Fowler-Armstrong is one of seven children born to Gordon "Dick" Johnson and Zola May Warren Johnson of Little Rock, Arkansas. Fowler-Armstrong received her public school education in the Little Rock School District where she attended Stephens Elementary and Gibbs Elementary. She graduated from Dunbar High School/Junior College and went on to earn college/university degrees at Philander Smith College (B.A., elementary education) and the University of Arkansas at Fayetteville (M.Ed, elementary education). Shortly after her graduation from Philander Smith, she married William Harry Fowler. This union produced five daughters.

Prior to selecting public schoolteaching as a career, Fowler-Armstrong experimented with several occupations. She worked as a secretary for the noted black physician Dr. G. W. Ish, as a typist for a black newspaper in Little Rock, and as a secretary at the federal Pine Bluff Arsenal. Once she decided to become a teacher, Fowler worked in the Little Rock School District from 1956 until her retirement in 1984. Her experiences in the private sector helped to make her an excellent communicator and teacher, and in 1965 she was one of four black teachers selected to help desegregate the Little Rock School District. She excelled as a teacher in the desegregated environment, and in 1979 she participated in a national contest sponsored by the International Paper Company and won an Award of Excellence in the Teaching of Economics from the company and was recognized for her efforts by Arkansas governor William "Bill" Clinton.

Thomas Brannon. Born on a plantation near Union Spring, Alabama, in 1935, Brannon is one of two sons born to John and Arphelar Brannon. He began his often-interrupted public school education in Elba, Alabama. Following one year in Elba, the Brannons moved to Enterprise, Alabama, where Thomas attended the Enterprise Elementary for Colored for two years. The Brannons left Enterprise for Wrightsville, Arkansas, where Thomas completed the fourth grade at J. C. Cook Elementary. His family then left Wrightsville and settled in Little Rock, where Thomas attended the Capitol Hill Elementary School for a year. The Brannons then moved to North Little Rock, where Thomas completed the sixth grade at the

Hillside Elementary School. Due to the frequent moves, Thomas had become tough, streetwise, and undisciplined by the time he enrolled in Jones High School in North Little Rock.

At Jones High School, Brannon came into conflict with Elza Hunter, the school's principal. Hunter was an experienced educator who not only stressed academics but also self-discipline. Subsequently, that "Brannon Boy," as Thomas had become known because of his unruly conduct, repeatedly clashed with Hunter until he was transferred to Dunbar High in Little Rock. The rules of conduct were strictly enforced at Dunbar, and Brannon's stay there was a short one. He was then enrolled in Little Rock's Catholic High School for Colored. His experiences at Catholic High, his first with white teachers, was not a pleasant one, due to his independent spirit and behavior, but it forced him to realize that he had a friend at Jones High in the person of Elza Hunter, the principal. He returned to Jones High where he completed the eleventh grade. Brannon, still rejecting strict discipline, then decided that he did not need a high school education and, ignoring the advice of Hunter, dropped out of school and joined the navy. His naval experience made Brannon recognize the need for a good education and after his honorable discharge in 1953, he returned to North Little Rock. With the help of Hunter he enrolled in Shorter Junior College where he earned an associate degree. He went on to earn a B.A. at AM&N College at Pine Bluff, Arkansas (1960), and an M.A. from Adelphia University in Garden City, New York (1970).

Following his graduation from AM&N College, Brannon decided to pursue a teaching career in Arkansas, but because of the desegregation furor that characterized public education in Arkansas in the early 1960s, it was difficult for blacks, especially young black males, to find employment in school districts that were going through the desegregation process. Brannon, however, applied for a vacant position in the Lonoke School District. He was granted an interview by the white superintendent but did not wait for the result because he was told by the superintendent during the interview that "if you are hired and are around any group of Coloreds talking about attending our school (white school), you run and get away as soon as possible." Brannon eventually found employment at the all-black Childress High School in Wynne, Arkansas. Because of his open and consistent criticism of the principal at Childress, Brannon's stay there was a short one, 1960–1962. From Wynne, Brannon moved to Marianna, Arkansas, where he had found employment in the Lee County School District, where he taught junior high social studies, 1962–1963. At the end of the 1963 academic year, Brannon moved to Long Island, New York, where he taught in several public schools before retiring from the Central Islip School District in 1994. Following his retirement, Brannon moved back to Arkansas where he has become an active member and treasurer for the Retired Educators of Little Rock and Other Public Schools.

Index